The effective sales manager

The effective sales manager

Practical solutions to sales management problems

John Rock

Longman Professional

Longman Professional
A Division of Longman Cheshire Pty Limited
Longman House
Kings Gardens
95 Coventry Street
Melbourne 3205 Australia

Offices in Sydney, Brisbane, Adelaide and Perth.
Associated companies, branches and representatives throughout the world.

First published 1992

Edited by Louis de Vries
Designed by Jan Schmoeger/Designpoint
Set in 11/12 Monotype Plantin
Produced by Longman Cheshire Pty Limited
Printed in Hong Kong

National Library of Australia
Cataloguing-in-Publication data

Rock, John.
The effective sales manager.

ISBN 0 582 87564 1.

1. Sales management. 2. Sales executive.
I. Title
658.81

To Wendy

Contents

Introduction

Over the years, the job of selling has undergone enormous changes. The days when the only key results areas for sales people were the ability to get on with others, sell yourself, get round and see the customers and ask for the order, have long since disappeared. Irrespective of how technically complex the product, the job of selling in the 1990s requires a large portfolio of skills. These include: analysis, problem solving, selling technique, interpersonal relationships, communication, presentation skills, financial skills, planning, negotiation skills and time and territory management.

This is not altogether surprising given that advances made in computer technology permit vast amounts of data to be produced, potentially leading to much more information being available about our own and our customers' businesses. (Potentially, because the data produced can create more confusion than information!)

More effective communication systems mean that suppliers and customers are much better informed of what is going on in the rest of the world, providing another dimension to the decision-making process.

At the same time, the art of managing companies has developed so that individuals are more accountable now than ever before, including those who make purchasing decisions. One discipline which has made great strides in its professionalism is that of purchasing, or supply. This has partly been through training and partly because the quality of people appointed to purchasing roles has risen in recognition that they can contribute very substantially to the bottom line of the company. The purchasing position is hardly ever any longer the place where loyal old-timers are put out to pasture while awaiting their retirement.

The salesperson of the 1990s must know how companies operate and how they make profits, and must be able to put up competent financial arguments in favour of his or her products. (For ease of communication, instead of using 'he or she' or 'her or his' etc. on each occasion, only the masculine form of the pronoun will be used in this book. In doing so, it is recognised that reference is made to sales people and sales managers of either sex. Fortunately, the number of women in sales is increasing, although far too slowly, especially slowly in sales management. Those women who choose careers in sales management are generally very effective. They tend to be high achievers, and with sexual difference ability profiles showing very little difference, it is not surprising that female sales managers frequently outperform the average male sales manager.

As a result of the need for higher skill and knowledge requirements in the selling job, enormous amounts of money have been invested in training sales people. This is a very necessary thing.

However, what companies all too often fail to realise is that a major determinant of the effectiveness of the sales force is in fact the effectiveness of the sales manager. There is absolutely no point in investing money in training the sales people if they are poorly directed, unmotivated, undisciplined, not sure what the goals are or how they are doing. Furthermore, selling is an active profession which relies heavily upon skills. Training serves a critical role in establishing what those skills are and how to acquire them. It can also start to help individuals develop skills. But unless what happens in the training room is consistently and frequently reinforced, the skills will never develop. Otherwise, in six months time the sales people will remember attending the training course, they may even remember vaguely what it was about, and perhaps the odd point which they have integrated into their jobs. However, most of it will have been lost, together with all the money that the company has poured into training.

Sales managers also know that it is virtually impossible to find the right sales people to fill sales positions. As a result, all sales forces compromise. They generally have a few strong people and quite a few weaker ones. Sadly, that situation is frequently tolerated. Experience shows that the weaker can be considerably strengthened under the expert management of a competent sales manager. Failure to do this entails a loss of productivity for the company, and a failure of its obligations towards that employee.

Given that sales managers are such important people, it is quite strange that relatively little thought is given to their appointment, their induction and their ongoing training. The large majority of sales managers are appointed on the basis that they were very competent in performing a selling role. In some cases, especially those working for companies which operate strictly systems such as the Hay Scheme, the successful salesperson is promoted because it is the only way of rewarding him financially—for otherwise he would leave. The problem is that the real job of a sales manager requires a number of very different skills from those of a salesperson. Even the type of person who is most likely to succeed as a sales manager may not be the same as a successful salesperson.

The overall result is that far too many sales managers are not performing effectively in their jobs. This book was written with one clear objective in mind: to provide a very practical guide as to what sales managers should be doing, and how they should be doing it. It is based on many years of experience gained from sometimes making mistakes, sometimes getting it right and from observing what works across a very wide range of selling situations. The reader should be able to short-circuit several years of hard knocks, and pick up some practical solutions on how best to manage the sales force.

1

The role of the sales manager

Am I barking myself instead of leaving it to the dog?

Sell or manage?

The role of the sales manager is to produce agreed results for a specific area of operation through a productive, effective and satisfied sales force.

The key to the role is the words 'through a ... sales force'. The real sales management job is to manage sales people, not to be a super salesperson. The degree to which sales managers 'sell' or 'manage' is variable. There are sales managers, especially in smaller areas of operation, such as the smaller business volume states, or small market segments, who are called sales managers but do not have any staff reporting to them. This book was written primarily to assist those sales managers who have a sales staff reporting to them.

Yet many managers who do have several sales people reporting to them actually spend a significant part of their time selling. It is not possible to say in principle whether this is right or wrong. There are certain cases where it becomes necessary. However, too many sales managers hide behind the difficulty in defining whether they should sell or not, and in fact spend far too much time selling, and consequently far too little time managing.

It is justifiable for a sales manager to sell when the sales department is very small, with perhaps only one or two sales people reporting to the manager. In this case, the sales manager is hardly going to find managing two people a full-time job, and it is probable that a number of accounts will be allocated to him. However, he must be very much aware of the sales management role he should be performing with the people who do report to him, and it will be useful in such cases for the manager to try to compartmentalise the two aspects of his job.

Sales managers frequently sell to large or key accounts. This can happen both at the state level and the national level. The rationale for this is twofold. Firstly, selling to such accounts requires considerable skill and is very important to the company because key accounts produce most of the sales revenue and plant loadings (even if they don't produce much of the contribution to profit!). Secondly, the business at these accounts is generally large and customers handle such purchases within their own organisation at a relatively senior level. There is a perceived need to meet this seniority by fielding a senior salesperson from our side. That means either the state sales manager or the national sales manager. It sometimes means the sales director.

There is some justification for both of these reasons, but it is limited and must not be used by sales managers as a crutch for not getting on with the job of managing. Sales managers who were appointed from a sales position in which they were successful, especially those who were put into the job without induction training or preparation for a sales management role, will tend to want to keep on selling because that is what they know and what they are good at.

As long as they continue to do that at the expense of their sales management duties, the situation will be self-perpetuating. The sales manager sells because the sales people do not have the skills or experience. While he is doing that, the sales people never get the chance to develop their skills and experience, so the sales manager has to keep on selling. Eventually the brighter sales people get fed up and leave, joining an organisation that is prepared to help them reach their full potential. The sales people who stay lose their motivation because they realise they are second class sales citizens. The sales manager collapses from exhaustion trying to handle all the major accounts and putting out all the bush fires which result from the poor standard of work from an unmotivated and ineffective sales force.

It clearly does not work. Sales managers must make a concerted effort to develop their sales people and introduce them into key accounts, and eventually hand over to them the running of those accounts. Apart from the need to cut down the pressure on themselves, and the need from the company's point of view to develop the skills of the sales people, unless the manager has trained his staff to the point where there is at least one person competent and skilled enough to take over from him, he could very well find that his career might have to stop where it is. The company cannot afford to move him out of the position. Plenty of sales managers have dug themselves into that hole. Don't believe that such a position provides any security to you if the current position of sales manager satisfies your career ambitions. No one is really indispensable, and the company may very well be concerned that you are not developing your staff, and thus blocking the people whom the company expects to take leadership roles in the future. As a result you may find your career has taken an unexpected direction sideways, down or out.

The sales manager and key account planning

Key account management calls for multi-level selling (see Chapter 13). In other words, it recognises that major accounts are so complex that their correct management requires contacts between a number of functions and at a number of levels in both the customer's and the supplier's organisation. The sales manager can certainly be expected to play a role in this process. Playing a part in the account and running it, however, are two different things.

There may be a need for the sales manager to be involved to satisfy the ego requirements of a senior executive who is handling purchasing. However, beware of ego-tripping yourself. Can you build up the status of your sales people in the customer's eyes, so that they are acceptable? Experience suggests that under the following circumstances they will generally be acceptable to most senior people:

- They do not have 'sales representative' or something equally inappropriate on their business card.
- They are knowledgeable about your company, business and the market.
- They behave in a mature and competent way.
- Most importantly, they can make decisions.

The key issue here is the one of being able to make decisions. No one likes to deal with someone who can't make the decision. The tendency will always be to seek out the person who can. But at the end of the day, if you are afraid of allowing your sales people to make decisions—within certain guidelines to be sure—then you need to ask yourself what the function of the sales people is. If you are the only one who can make a decision, or if even you can't make it, then your sales people are effectively relegated to the job of 'go-for', where literally all they do is service the account. If that is true, then ask yourself the question of whether you have actually faced up to that, and what implications it has for the type of people you employ in that position. Maybe you are paying them far too much for the job you really expect them to do. Maybe they are frustrated because you have not levelled with them, and they still have an expectation that they are responsible for selling.

If you are handling key accounts yourself, ask yourself the questions in the following checklist, and answer them honestly.

Questions you should ask yourself if you spend a lot of your time selling

- In the structure of the sales department I have, should I really be handling all these accounts?
- Why am I handling them myself?
- Is there a way I could hand over either the partial or complete running of some or all of these accounts right now?
- If not, what do I need to do to be able to hand over at least some, preferably all, the responsibility for these accounts in, say, six months or a year?
- Is there a way of delegating, using guidelines, all or some of the decision making at this account?
- If not, why not and what can I do about it?
- How is the status of our sales people perceived at key accounts?
- What can I do to try to raise their status in customers' eyes?
- Do I tend to enjoy the glory of being the sales manager when I visit customers?
- Are there times when I should concentrate more on taking a back seat and let the salesperson assume more responsibility?
- Do I devote as much time as I should to managing the sales team as opposed to selling?
- Do I really see my job as producing results through others?
- Am I dedicated to the principle of producing results through others, or do I tend to pay lip service?

In summary, although in an ideal world, sales managers should not have accounts, should not handle accounts and should not accept as part of their role a specific selling component, in reality they will. However, they must ensure that they do no more selling than is absolutely necessary, and they must work towards divesting themselves of as much selling as they can by both building up the skills and the status of their sales people so that customers will accept them as the person responsible for managing their account.

Activities the sales manager performs

Given that we have succeeded in maximising our managing time versus our selling time, it is time to examine the sorts of activities the sales manager is involved in.

Typical sales manager activities

- Identifying the job to be done and deciding on the right number of positions, and how they will interrelate (getting the right organisation).
- Specifying the job descriptions and the key activities for each position, and setting standards of performance.
- Identifying the knowledge, skills and attitudes required.
- Recruiting or selecting from within the organisation the right people, training them, both induction training on appointment and on an ongoing basis according to identified training needs.
- Appraising staff.
- Translating the marketing strategies into a plan for the region or segment and setting direction for the sales force leading to plans by account.
- Budgeting and forecasting.
- Monitoring performance against key objectives for the department, sales revenue, sales volume, contribution, sales costs, market share, promotional funds, debtors, forecasting etc.
- Reporting, up the line and across the matrix.
- Human resource development planning.

This can be expressed in a flow chart (see Figure 1.1 on page 6). The ease with which all those steps happen will depend on the ability of the sales manager to wield a series of interpersonal skills.

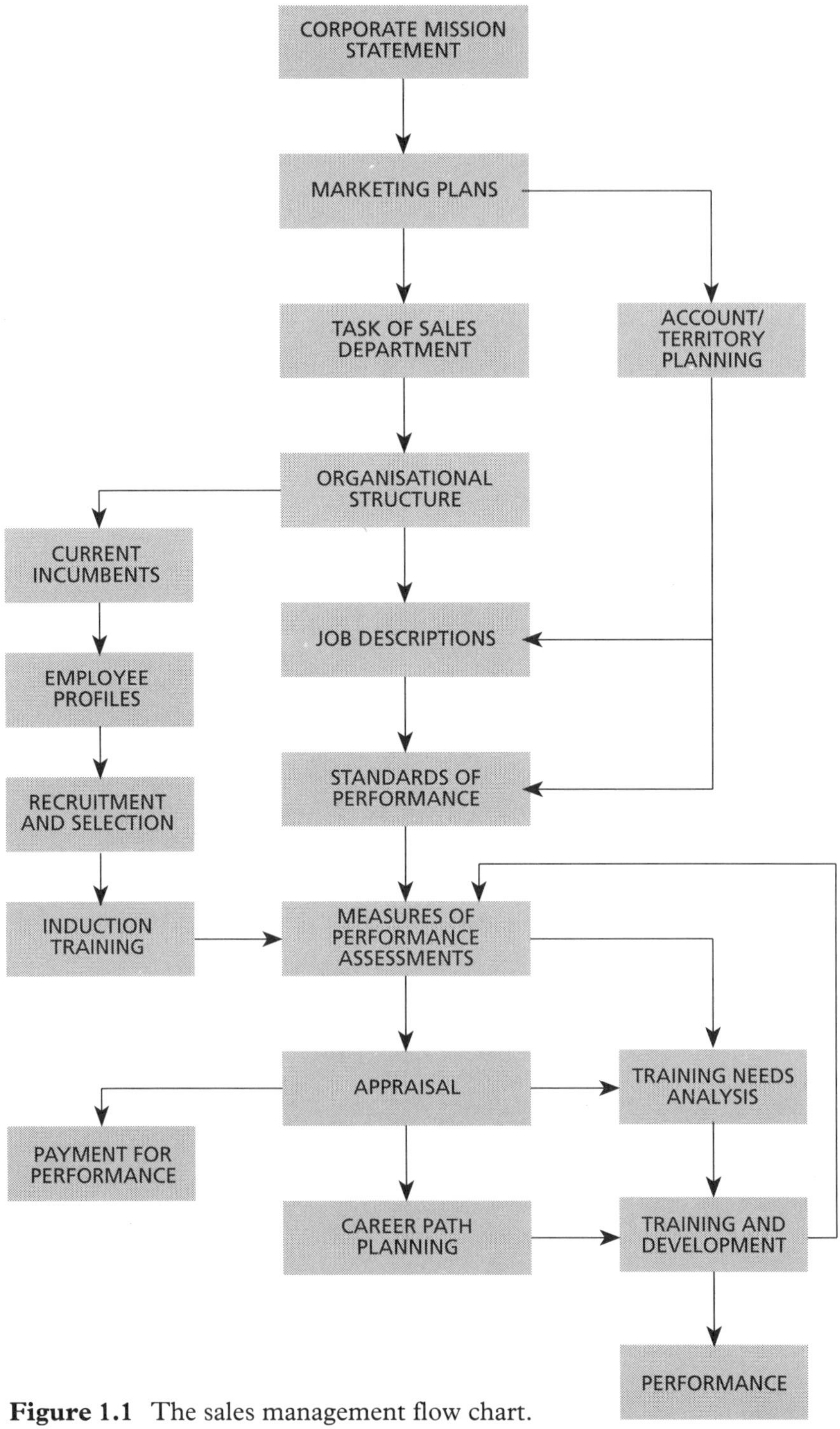

Figure 1.1 The sales management flow chart.

Interpersonal skills the sales manager needs

- motivation
- leadership
- communication
- delegation
- team building
- counselling
- diplomacy
- assertiveness
- the ability to ignore one's personal prejudices
- establishing the right personal relationships with individuals.

Apart from these interpersonal skills the successful manager also needs a portfolio of technical skills.

Technical skills the sales manager needs

- organisational
- planning/analytical
- problem solving
- financial
- presentation skills
- selling skills
- negotiating skills
- training
- time management.

What the sales manager should avoid

Success also depends on the degree to which the structures exist in the company to facilitate these steps, and the amount of information which the sales manager can access to help manage.

The list above, describing the activities of a sales manager, is very theoretical. It is correct and it is practical. The only problem is that it is interrupted by another list of things which sales managers inevitably get involved in, but which detract from their ability to address those critical activities on the list.

Things which interrupt the sales manager's real job

- solving problems which should have been prevented
- answering routine customer enquiries
- chasing deliveries
- putting out bush fires
- attending unnecessary or overly lengthy meetings
- handling complaints
- picking up someone else's telephone
- doing other people's work, such as selling!

This is the list we should be trying to avoid, since it quite unproductively eats into the time we have to do our real job. It will be clear to the reader by now that the job of sales manager, if it is done correctly, is very demanding.

Sales is different

It is worth observing that the three areas of operation in a company which are constantly and immediately under the microscope, are sales, distribution and production. When they make a mistake, everyone knows about it immediately. Who knows whether the corporate strategic planning department ever gets it right?

But in the area of responsibility of sales managers, the factors affecting the result are unpredictable and hence much harder to control. It is also harder to manage sales people than anyone else. This is because they are out doing their job on their own most of the time. (Well, they ought to be, and that is another issue we will be discussing later. Industrial sales forces are very low in productivity in Australia, and that can be addressed by forcing them out into the field.) In many cases, sales managers actually have no idea at all what their sales people are saying to customers. They do not know how they plan or handle a sales call when they are on their own.

And the sales people, unlike the rest of us in the office who reinforce each other's warm view of the world, are constantly being challenged by customers, threatened by the reported strength of the competition, and told that they have to do more for the customer. Sales people are particular types of people. They tend to be more emotionally labile, because if they are not, they will not be able to react to different customer situations. They also tend to be sensitive for the same reasons. As a result of all of this, sales people go through wider swings of 'highs' and 'lows' than employees in other disciplines, and the sales manager has to be able to recognise and manage it.

Types of sales manager activities

It can be useful to divide into three types the tasks that sales managers perform: people management, sales manager tasks and general tasks.

People management includes all the activities involving either individuals or the team.

Sales manager tasks are things the sales manager does which only he can do, such as approving expenses, signing off the budget, deciding on the right organisation, recommending to marketing a change in distribution.

General tasks are those on the second list above, which sales managers often do, but which could easily, and usually should, be performed by others in the sales team, either an external salesperson, internal sales staff or a secretary.

The ideal mix of these activities will vary with the structure of the particular job concerned. For a sales manager with seven sales people reporting to him, most of the time must be spent in people management, whereas for a sales manager with only one or two sales staff there will be a greater percentage of sales manager tasks.

Getting the mix of activities right

One of the problems is that of the squeaky wheel. The things which cry out for action are not usually those which in the long run will produce the results. Tasks fall into four categories (see Figure 1.2).

It is clear that urgent and important tasks will be attended to first. Those that are neither urgent nor important will probably never be done. The ones that are urgent but not important will tend to take priority over those that are important but not urgent.

IMPORTANT OR JUST URGENT?

IMPORTANT	3RD (2ND?)	1ST
NOT IMPORTANT	4TH	2ND (3RD?)
	NOT URGENT	URGENT

Figure 1.2 Too often tasks that are urgent but not important are attended to before those that are important but not urgent.

Sales managers keep putting off a significant part of the most important management activities because they are not urgent. They ignore the need to communicate properly with their people, or to get out in the field with them and observe how they are going. They don't keep records on the items that will be raised in the next appraisal.

It requires enormous discipline to achieve the right balance of activities. The manager who does not, will always be rushed off his feet and fighting fires, because *the key issue in sales management is producing results through other people*. It is those activities, the people management activities, where the sales manager must allocate more of his time.

As an exercise, given the size of the sales team you have and the sort of business and area you are in, make a list of what you consider should be the percentages of your time allocated to the three activities, people management, sales manager tasks and general tasks.

For a manager with seven external sales people, two internal sales staff and an assistant/secretary, the time allocation should be something like this:

- people management: 65-75 per cent
- sales manager tasks: 15-30 per cent
- general tasks: ideally very little, but realistically 5-10 per cent.

To help you decide what kind of activity falls into which category, examine the checklist on pages 11–12.

Now sit down and write what you believe the time allocation would have been in the last month. You will probably already see a discrepancy.

Finally, for one month keep a time log. Have it on your desk and divide it into hours. At the end of each hour or whenever it is convenient, but certainly at least once a day, write down in the time log to which of the three categories that hour or time period should be allocated.

At the end of the month, add it up and it can be virtually guaranteed you will find still another discrepancy, even from where you thought you were spending your time.

The rest of this book is devoted to looking in detail at the key results areas for sales managers. It will not come as a surprise to you that most of these will have a high component of people management, although we will also be addressing some of the sales manager tasks.

Although each subject will be treated as a discrete entity, in practice you will start to find that all the aspects of sales management interrelate. If you do not appraise well, staff will be disillusioned. If you do not train and develop them properly, results will be down, and appraisals will start going wrong. If you fail to communicate, morale will slip and the error rate will increase. To be a successful sales manager, you have to be good at the whole wide range of activities which are the role of the sales manager.

Checklist of category of activities for sales managers

Which category of activities do the following fall into, people management, sales management tasks or general tasks?

1 Calling on an account with one of your sales people to show that your company's senior management is interested in him.
2 Explaining to a salesperson a task that you are about to delegate.
3 Preparing a justification to the sales director for adding another salesperson.
4 Analysing in detail a salesperson's sales performance to find out why the overall territory he is responsible for is down.
5 Accompanying a salesperson on customer visits to observe how he is going.
6 Designing a short training session for the next sales meeting.
7 Getting the figures ready for the next sales meeting.
8 Signing a salesperson's expenses.
9 Explaining to one of your people why they are receiving a certain salary increase.
10 Making a call to a customer where the business has been lost.
11 Attending an industry conference to learn the latest developments in the industry.
12 Interviewing a prospective employee.
13 Designing a sales incentive scheme for a current campaign.
14 Monitoring the cost budget for the sales department.
15 Asking one of your people what he thinks about an idea you have for his area of responsibility.
16 Phoning production to find out when a product will be available for delivery.

17 Having a chat in the pub about the personal difficulties one of your people is having at home, and how that has affected his work.
18 Taking the buyer of the largest account out to lunch to have a one-on-one talk about the business.
19 Phoning one of the customers you knew well when you used to handle the territory, to find out whether the salesperson currently responsible is doing a good job.
20 Encouraging a salesperson with a sales problem to tell you how he would handle it and why.
21 Telling a salesperson with a sales problem what he should do.

The answers

Not too much in this world is black and white, and there may be more than one way of looking at some of the above questions. It is less important whether you agree with the answers given than the fact that you are thinking about the activities and remembering that you must spend most of your time on the people management.

PM = People Management
SMT = Sales Manager Task
GT = General Task

1 SMT
2 PM
3 SMT
4 SMT, and when you talk to the person about it, then PM
5 PM
6 PM
7 SMT/GT, you may be able to delegate that to someone else
8 SMT
9 PM
10 GT
11 SMT
12 PM

13 PM/SMT. Designing it could be considered as a task, but as a motivational technique it is also people management
14 SMT
15 PM
16 GT
17 PM, but the pub is probably not the ideal venue
18 GT, why go on your own? Take the salesperson with you next time!
19 Never do it. It is your job to go out with sales people and observe them. The customer will have different criteria for judging the salesperson anyway.
20 PM
21 SMT.

2

Getting the right organisation

Introduction

This is a subject to which most sales managers never really give much consideration, and that is because they are normally given an organisation when they take over the position. Many sales departments have just evolved and rarely does anyone question whether or not we are organised in the best way, because that is the way it has always been. This is particularly so within a state organisation. At the national level, there are sometimes considerations of whether the state sales forces should report to a state manager or directly to a national sales manager.

The organisational structure is often a function of the type of business and the way that company developed. There are, for example, some very centrally organised companies. They usually have one centrally located production unit which supplies the whole country. Examples might be companies in the food industry, petrochemicals, electronics or mechanical equipment. Such companies have evolved with a lot of central control, and the local sales forces have little autonomy.

On the other hand, there are companies whose business comprises a number of smaller manufacturing sites which have grown up all over the country. In many cases they were independent, and over the years have been bought out and merged into a large company, but still with a very decentralised structure. In other cases, the products are expensive or difficult to transport and manufacturing sites have been placed close to the customers who need the product, both for convenience and for cost savings. Examples would be packaging materials for the food and beverage industries, or the final preparation of explosives for the mining industry.

There is, however, a trend for the sales forces to become more centrally managed within any strategic business unit, and sometimes even across them. This is partly because there continues to be rationalisation within Australian industry, and companies are beginning to use their total purchasing power as a negotiating tool. The price of one $10 million contract tends to be lower than for twenty contracts at $500 000. When the customer is grouped into a national organisation, the supplier needs to respond in a similar way.

Another point is that with the speed of effective communications nowadays, what you do in one part of the country today is known all over the rest of the country tomorrow. Ask anyone who has sold to Coles how long it takes for the special deal their manager in Tasmania did with them yesterday afternoon to be mentioned in Brisbane or Perth. Not long!

Clearly, there is a need to ensure consistency in tactics and approach throughout the country, and unless there is a very strong centrally based organisation, that becomes very hard to achieve. The complication of having state managers to whom state sales managers report in any business sense at all, is such that it rarely works. It adds to the communication lines, causes conflict and encourages parochialism.

Structuring the sales department from scratch

Even though most sales managers inherit a department, it is a good idea to go through the exercise of deciding how you would have structured it if you were starting from scratch. Nothing is set in stone for ever, and if you determine there is a better way of organising the department, you can work towards it. If you do decide to make changes, remember that the human being is in fact a very conservative animal and resists change and usually feels uncomfortable about it. You should therefore manage change very carefully. Try not to make changes too dramatic or abrupt. Go step by step, do not leap!

The parameters you will be working with will in general be the number of external sales people, and the 'type' of sales person. Should they be representatives or account managers? This will depend on the nature of the selling job and the customer mix you choose to service. How will you organise them—by industry, customer type, customer size or geographical area? What mix of internal to external sales people will you have? What is the role of the internal sales people to be? What is the level of clerical, secretarial or administrative support?

The starting point will always be to identify accurately the job that the sales department is to perform. What are the results you are expected to achieve? This will depend on the marketing plans for your company. Make sure you understand exactly what you are expected to achieve and what the broad strategies are for achieving it. Only then can you start to look at the details of how you might best organise the department. If there are different business segments for your business, you will need to know the plans for each segment. For example, you may be selling your products to the large supermarket chains, to independent grocery stores and through pharmacies. In this case, you need to know what is expected from each of these areas. Or you may be selling to an industry where there are 400 customers, but where fifty of them take 90 per cent of the volume. In this case, do we just go for that 90 per cent, or do we want to try to service the whole lot? And if so, is there a better way than doing it ourselves, such as appoint a distributor who is selling a much wider range of products and who can therefore justify calling on those smaller accounts where we would find it hard to justify?

These issues are in fact really marketing issues and should be addressed by those with the marketing responsibility. In larger companies there will be a marketing department which should be addressing these questions. In smaller companies there may not be a marketing department as such, but certainly someone in the organisation must give thought to these issues.

Defining the sales job

Determining the number of calls to be made

A good way to look at the sales job to be done is to start off by listing the customers we will be servicing and dividing them into categories. Initially that may be in general categories. Using the previous example, you would separate the supermarket chains, the independent grocery accounts and the pharmacies. At some stage you will need to decide whether you will need dedicated sales people for each of these broad categories. Then, within each of these categories, you may separate them into types of visit. Clearly, the length of visits and the degree of planning and preparation, and the experience required to handle an account buying $5 million from you will be different from an account which is small, uncomplicated and buys only $100 000. There may be technical skills required at certain accounts, but not at others. You will need to decide on your own parameters, which will reflect the needs to satisfy the customer mix you are selling to. Do not at this point express it in terms of the people you have or their job functions, but rather the type of servicing the customer will require.

The type of servicing can be categorised as follows:

- *Category A*: large account, critical to success, full account management (including full planning and multi-level selling), good technical skills, mature salesperson, good presentation skills and negotiation skills
- *Category B*: fairly large account, desirable that we get the business, two or three contact points, some account planning, good technical skills, good negotiation skills
- *Category C*: we want the business, but are not prepared to devote high level of resources, shortened version of account plans, low level of technical skills, basic negotiation skills only
- *Category D*: will provide only minimal service and support.

For Categories A and B, you may need to list the customers individually; for the other two categories you really need to know only how many of them there are.

Now you can start deciding what the call frequency is you require. That is why you should list the customers in the first two categories, because it will be hard to generalise for these accounts. Work the calls out on the basis of the frequency and then multiply to give the number of calls in a year. For example, a call frequency of once every six weeks means eight visits a year.

You can either define a visit to the customer's premises as one call, irrespective of how many people are visited, but then later in the process reflect the lower call rate per day, or you can identify a call as to each individual in the firm, in which case you will have a higher call rate per day. It really does not matter which way you do it, so long as you keep the same convention throughout. I have a preference for counting each contact as a call because you can build it up at the large accounts, with say one call on marketing a quarter, purchasing every week, production once a month, technical department once a quarter, etc.

At the end of the exercise, you will have identified how many visits in a year you need to make for the four categories you have chosen. Of course, there will be unplanned visits, and contacts made at liaison and review meetings, but this method gives you a good guide to the sort of planned regular sales presence you require out in the field.

Setting call rate productivity standards

You now need to set some standards for the productivity of your people with respect to visit schedules.

At this point there tend to be significant protestations from those sales people selling in the industrial areas. It goes something like this: 'It is the quality of the calls that matters, not the number you make'. We all know that! No one is trying to say that we should be making more calls if it means the quality of the calls we make decreases. Neither should we be making unnecessary calls. However, everything else being equal, the more calls a sales force makes per salesperson, the more cost effective it will be. Most sales people are paid a straight salary, and are thus all fixed cost. We pay for them whether they produce or not (maybe not for too long if they don't, but as a matter of principle). To put it quite bluntly, the productivity of a large number of Australian sales forces is so poor that it ought to be possible with better management of the sales people to do the same overall sales job with fewer people.

The number of calls you might expect your people to make in a month will depend on the type of call, the type of customer and the geography of the territory. Compare a 'route' salesperson calling on deli's in a compact area of a city with easy parking, and a person selling mining equipment to very large mines located at inaccessible sites all over Australia. The variation might be from 200–300 calls a week to only ten or so a month in these extremes.

Most of the companies selling to the retail trade, whether it be grocery, hardware or pharmacy, are fairly well managed in this regard. In many cases, for representatives calling on stores there is a fixed cycle of visits. In certain companies it is even computerised. In such cases, the problems are less whether the right number of calls is being made, but more the quality of the calls or even the need. Representatives in such an automated system must be sure that they have a reason for calling and plan what they are going to say, rather than turning up because that's what the computer tells them they should do.

The real problems of call rate are in the less programmed industrial selling area. In many cases, the sales people only make an average of fifteen or twenty calls a month. One way of looking at that is to say that the salary overhead of the salesperson—what it actually costs the company overall to employ that person—is around $70 000 a year. Each sales call then costs around $400!

In fact, most sales forces selling in this area accept that their productivity should be higher. Interestingly enough, many sales managers do not know actually what the call rate of their sales people is, and tend to express surprise, or even horror, to hear their sales people admit to such low rates. Account managers selling to industrial accounts, should aim for at least thirty calls a month, and that is counting a call involving purchasing, production scheduling and the technical manager as just one call! That would bring the cost per call down to $200.

Improving sales productivity

Why is that such sales people manage to make so few calls? There are several reasons. Fundamentally, they lack the internal support functions or information systems to enable them to get out into the field. At the same time, it can be quite comfortable in the office. It is easy to be busy all day long (busy, not necessarily productive), less lonely than on the road, and less stressful than being told how good the competition is.

One problem leads to another. If the sales people have to handle some of the support tasks which others should be performing, they will come into the office every day, and sometimes twice a day. In Sydney this can mean two hours or more a day of unnecessary driving. That is 25 per cent of the allocated hours of work (we know sales people put in much more than the thirty-seven or forty hours most people work).

You may be asking what this has to do with the question of organisation and why it is not addressed in a separate chapter on sales productivity. The answer is that you may be better off investing in better systems and internal support and having fewer external sales people. The most expensive of your sales staff are the external people, and it is quite ridiculous to be paying higher salaries to let them do what are basically clerical or administrative tasks.

Try to structure things so that sales people do not come into the office more than two or three times a week. Provide them with car telephones, good internal support staff, and the right information systems to get the right information on deliveries and order status. Make sure that the internal people are competent to get the quotes right, or can handle the customer on the phone and handle basic enquiries. It is hard enough to get good sales people. When we do find them and train them, it is a waste of one of our most valuable resources when they are stuck in an office or a car.

You need to decide what is a reasonable call rate, given the ideal situation and then given the current situation. If there is a significant difference, you will have to start planning how you can change the organisation and the systems to get closer to the ideal. For a start, the internal sales people should report to the sales manager and not to accounts or administration or some other area. Call them 'internal sales', too, not 'order entry'. It helps if distribution reports to marketing rather than to production, because the flow of information is better, and the need to respond to the customer is understood more clearly. There is even a case for production planning to be considered as part of the marketing function too.

Deciding how many sales people you need

To help set the standards, you can work out the time available for selling. You start with fifty-two weeks available, less four weeks annual leave, times five days a week. This gives 240 days. Take off the public holidays, say eight, then sick days at an average of five; training courses, conferences another eight. This leaves 219 days. Monthly sales meetings, 'quality time' (see Chapter 9), 1.5 days a month, leaves you with 201 days. Report writing, necessary general administration, half a day a week. (If you think more, examine your systems and reporting procedures. Do you really need them?) Half a day a week for forty-eight working weeks is twenty-four days. We are now down to 177 days.

Let us assume that we are talking here of an account manager in an industrial company calling on clients in the Category A above. You may consider that, given the territory of the whole metropolitan area, including driving time, planning and making the call, an average of three hours a call is reasonable. With 177 days at eight hours a day, this would give 472 calls, or ten calls a working week per salesperson. Or, that with 177 days, there are effectively 3.7 days available in the working week, and that on three days it is possible to make three calls a day, and on the other day one call, again giving around ten calls a week or 480 calls a year per salesperson.

You may decide that the average for Category C accounts would be 1 hour 45 minutes, including driving, planning and the call. This would lead to 810 such calls a year per salesperson.

If you now look at the total number of calls of each type you have identified as being required, it will give you an idea of the numbers of sales people you need to handle each category. An example is given in Figure 2.1 on page 22.

Improving call rate productivity

At the same time, you should measure what the current productivity is for each category. If there is a divergence, you can look at some

	Type of account			
	Category A	Category B	Category C	Category D
Number of accounts	15	40	60	40
Visits/month*	8	4	1	.5
Total visits p.a.†	1320	1760	660	220

* One visit is considered as one function, such as purchasing or technical.
† Assumes 11 months available for visiting and one month shut down.

	Category A	Category B	Category C	Category D
Visits per selling day	4	5	5	6
Full days selling time available	142	160	185	200
Visits p.a. available per person	568	800	925	1200
No. of people needed	2.3	2.2	.7	.2

Selling time available

Account manager 'A' accounts		
Days in a year		365
Working days		260
Annual leave	-20	240
Public holidays	-10	230
Training	-7	223
Conferences	-4	219
Sick days	-5	214
Planning/admin. meetings 1.5 days a week x 48	-72	142
Full selling time (days)	142	
Visits/full day	4	
Total full visits/p.a.	568	

Note

1 The planning and administration needs, office time, will be different for different category accounts, so that the full selling time available will differ.
2 You will have requirements of fractions of people. You must then decide how to split up the work load.
3 In this case your total need is for 5.4 people. You may settle for five and give 'D' accounts to a trainee.
4 Then you would need to decide whether to have two people for 'A' accounts, two for 'B' account and one for 'C' accounts, or have a mix of 'A', 'B' and 'C' for each of the five people, or a hybrid of these options.

Figure 2.1 Calculating manning needs to service accounts.

of the factors we have been discussing to see if you can make the sales force more productive.

Once you are satisfied that you have optimised the call rate, if you appear to have too few people, either put up a justification for more sales people (likely to be knocked back), or compromise on the level of customer contact. At least you can go back to your working documents and decide where you want to reduce the contact schedules. You may decide to maintain Category A, but reduce B and C, for example.

You will never end up with even numbers. You may find, for example, that you need 1.7 people for Category A, 1.5 for Category B, 1.1 for Category C and 0.5 for Category D. Now is the time to start looking at the individuals you have. If you have four people—two good mature people, one with some experience and one new—you may decide to use one of the good people for Category A and the other for some A and some B. The third person might handle the rest of the B accounts and the fourth person might handle the C accounts. You could then consider letting one of your internal people handle the D accounts as a training role, initially largely by telephone. Alternatively, you may decide to give each of the first three people a mix of A and B accounts split by geography or area, and the fourth the C accounts.

Summary

There are no fixed rules. The important thing is to relate the whole structure to the business priorities as expressed by marketing, and then to allocate the accounts according to the business needs, the individual development needs, the particular strengths and weaknesses of members of the team, and what is expedient at the time.

You should try to keep stability in the customer base. Customers judge badly those companies where the salesperson calling on them changes regularly. Ideally a salesperson should handle an account for at least two years.

There is a great temptation to let the organisation be determined by the employees we have. This is very much letting the tail wag the dog. We must decide what the optimum organisation is as the first step. We may then have to compromise in certain regards because of the mix of people we have. Recognise that this is what is happening and have a longer-range plan to get to the organisation we really need. People come and go in any case, and we must inject some direction into the operation rather than let it drive us.

Some golden rules

Do not create spans of control that are too large. No one can effectively manage more than six or seven people. While it may be desirable to have a flat organisation to prevent it from becoming a civil service-like hierarchy, with too many chiefs and no Indians, neither should we have such wide spans of control that there is no effective management.

Ensure that if you have to introduce intermediate levels of management, such as field supervisors, or sales supervisors, they are real and not Clayton's positions. This means delegating to the next level down from the manager, all the managerial and as many of the business accountabilities as possible. Any manager is only really a manager if he has the delegated authority and accountability for the people who report to him. He should be the one who has the prime responsibility for recruiting the people who report to that position, and for appraising them. These are two functions which the sales manager occasionally tries to hang on to himself. How can a sales manager appraise a sales representative who reports to a field sales manager, when he never has anything much to do with the representative on a day-to-day basis? Yet it happens. The field sales manager is the one who spends the time with the representative, coaches him, makes visits with him, sees his reports and controls his activities and supervises him on a day-to-day basis. That field sales manager must also appraise him, counsel him, recommend him for promotion, and if necessary fire him.

Make the reporting lines simple and clear. Sales people do not respond well to matrix organisations. In an organisation where a salesperson reports to a sales manager, but takes business direction from a product manager in a direct dotted line, there will be rows. The product manager will complain about the ineffectiveness of the salesperson. The sales manager has no control over what the salesperson is doing in a business sense. Everyone spends too much time trying to communicate and failing, and the salesperson has demands for his time from two different people. It is much better to have clear reporting lines.

Ideally, the sales people should respond to a sales manager who may respond to a national sales manager. The business direction should in principle pass from the marketing people to the senior, say national, sales manager. The national sales manager would then agree that the overall strategies are achievable, and would then interpret them into sales tactics (activities) to the sales force. Marketing is 'strategic' and sales is 'tactical'. In an ideal world, marketing should not need to get involved with day-to-day issues.

In practice, of course, issues are always coming up which are not covered by the guidelines agreed to between marketing and the senior sales manager. In that case, either the matter should be handled up the line between the senior sales manager and marketing or directly between the salesperson or the state sales manager and marketing. What is best depends on the type of business. There are many relatively superficial matters which are better dealt with directly to save time and avoid burdening the national sales manager with trivia. But there are more important issues which would be more appropriately handled up the lines of command. In most organisations, people will intuitively know what is best most of the time. It is in the cases when they don't, that the bickering will start (see Chapter 15).

There will be some organisations where there are several businesses, strategic business units, which are being handled by an integrated sales department. The SBU's may be very diverse and have quite different marketing issues. The sales managers cannot be expected to know the businesses well enough to provide business direction on all of them. In such cases, the sales people are going to have to take their business direction from the SBU. Mostly, a salesperson will work with only one SBU anyway.

There are two ways of organising sales in such cases. You can have the sales people reporting to the SBU in a total sense, which means either to product manager or a profit centre manager, often a manufacturing unit site manager. Or you can have the sales people reporting to a central sales organisation and have them take their business direction from the SBU. Neither system is very satisfactory, but that is life.

Whichever way you go, the thing to recognise is that allegiance will always go where the bread and butter is. The boss who appraises you and signs your expenses, the one who recommends you for promotion and decides your salary increase, is the one who owns you. We are, after all, pretty basic creatures!

My recommendation would be to opt for a strong central sales organisation. The reason is that in the case where the sales people report to product managers or site managers, they will not be professionally managed by people who understand what selling and sales management is all about. There will be variable standards across the company, little dedication to training and development, and a poorly developed sales professionalism. In the introduction of this book it was stated that the effectiveness of a sales force is very largely dependent on the way that it is managed. The most effective manager of a sales force is a professional sales manager.

Internal sales

In organising the internal sales organisation, integrate it as much as possible with external sales and get people working together. Where possible, have internal sales people working with the customers of just one or two external sales people. Encourage both parties to have joint ownership of the customers. Involve the internal people in sales meetings. See them as an integral part of the sales force and make sure that they know that you see it like that. Get the external sales people to take the internal staff out with them to get to know the customers. Build interest in the internal sales positions. And give recognition.

The fact is that internal sales people often have more frequent contact with customers than external ones. If you treat your internal people as administrative clerks, then that is what they will be. They will not show involvement or initiative. And you will suffer from the same levels of staff turnover as the traditional administrative jobs, such as at the banks, which are very high indeed.

Once you can get a stable, effective internal sales group, your external people will begin to develop a bit more confidence so that they can go out and visit a customer without having to supervise everything in the office. It is a sort of crisis of confidence. To achieve this level of cooperation, you must ensure that your external sales people understand the ground rules and are prepared to give the internal staff a chance. They have to learn how to work with the internal people, to involve them and to share a bit more. The result is a much more effective and harmonious team.

One last point is that whatever organisation you end up with, it is most important to have clear job descriptions for each position, and clear reporting lines. Ensure that the sum of all the job descriptions, including the job purposes and the key accountabilities and tasks describes completely the total job the sales department is to perform.

3

Job descriptions and measures of performance

Why job descriptions are so unpopular

Most medium- to large-sized companies have as a policy the writing of job descriptions for all employees. Despite that, or maybe because of it, the job description is one of the most unpopular pieces of paper around (beaten only by the appraisal form). It has been abused and blamed and comes in a hundred different varieties from half a page to twenty pages.

This does not mean that the concept of job descriptions is bad; it simply means that companies are bad at using them.

The job description is the basis of the whole of sales management. Without defining the jobs that individuals are to do, how can we go out and recruit the right people? How can we be sure that the total job of the sales department will get done? How are we to be able to identify the training needs of individuals and the group unless we know what it is they are supposed to be doing? How can we develop them and train them? And then how can we appraise them, or reward them for a job well done?

If they are so important, why have they got such a bad reputation? It is possibly because their role in the company is not understood. Many people still see them as restrictive, with an almost union-like undertone of demarcation. 'If it's not in my job description, then I'm not going to do it!' Surely we have progressed a bit further than the film *I'm All Right Jack.*

Others do not see the need for job descriptions. They do not understand how they fit into the whole management structure. Another reason for their unpopularity is the quality, or lack of it, of the job descriptions. Many are written in 'personnelese' and go on for pages. They are as hard to understand as a legal document. They are hard to read and go into so much detail that it is impossible to get one's mind around the essence of the job. Others include petty items and motherhood statements which are peripheral to the key results areas. If there is one thing that should never get into job descriptions, it is all that stuff about keeping the company car clean. We know that we should look after the company property, and if we don't, we can expect the sales manager to say something about it. However, it is not the sort of thing which should clutter up a job description.

Individuals have a right to know what their job is and what is expected of them. They want to know what their responsibilities and accountabilities are and what their authority is.

One of the most common responses when people are asked if they have a job description, is: 'Yes, somewhere there is one, but it is probably out of date by now'. It is not taken seriously, it is not used, it is not a live document. It has as much relevance to the lives of most people as Latin.

Revitalising the job description

For the job description to regain the position of respect it deserves, a few things need to happen.

- Managers must understand how important they are, and in turn they must ensure that the sales people understand that too.
- Job descriptions need to be made relevant to the essence of each individual's job.
- Job descriptions should be written in normal English, and they should be concise.
- They should be used when a new person starts, and made part of the induction training.
- Job descriptions should be kept up to date and reviewed at least once a year.

Ideally, they should be written by the incumbent for the job and then agreed to by the manager. This is not always possible, and clearly in the case of people joining the company, the job description must be written first. If you are updating your job descriptions, or writing them for the first time, sit down with your sales people individually. Explain what the job description is, why it is important and how it is to be used. Discuss with them what they see as their main job purpose and their key accountabilities and tasks. Then get them to go away and write their own job description. You may encounter some disturbing discrepancies, but better they be identified than unknown. If you have several people in essentially the same position, you will need just one job description common to all incumbents. This should be true throughout the country. At least you can then take the best from all of them and issue a job description which they have all contributed to. Ideally, there should be consensus, but the sales manager will remain the final arbiter. They should be used and referred to. The manager should encourage the salesperson to look at the job description before appraisals. He should refer to them in 'quality time' (see Chapter 9). They must become live documents.

The flow of job descriptions, as with so many things in companies, should be from the top down. The manager must ensure that his own job description is appropriate and up to date. He ought to have a copy of the job description of his immediate supervisor before he starts. The sales manager's job description will define the job to be performed in his area of responsibility. Much of it will of course be delegated to the people who work for him, such as the selling, for example. The job descriptions of all the people who report to him should flow from his own job description. This will be the first step after getting the right organisation. The sum of all of the job descriptions of the people who report to him should equal the sales manager's job description.

It is also a good idea to have a copy of the job descriptions of people with whom the department has a significant dotted line relationship, such as distribution, product managers, credit manager etc.

What the job description should look like

The format does not matter. It should be as clear and precise as possible. As long as all the main points are covered, the shorter the better. Try to get it all on one page, and never let it go beyond two.

The following items must be included in job descriptions:

- job title
- reports to
- supervises
- key job purpose (one or two sentences only)
- main duties, accountabilities
- authority.

It may be advisable, depending on the circumstances, to make a statement about one or more of the following points:

- job location
- department
- special relationships (strong dotted line relationships).

Some job descriptions include a range of remuneration parameters. Many managers shrink from the thought, but it is hard to see why.

With respect to their perceived inflexibility in some quarters, job descriptions can be as flexible as the manager's style and his ability to motivate the team. The job description is to define what the key results areas are, not to specify every single thing the incumbent might be called upon to do. If the content of the job changes such that there are significant things which the job will entail in the future, then the job description should be changed to reflect these.

Because they give people clarity of what is expected of them, job descriptions provide both direction and security. They are a basic communication tool. They form the basis for agreeing on performance and hence remuneration, and career progression. They take subjectivity and misunderstanding out of the game. They are the fundamental building block of our relationship with each member of the team.

Measures of performance

The job description tells each person what the job is about, what his purpose in the organisation is. It defines the sorts of activities people should be spending their time doing.

What it does not do is tell people to what standard they should be performing these activities. This is important when it comes to both appraisals and to identifying training needs. It is clearly essential in a sales organisation which spans several locations, that there be a commonality across the network in judging what constitutes satisfactory or good performance. Most companies claim to have a payment for performance scheme. Without this commonality, one could be doing the same job to the same standard in two different locations and be judged quite differently.

The principle is easy enough to state and to understand. What is much more difficult is to define the standards of performance so that subjective interpretation by the sales manager is precluded. Strictly speaking, this is impossible. However, agreeing on some performance criteria is much better than having none at all. The measures of performance will flow from the activities or key duties as described in the job description. Achievement of sales budget, volume, sales revenue dollars or contribution will also play a role. Many sales managers use this as the only criterion. In some very simplistic sales situations that may be valid, but in most cases achievement of budget alone is a very limited way of assessing individuals. This is because achievement of budget is also subject to factors outside the individual's control. These might include a change in exchange rates allowing import competition, poor weather creating low demand, plant breakdown causing non-availability of product, a marketing decision to not follow lower prices from the competition etc. It is very disillusioning when sales people are judged on adverse factors beyond their control—especially if their financial reward depends on it.

Furthermore, using such figures exclusively has two other problems. Once you have missed budget it is a bit late to do anything about it. Simply looking at the figures is not in itself a diagnosis. You can certainly tell that something has gone wrong, but you do not know what.

For all these reasons, it is most important to look at the key results areas in terms of figures, activities and skills, and then set some standards.

The setting of standards is closely tied up with assessing training needs and appraisals. In Chapter 7 there is a list of possible criteria you would use for assessing sales people, in terms of the knowledge and skills required. These derive directly from the requirements of the job as expressed in the job description. However, before you can start using these types of forms to assess training needs or to appraise, you must have defined some standards.

Expressing standards

The best way to take subjectivity out of anything is to quantify it. Who knows what 'often' or 'frequently' means? We all know what 'always' means, or 'no more than two instances', or 'every week'. The sorts of things which might appear are:

- *Excellent*: All account plans were prepared by the agreed date, and accepted without any revision.
- *Good*: All account plans were prepared by the agreed date, with 50 per cent accepted without revision and the other 50 per cent only requiring minor revision (one objective or strategy).

- *Poor*: Up to five account plans were prepared up to one month late, the rest on time, and/or more than 50 per cent required minor revision, or up to three of the plans required major revision (more than one objective or strategy).
- *Unacceptable*: More than five plans were up to a month late, or any plans were more than a month late, or more than three of the plans required major revision.

This may seem a lot of work, and it will certainly tax your mind, but at the end of the day it does save a lot of argument, allows fair comparisons across the whole country, and lets the sales people know exactly what they are aiming for. When we come to discussing appraisals (in Chapter 7), this will become particularly evident.

One of the principles of business is to concentrate on the few key things which really make a difference. It is true from corporate strategic planning and through all a company's activities. There is a limit to how much anyone can effectively address at any one time. Part of the process of the strategic planning process is to define what those few really key issues are, and then go after them. It has been shown time after time to be the most successful way of running a business. Maybe governments should take it to heart too!

The same is true of the salesperson's job. You do not need a large number of criteria for which you are writing standards of performance. That is another reason for making the job description as short as possible. Otherwise you start to include less important things and focus is lost on which items are the really critical few. You ought not to be writing standards of performance for more than twenty items; you should be aiming for ten.

If you can involve your sales people in the writing of their own standards, you should do so. There will be more commitment. Your role must be to end up with the standards you set. You cannot afford to compromise. If there is a gap, then you must persuade, and if that fails you must arbitrate.

The right time to introduce a person's job description and standards of performance is when they join, in which case they will be presented as a fait accompli. This way there is full understanding from the very start. Job descriptions will be one of the first things you will talk about in the induction training program for new staff.

4

Recruitment and selection

Introduction

Although recruiting a new salesperson, or for that matter an order taker or secretary, is not something that the sales manager has to perform very often, it is one of the most important. A company is only as good as its people. After all, they are the ones who develop new products, set new directions or open up new markets. People are the most important resource of a company, bar none.

It stands to reason that the more suitable the people we employ, the more effectively they will perform, everything else being equal.

The cost of a poor recruitment decision is enormous. Firstly, there are the direct costs incurred again if the first decision is wrong. Then there is the time of the manager involved, which would have been better spent doing other things. There is the possible harm done to the business in the meantime, the orders lost or the damage done to customer relationships and loss of credibility for the company. There is usually a drop in motivation of the whole team. As far as the sales manager who made the poor decision is concerned, he loses the credibility with his team and with his bosses.

That assumes that the poor recruitment decision can easily be reversed, by simply getting rid of the person who was incorrectly employed. With legislation moving the way that it is, it is becoming harder and harder just to get rid of people. It is not just a legal issue, either.

There is also a moral issue at stake. If we make a mistake and remove the individual, either to another position which he did not apply for and probably does not want, or we sack him, we have destroyed that person's confidence in himself and possibly caused considerable financial and social embarrassment to him and his family. We may ease our consciences by providing a 'generous' settlement, at heavy cost to our bottom line, but the individual may spend months looking for another job. If he has left a secure job in the first place to join us, he will be feeling pretty sore.

Typically the decision to get rid of someone is not taken immediately. They are given a period of time to 'prove themselves', and then when they fail to deliver after a couple of years, that is when the axe falls. Frequently, getting rid of people is necessary, but let us try to ensure that if it is, the fundamental reason is not that we made a bad recruitment decision in the first place.

Good people are hard to find

As we discussed in the introduction, the sales job is becoming more and more complex, requiring increasingly higher levels of a wider variety of skills. Inevitably we are not going to be able to have a team full of star performers. However, we must be aiming as high as we possibly can when we recruit.

Sales people must be able to sell, plan, analyse, present, negotiate, organise, manage their time, communicate, and establish relationships. They need to understand business, their market, the customers, their products and how to get the best out of them.

It is hardly surprising that the need for such people greatly outstrips the availability.

Given what was said about the importance of not making a poor recruitment decision, if we are now saying that there are not too many of the right people out there, it seems as if we have set ourselves an impossible task. In fact, if you ask some experienced sales managers, they will probably tell you that it is impossible!

What it does mean is that we could face the situation where at the end of a recruitment campaign, there is no candidate suitable or capable of being developed within a reasonable time frame. Time after time in this situation, the sales manager has finally relented under the pressure of not having a full complement, to just take the best of the bunch and hope it works out in the end.

It very rarely does.

Sales managers are reluctant to believe it, but if you cannot find a suitable person, do not appoint anybody. Otherwise you will be making a rod for your own back, or for someone else's, if you are lucky enough to get moved into another position. Try again, or try a different avenue. Maybe reassess whether you are offering the right remuneration package. However, do not employ someone whom you know at the outset is not the right person for the job. It is bad for business, bad for the individual and in the long term it is bad for you, the sales manager, too.

Selecting from within

So far we have been talking about recruitment. However it is usually a better strategy, if you can, to select from within your own company. Part of the whole practice of human resource development is the recognition that it can be very difficult to source the right people from outside the company. A better strategy is to appoint people in fairly junior positions who are capable of development into more senior roles. It is often argued that this strategy does not work, because the bright ones get impatient and leave after we have trained them. That we cannot always have ready a position for them to advance into when they want it.

It is true that there are some classic examples of Australian companies which have provided the managers for a whole industry, often even for companies that compete with them. However, this has been because the human resource development has only been followed part of the way. It is not just a question of employing a number of bright young people; they must then be effectively managed. They should be made aware of the career paths available to them; they should be developed towards the next step and be given feedback on their progress. They must also be given a realistic assessment of when the next move may happen. In the meantime, the company should look after them financially. In the long run, it is far more cost effective to do this than have an ad hoc approach to career planning.

The implication is that at each level we need to have a balance of people. It is bad to have no one who wants to advance or is capable of advancing. Equally well, it is a disaster if everyone at any particular level wants the next job up. Should you be hiring just an internal salesperson, or should you be hiring someone who can grow into an external sales position in a year or so? Do you want an account manager, or do you want a possible replacement for your own job?

Selection from within is generally more motivating for the whole company. It shows that there is a point in giving your best. Appointments from inside take less time to get up to speed.

Recruiting from outside brings new blood to the team and the company. It can bring new ideas, different ways of doing things, a breath of fresh air. It stops organisations becoming inbred. (The Japanese system of working in different functional positions within the same company for life is great for reaching consensus, but bad for bringing in new ideas. The Western way of sticking mainly to one discipline but moving from company to company makes consensus harder, but cross-fertilisation of ideas much easier.)

We need a mixture of recruitment and selection in any organisation. In any case, the overall approach is conceptually the same.

Why does it go wrong so often?

Perhaps it is because most managers do not have to recruit very often. Maybe it is because they have never been given guidelines on how to do it. The fact is that very few managers follow a systematic step-by-step approach to recruitment and selection.

One of the most common sins is that in the interview, the employer does most of the talking. Now, how can you expect to find out anything about a candidate if you are doing all the talking?

Too little thought is given to the type of person we really need. The sales job is undergoing continuous change. It is quite different today from even ten years ago. How many managers just pull out the same advertisement that was used the last time? When was that first written? 1983? We can always change a few of the words to correct for changes in the name of the department, and she'll be right!

What about the need for balance in the team we discussed in the previous section? The process requires thinking the recruitment campaign through from start to finish, each time you do it.

There is a tendency to concentrate on the positions people have had and what the job they did was supposed to be about. However, there are not enough probing questions asked about what the individual actually achieved in that position and how they achieved it.

The most common errors

The following are some of the most common errors made in recruitment and selection:

- Not taking into account the need to balance the team.
- Failure to reflect the changes in the sales job in the characteristics of the ideal candidate.
- Failure to strictly follow a procedure.
- The manager's belief in his innate ability to sum up people at first sight.
- Subjectivity allowing prejudices and personal likes and dislikes to influence the decision—his eyes are too close together and therefore he must be untrustworthy.

- Not enough probing as to how people performed in previous jobs and what they achieved.
- Not probing enough when talking to referees.

Eight steps

Taking a systematic approach will reduce the risk of making recruitment errors.

The following are the eight key steps in the process:

1. Define the job to be done, including key results areas and activities. In other words, ensure that the job description is valid.
2. Develop an employee profile. What are the skills, knowledge and attitudes required to do this job? What is required to balance the team? What is required to satisfy future staffing needs? What are the technical factors and the motivational, emotional or personality factors we are looking for, the 'can do' and the 'will do' factors?
3. Decide how to locate candidates. Advertise? Agency? Recruit or select?
4. Telephone screening.
5. Applications and resumés.
6. The job interview.
7. Making the decision.
8. Checking references.

The eight steps are now examined in detail.

Defining the job

This may sound very obvious, but what the job entails keeps changing, and frequently the job description does not reflect all these changes. The job description has to be the building block of the whole management process. It is essential to define each individual's job (see Chapter 3).

Review the job description of the job when it was occupied by the previous incumbent, and then ask yourself if there have been any changes. It is a good idea to note the date when a job description was prepared so that you know how long it has been since it was written. Be sure that the job description includes a main job function together with key tasks and accountabilities. You may consider that the fact that you are about to recruit someone is a good opportunity to check that you still have the right organisation and allocation of duties.

If this is a new position, it is essential you write a complete job description.

Employee profile

While most large companies and many smaller ones will have job descriptions of some sort or other, very few ever give consideration as to what the profile of the successful candidate should be. The profile will include a number of elements.

It will define what are the qualifications necessary to perform the job as described in the job description. These may include academic achievements, knowledge of the technology base of the industry, knowledge of the market or even the customers. It will also refer to the technical skill level required, such as selling skills, negotiation skills or planning skills. These may often be expressed in terms of years of experience in certain types of job function, but they are issues which will need to be verified with each candidate later. These factors can all be summarised under the heading, 'can do' factors, and they define whether the candidate is likely to be technically capable of doing the job. Remember that if you are looking for someone capable of advancement, this also needs to be reflected in the 'can do' factors.

Then there is a second group of factors which we will call the 'will do' factors, which tell you whether the person is likely to do the job in your company, with your products in that position. They are more about the individual's personal motivation factors, about the sort of person he is, his maturity. Will he fit in? Does he have the drive and commitment we are looking for?

The need for balance in the team

It is also in this profile where we need to look again at balance in the team, this time in terms of the sorts of personalities we employ. We need to make sure that people will fit in to the 'culture' of our organisation. If we are a very conservative company with a de facto dress code of neutral coloured suits, we would think twice about someone who turns up at an interview looking like something out of an Italian fashion magazine. By the same token, if we are a company that concentrates on sporting events and promotions, and we tend to be hard-living, fun-loving people, the candidate whose major interests are classical music and bush walking is not going to fit in.

On the other hand, there is a real danger that a sales department can move towards a group of clones. That way they are all similar in personality and are likely to get on well as a team. The sales manager rightly believes that he was one of the best sales people the company ever had. To continue the dynasty, the only thing he has to do is to hire people who are as much like him as possible. Again, it is comfortable from most points of view.

The trouble is that it becomes very incestuous and leads to a flabby and boring sales department. I once knew a sales team in Sydney. They were all the nicest people you had ever met. They were polite, rather passive and there were never any fights or arguments. In fact, there was not much of anything at all. The manager wanted to employ yet another 'lovely' person when a vacancy came up. He was persuaded to hire a rather more assertive and questioning individual to stir everyone up a bit, including the sales manager.

Deciding on the factors for the employee profile

In a suggested format for the employee profile (see page 57), there are three columns: 'essential', 'preferred' and 'undesirable'. The form was not designed just to tick. You need to state what is essential, what is preferred and what you do not want. For example, under sales experience you might say, under 'essential', two years in any industry, but under 'preferred' you could put 'four years in the textile industry'. You might say that Higher School Certificate is essential, that a trade qualification is preferred, but that a university degree is undesirable because it would suggest a person of career and salary aspirations which we could not meet.

There is a tendency to say that we are looking for ambitious self-starters who are financially motivated, but that may not be right. You need to look at what sort of company you are, what your 'culture' is, what type of customers you have and whether you pay well enough linked directly to results to satisfy this money-hungry ambitious dynamo. Frankly, most people like that will cause severe fatigue and disruption in the large majority of Australian businesses.

Try not to request personality profiles which have an unlikely combination of factors. For example, it is rare to find people who are both ambitious and not financially motivated, or motivated by power but not status conscious. Be realistic and recognise that there are certain traits that are more likely to go together. Be careful too about what you really need in terms of experience. If you are a small manufacturer of computer hardware speciality products, trying to build market share on the basis of a no-frills service at a no-frills price, would a person from IBM have the right experience? You would probably be better off taking a salesperson with sound numeric skills who had successfully introduced a range of imported pumps and valves from Taiwan, because he knows what it is like to come from nowhere as a small guy. The IBM person may never adapt to a very different selling situation even though he may know heaps about selling IBM computers.

The example on page 57 shows a menu of factors to choose from. You need to make up your own lists, adding and subtracting from this one according to your needs.

It is worth spending a bit of time on this step, because if you get it right you can then more accurately target the questions in the interview to find out whether the candidate is going to meet your needs.

One last word of warning. A friend of mine had found it very difficult to recruit the right people. So he decided to try a totally different tack. He asked each of the candidates in the interview to sell him his cheap ballpoint pen. (The company was involved in the manufacture of chemicals). One candidate picked up the interviewer's cheap pen, looked at it disdainfully and put it down. Then he reached inside his own jacket pocket and pulled out a gold-plated Cross pen, saying, 'A man in your position does not need a poor quality pen like that, what you need is a fine gold pen like this'. He then proceeded to make an excellent impromptu sales presentation on the pen. My friend was so impressed he hired the guy.

The only problem was that the man was so lazy he would not get out of bed to go to work in the morning and he tried to break every rule in the company's book in order to make sales. Eventually he was sacked. The mistake my friend made was to look at the 'can do' factors only. If he had looked at the 'will do' factors too, he would never have made the mistake.

Locating prospective candidates

The following are the three main options:

- Select from within your own organisation.
- Recruit, handling the whole project yourself.
- Recruit, using an agency.

You may elect to try a combination. For example, you may suggest that a couple of internal candidates apply for the job when it is advertised and be considered on their merits against external candidates.

If you decide to handle the selection yourself, you will find it takes a tremendous amount of time. It usually also means that you will be advertising it under the company's name, so that no anonymity is possible. The alternative, if you want to retain anonymity, is to ask for resumés to be mailed to a post office box number, in which case you will be lucky if anyone applies at all. Or you could hire a temporary phone line, which is totally impractical. If you do decide to handle it yourself, it is more important than ever to follow the eight steps rigidly.

To do it yourself has two main advantages. First, it avoids the problem of communication failure with the agency, which has been known to discard the best potential candidate because the agency's understanding of the brief was poor. If you have no experience of the agency, you can never be quite sure how professional the consultant is who will be handling your work. I have sometimes been appalled to discover that people whom I know personally have been working as consultants for reputable recruitment agencies, when I also know they are not qualified to do that kind of work, and have had virtually no training or guidelines set down before they were thrown loose on the clients! In some cases, they were only fill-in jobs while the individuals were looking for permanent jobs.

The second advantage is cost. Recruitment agencies are not cheap. The fees they charge vary, depending on the level of the position in the organisation and the agency. As a rule of thumb, head hunters at the top executive levels can charge up to 25 per cent of annual salary. Agencies which recruit through advertising and the usual process will charge 8 to 10 per cent for clerical staff, 10 to 12 per cent for the junior or more straightforward sales positions, 12 to 15 per cent for more senior sales positions and account managers, and 15 to 18 per cent for sales managers. Of course, it is the employer who pays the fees.

Agencies do have some advantages, however. They allow anonymity. They save the sales manager a lot of time in screening, collecting resumés and other information, and in holding initial interviews.

If your company is well known and large enough to have its own personnel department (an animal that is fast disappearing in its traditional role of ten years ago), you can effectively use it like an agency, to take the hard slog out of the project, and then take it over at the short-list stage.

In some cases, however, recruitment agencies can also act as superior draw cards, especially if they are a well known and reputable agency. This can be useful if your own company is not so well known.

If you use an agency, there may be a couple of other choices. For example the recruitment agency may advertise the job under their own banner and then present you with a short list of candidates after they have done the first round of interviews. As long as you monitor what is happening, that can work well.

In fact, managing the project together with a good agency will be the best way to go for most large companies.

Tips on managing the recruitment agency

1. Pick your agency carefully. Ones you have dealt with before are more likely to suit you. If you have not dealt with one before, ask your contacts which agencies have produced good results for the type of job to be filled in your geographical area and in your industry.
2. Ask the agency how they propose to approach the project and observe whether they seem to have a coherent and logical plan.
3. Find out which consultant will be handling the assignment, and check what sort of experience the person has in recruitment work and the qualifications they have for such a job.
4. Don't be afraid to ask for references if you feel you need to.
5. Once you are satisfied that the agency is competent to handle the assignment, brief them fully about the job, your department, the products you sell, the types of customers you sell to and the 'culture' of the company.
6. Give them a copy of the job description.
7. Go through the employee profile with them in detail. Even though you are delegating the time-consuming screening and initial interviewing to the agency, you must still prepare the employee profile yourself. Unless you make this an integral part of your briefing to the agency, they will probably go out and hire the wrong person. Go through it in detail and make sure they understand what you mean by each point and where your priorities are.

8 At this point, you will need to agree with them how they are going to try to locate a candidate for you. There are a number of options. If the position is a senior enough one, the agency may head-hunt someone. In other words, they will have a list of people who they know are good performers for a range of jobs, and they then contact these people and ask them if they would be interested in being considered for your job. It is a form of de facto poaching, but is used quite extensively in the United States, where no one seems to mind. Most executives who consider themselves half-way decent would feel miffed if they were not approached by a head hunter several times a year.

9 Most agencies are supposed to have registered a number of people who have expressed a desire to either find a job or change job. Sometimes they are individuals who have applied for a job with the agency, are considered good people, but who for some reason or other did not get the job they applied for. Many of the people on those lists are unemployed. In a recession there can be some very good people in this position. In more buoyant times, the chances are that the best candidate is probably fairly happily employed somewhere else and therefore not on anyone's list. However you should make sure that the agency does scan their files before you start advertising. It can save a lot of time and money if there is a good candidate there. My experience is that consultants will often forget to look through the files, and you should make a point of prompting them.

10 The other option is advertising, and you need to agree on which newspapers or magazines to use, the position of the advertisement and when it will appear. Be careful about the wording. After all, this is your selling document for the job.

11 Ask to see the interview questions they are going to ask each candidate, designed to draw out whether the candidate will meet the employee profile you have devised.

12 Scan the application forms and resumés just to make sure they have not neglected someone you think could have been interesting.

13 Insist on doing the final interviews of the short-listed candidates yourself.

14 It is fine for the agency to check general references, but once you have made a decision on the candidate of choice, do a reference check yourself. There was one case of an agency in Sydney which had made reference checks, but had not found out that the candidate they were promoting had served a two-year prison sentence for embezzlement.

Running your own advertisement

The main difference in most of the steps in the recruitment process between using an agency and doing the whole thing yourself, is that in using an agency you are getting rid of a lot of the leg work. You still have to put in a lot of the thinking. Even if the agency is running the project, you will need to vet the advertisement to be used. They will propose copy and you will agree or not. When you run your own campaign, you write your own advertisement.

The success of a campaign will be largely dependent on the ability to attract a number of good candidates. The only chance you have is through the advertisement. You must see it as your selling tool. The best candidate may very well be currently employed and not actively looking for a job. Even so, most sales people scan the positions vacant, including your own sales people, and probably you too! As far as possible, try to be creative. Make your advertisement stand out if you can; it has to attract the eye of the person who is scanning rather than searching desperately.

If you are a well known and prestigious company, a well known leader in your field, use the company logo. State clearly and briefly what the job is and what are the key things you are looking for in the ideal candidate. Make the job sound attractive; you are 'selling' it as hard as you can. Don't try to put in too much information, rather make the advertisement clean and concise. Give a name to contact with phone and fax, as well as an address for resumés. The contact point should either be yourself or the person handling it from your own personnel department.

Should you ask people to phone or write? There is little proof that one is better than the other. You will get more responses by telephone but overall they will tend to be poorer in quality. Some take the view that if a person is really interested, he will be prepared to write. On the other hand, there is the case of the person who is relatively happily employed at the moment, who may be prepared to investigate further if there is a quick call he can make, but is certainly not going to bother to send off a resumé. On balance, in most cases it is better to provide a phone number.

Since many employed people read the newspaper over the weekend, and will forget about your ad once they get into the hurly burly of the next week, it is often a good idea to give a weekend number too. Your home number on Saturday and Sunday afternoons between midday and 6 p.m. can work quite well, and is not really too much to ask you to give up if it means getting the right person.

Pick the newspaper (or trade magazine) and the day carefully. Decide where you want the advertisement to appear, and if you can afford a display, so much the better.

Telephone screening

The purpose for screening is really to screen out those who are not likely to be suitable candidates. This is important if there are a lot of applicants. You do not want to waste their time or your time if there is really no hope that they could ever do the job. This is especially true when there are large numbers of applicants, such as in a period of high unemployment.

You should design a telephone screening form, something like the one on page 58. It should include both things which are essential for the job (check against your employee profile), and any items which would cause the candidate to be excluded. The form should start with the person's name and contact telephone number. It should also ask whether the person is currently employed and what job he is doing. The rest of the form will depend very much on your own criteria.

Keep the form by the telephone and fill one in for each and every caller. Go through the form in the same order each time. If at the end of the questions you determine that the caller does not qualify to be considered, terminate the matter right there and then. 'I am sorry, but your qualifications and experience do not match up with the requirements for this particular job, but I would like to thank you for calling.' Do not prolong the conversation, and do not enter into any discussion on the matter. Try to always use the same words in rejecting applications, and then place those rejected telephone screening forms in a folder together. This is just to protect the company's interests in the unlikely event that some smart person wants to take the matter further. It has on rare occasions happened that people have tried to cause trouble under the anti-discrimination act (see later in this chapter for more information).

Applications and resumés

Apart from assessing initially whether an applicant's experience and qualifications justify him for inclusion for consideration, the resumé should really be seen as a selling document.

You should take into account the way the facts are presented, how neat the document is, language, grammar and spelling, and whether the document succeeds in selling the individual. Sometimes the resumé can tell you quite a lot about a person. If it is too long and detailed (I have seen resumés twelve pages long!), it suggests a person who has a mania for detail. This could equip him well for accountant or company secretary but is not a good omen for someone in a sales position.

One of the problems with resumés is that applicants can now pay a modest fee to have them written professionally. The word 'professionally' here should have the meaning of 'provided in exchange for money' rather than necessarily of a professional standard. Some resumés prepared by so-called professionals are of a lamentably poor quality. If you believe or know that the resumé was prepared by someone other than the applicant, its only use is the assessment of whether the 'can do' factors suggest this person should be given further consideration.

The job interview

Selecting candidates for interview

At this point you will have screened out some, and you will have some promising applicants whom you will want to invite to interview straight away. Then in the middle there will be a group of 'possibles' whom you should leave in abeyance until you have dealt with the 'hopefuls'. If you need to delve further into the 'possibles' category you can do some more telephone screening and then arrange interviews for the best candidates as you assess them after the second screening.

Application forms

The main purpose for application forms is to collect information on candidates in a consistent way, so that the interviewer does not have to deal with information presented in all sorts of formats. They also may ask questions which are not addressed in resumés, since the latter are selling documents, and no one in his right mind is going to volunteer any negative information about himself. Finally, if an applicant is successful, the form serves as the basis for establishing the personnel file consistent with the required company records.

Application forms can either be sent to those invited to interview, giving them time to fill them out and either mail them back or bring them to the interview. Otherwise applicants should be asked to arrive at a time which allows them to fill out the forms before the interview starts. An advantage in having them mailed back is that the interviewer has a bit more time to study the completed form and then decide which areas require more probing. In any case, the interviewer should give himself a few minutes to study the completed application forms before the interview commences.

Most companies will have a standard company-wide form designed to cover all positions. They are variable in how easy they are to read, and to what extent they collect the sort of information the sales manager needs. You may decide to add a supplementary page for your own purposes. You should vet all application forms carefully to ensure that they do not contravene any anti-discrimination legislation.

Things to look for in studying completed application forms

- Career progression—to what extent has the individual progressed from job to job, or moved sideways or even backwards?
- Stability—a reasonable time in each job.
- Any time gaps—were there any periods during the career when the individual was unemployed, and if so what did he do? Check that all the dates tie up, follow on.
- Highlight with a marker any points which are relevant to the employee profile.
- Mark any points with a 'Q' which you want to probe in more depth.

Arranging interviews

If possible, arrange the interviews for the same day or at least over a few consecutive days. This allows you to compare people more easily. Memories fade quickly. Allow plenty of time for each interview. You do not want to rush interviewees and you do not want to get behind and make people wait; it looks very unprofessional, especially as a first impression.

Preparing for the interview

The purpose of the initial interview is primarily for you to find out whether the candidate is suitable. It is therefore quite inappropriate for you to try to sell the job and the company to the applicant until you have established that he is a strong contender for the job.

Before the series of interviews starts, you should take the employee profile and construct a list of questions which you will ask each applicant, and which are designed to find out if the person meets the criteria.

The most reliable indicator of how a person is likely to perform in a job is how they have performed in their previous jobs. It is of much less value to ask hypothetical questions about how a person would handle situations which might arise in the job you are trying to fill. This is because they will answer the question from principles. They may well understand the principles, but this does not mean that they will adhere to them on the job.

Have a general list for all the candidates.

The list might include such items as the following:

- 'Describe a time when you successfully defended a major account under threat from the competition.'
- 'Give me an example of how you managed to secure business at a higher price than the competition.'

A full list of typical interview questions is on page 59.

You also need to ask questions which relate to their previous jobs. Include items about how they felt about the job. What they liked and disliked can often be revealing and answered more truthfully than the inevitable question as to why they left.

You are now ready to start the interview.

The interview

Start on time. It is the height of rudeness to make people wait and it makes you look most unprofessional. Hold the interview in a quiet room, preferably a meeting room rather than your own office. Ensure that there are no interruptions. It is best to have a low table between you and to sit at a slight angle rather than being directly opposite. Try to avoid the boss–employee across-the-desk-from-each-other situation. Avoid the light disturbing either of you, and try to ensure that one is not looking at the other profiled by a light window. In other words, have the light as even as you can.

There are some interviewers who believe that to get results you should put the applicant under pressure and see how he performs. Unless the job entails being subjected to constant pressure of that type (and I cannot think of any that are), then it is pointless to create that artificial environment. Applicants will tend to clam up and you will not learn much about them at all. If you are one of those who likes to turn the pressure on, stop and ask yourself whether you have any unsatisfied power needs!

Instead of being aggressive and confrontational, rather adopt a polite, friendly but correctly formal and business-like manner. You might start off by saying, 'Good morning, Chris. My name is Pat Wilson and I am the Sales Manager to whom the job advertised reports. The purpose of today's meeting is to explore with you a bit more your application for the position of Sales Executive. Please take a seat and make yourself comfortable.' Don't be overly 'matey' but create an environment where the applicant feels comfortable.

Start with the list of general questions that you have prepared. Go through them consistently. If in the course of the conversation the applicant answers one of the questions lower down on the list, mark that one off and then return to your place. Write down the key things which strike you as they answer, as it strains the memory too much when you come to making a decision between candidates at the end of the process.

In asking the questions, you should concentrate on the results they have achieved and more particularly how they achieved those results. The questions are general, but for each candidate you may refer them to items out of their resumé or application form. The question could be, 'Can you give me an instance when you regained business which you had lost to a competitor?' You might ask for an example while the applicant was employed in one particular position, or in some particular market.

Ask not just what they achieved, but how. 'This business you regained, how did you plan it? What was your strategy? What were the sorts of arguments you used?'

Look for evidence or proof of what you are being told. Don't forget that in this phase of the interview, they will be doing the selling. Give the applicant plenty of time to answer, and make your questions clear and unambiguous.

In the initial stages, you should refer only to the job in so far as you need to find out if the applicant has the necessary skills and qualifications. You should not in this first phase of the interview attempt to sell either the company or the job to the applicant. During this phase they should be doing most of the talking and you should be listening.

Be prepared to terminate the interview at any point. If you have established early on that the candidate is not going to be suitable, there is little point in wasting either his time or yours in prolonging the interview.

Don't forget to probe any inconsistencies in the application form or seek supplementary information.

At the end of the interview, thank the applicant and advise him of the next step and when he might expect to hear something. Then make sure that you stick to it. There may always be delays. The candidate to whom you want to offer the position may be away and you do not want to reject the others until after you have an acceptance from the preferred candidate. In such cases let the others know that there has been a delay and then set another deadline.

There may be two series of interviews. The first may be to form a short list, and the second to make a selection from that short list. In this case, the questions on the general list will need to reflect that, and some of the more penetrating questions will be left for the second series of interviews. In the case of handling the project through an agency, it is the second series of interviews which you will be involved in. You should make up your interview questions and conduct the interview exactly as has been described here.

Often at a second interview, the sales manager's own immediate supervisor will be present, in order to provide a second opinion. Whenever someone else is involved, be sure to brief them on the candidate and what has happened in the process so far, and agree with them on the role they will be playing in the interview.

Making the decision

In some ways this is the hardest part of all. So far, we have followed a structured and logical path. At the end of each interview you should look down the notes that you have made and try as objectively as you can to rate the answers against the employee profile criteria. You can make a short list of the key elements of the interview, such as: performance against the key items on the employee profile, 'can do' and 'will do' factors, as well as general presentation and the extent to which the applicant will fit with your organisation.

Try to write a score out of 10 for each of these items, and see how the candidates stack up.

There are two rather paradoxical issues in the decision-making process. It is the ability to do the job which you are looking for. You have to try to stop your personal likes and dislikes and your prejudices entering the equation. You must at this last stage be as objective as you possibly can be.

Yet at the same time you still have to make a subjective assessment of whether the person is likely to fit in with the rest of the team and the overall 'culture' of the company. It is quite possible for you to not really like a person and for the person to be quite different from the rest of the team, and at the same time still fit in. You must be very careful of the tendency for sales managers to choose clones of themselves when making the final decision.

Checking references

Written references are hardly worth the paper they are printed on. Anyone can write anything. Frequently, what you really want to know are the sorts of things which get left out of written references rather than included.

References are very important and should be checked before you actually offer the person the job. The ideal people to speak to are the former supervisors of the applicant. If the applicant is still employed it is not possible to speak to the supervisor in that job. You will then need to look at their previous job, or ask them if there is a person to whom they reported in their current job, but who has now left that organisation and would be available to talk to you. If the applicant has only worked for one company and is still employed there, that is the only avenue you have, and it will be important to try and track down bosses who have left.

For those who are applying straight from school or university etc., try a lecturer or teacher, or the president of a club to which the applicant belongs.

Personal references are of limited value too. They will tend to be biased and will not know the individual in a work context, which is really all you care about. You must try to speak to at least two or three former supervisors. If you contact just one, you will possibly get a skewed view. It is quite possible that the applicant happened to have either a very good or a very bad personal relationship with that particular person. If you contact three people and find that the applicant didn't have good personal relationships with any of the three, then start worrying.

Generally, people will not want to torpedo the chances of someone going for a job if they can avoid it, unless there has been some problem. It is not good enough to just let them talk about the applicant. They will attempt to hide the negative things as long as they do not have to prejudice their own credibility or honesty. For that reason you should have a list of questions which you will ask the referee. It only takes a few minutes of their time, and rarely are people reluctant to answer them. An example of the questions is given on page 60.

When you call the referee, state your name, position and company, and tell them that you have received an application from 'so-and-so' for 'such-and-such' position. Tell them that the applicant has given that person's name as a referee. Explain that you consider it important both for the applicant and for your own company that the right decision is made, and ask the referee if he would mind answering a few questions, in the strictest confidence.

He will say 'yes'. Then go through the questions consecutively, noting down the responses. Probe further if you need to. Listen very carefully to both what he says and what he doesn't say! Be wary of any guarded comments or hesitations; you may be wise to probe further. Make it clear before you start the nature of the job which is being offered, and exactly what will be expected of the incumbent.

The most powerful question of all is, 'Would you re-hire him?'

If all looks good, offer the applicant the job. Once he has formally accepted, advise the other applicants that they have not been successful.

Rejection letters should be as short as possible. There is no obligation to state why a person was not offered the job and you should not get drawn into any discussion or correspondence on the matter at all. The ideal letter just advises the applicant that he was unsuccessful, and thanks him for his interest.

Psychological testing

Psychological testing became very popular about twenty years ago. It is somewhat less in vogue today, but a few words need to be said about it.

It depends upon *trait theory*, which is a branch of that part of psychology which is sometimes called *personality theory*. The theory says that the personality of a person can be described as the sum of the degree to which a person exhibits certain traits. Understanding which traits a person possesses and to what degree, will give insight as to what sort of person he is and, more importantly, how he is likely to behave.

There are all sorts of trait theory. Some will measure introversion and extroversion on a two-dimensional scale. Others, like McClelland, look at elements such as 'the need to achieve' expressed as nAch, or the 'need for affiliation', rather unpleasantly called nAff! The Chandler and Macleod Humm Wadsworth test measures seven components, nowadays called self-control, self-interest, active/sociable, cautious/self-critical, introspective/imaginative, assertive/competitive, meticulous/detail minded. (The previous names which were used for these traits, and probably more familiar to some readers are: normal, hysteroid, manic, depressive, autistic, paranoid and epileptoid.)

With all of these theories, the elements need to be defined, and then to make them prescriptive in any way they have to be measured. Many find the whole concept quite problematical. How can you be sure that the elements you have defined are a complete description of the personality? If they are not, then there are other factors that will affect behaviour and the theory loses its power of prediction. How can you measure them? It is difficult to know what three units of 'need for affection' may mean relative to five. Is it a linear scale or not?

If one can accept that these theoretical concerns could be satisfied, one is then faced with the problem of determining what sort of profile is the best for a particular kind of job. Chandler and Macleod claim to have charted the personality profiles of people in various jobs against how successful they are. Some of the data could fall under the self-fulfilling prophecy banner, but there was one study which was blind (the supervisors did not know what the profiles were, and therefore they were not taken into account when making promotion decisions) and which does support the Humm Wadsworth test. The Humm Wadsworth test requires considerable skill on the psychologist's part in interpreting the data from the computer.

All I can say is that from my own experience, notwithstanding the concerns I have about the theoretical underpinning of the theory, Eva Wilton of Chandler and Macleod (sadly now in the USA) was able to tell me more about myself than even my own mother would have known! It was frightening.

However, such systems are not foolproof, and were never designed to be a decision-making mechanism. They are a useful input, but the classic Chandler and Macleod sales type, the HMP personality (hysteroid, manic, paranoid, or in the current nomenclature, high self-interest, active/social, assertive/competitive) personality may not be the right one for your company. It all depends on the type of selling job to be done and the industry where you are operating. Service selling roles would require a different set of characteristics from very overt selling jobs.

I have known people with a theoretically unsuitable personality profile who do a job outstandingly well.

Psychological testing can be useful as a piece of information as a part of the decision-making process, as long as it is not used as the decision-making process itself.

If you do send applicants for psychological testing, or your existing staff for that matter, if the consultancy offers a counselling service, as Chandler and Macleod do, it is most important to invest the small fee in sending the successful individual along. It lets the person feel that he has not invested his time for no personal gain, and the psychologist can give the individual valuable insight into his own personality. This may not lead to any changes, but it does allow one to understand one's own behaviour and manage it better. If a salesperson has a tendency towards being 'paranoid', knowing it may not stop him having feelings of 'paranoia' (as defined by Chandler and Macleod), but it may allow him to not react to it. That can make life easier for all concerned, particularly the salesperson.

Anti-discrimination law

In step with all the Western developed countries, even if a way behind some of them, Australia is moving towards providing legislation to reduce discrimination. There is both federal and state legislation to contend with.

The federal government and all states except Queensland and Tasmania, had introduced anti-discrimination legislation at the time of writing.

All states are bound by the following federal acts:

- *Commonwealth Racial Discrimination Act 1975* covering race, colour, descent or national or ethnic origin.
- *Commonwealth Sex Discrimination Act 1984* covering sex, marital status and pregnancy.

In addition to this, the federal government is committed to promoting 'equality of opportunity and treatment in respect of employment and occupation, with a view to eliminating discrimination'. As a result, six state committees and one national committee have been set up with an investigatory and conciliatory role, but no legislative status. The grounds for complaint in discrimination include race, age, colour, sexual preference, sex, marital status, religion, nationality, political opinion, national origins, disability, criminal record, nationality, medical record, social origin, trade union activities.

In New South Wales, the *Anti-discrimination Act 1977* makes it unlawful to discriminate in employment against a person on the grounds of their sex, race, marital status, homosexuality or physical or intellectual disability. This law covers all aspects of employment, including advertisements for staff, the selection process, promotion and working conditions, and it covers both public and private sectors.

In Victoria, the *Equal Opportunity Act 1984* covers discrimination in employment on the ground of status or by reason of the private life of the person. Status is held to mean sex, marital status, race, impairment, status of being parent, childless or a de facto spouse. 'Private life' concerns the holding of religious or political beliefs.

In Western Australia, legislation also refers to status and private life, with similar meanings as in the Victorian legislation.

In South Australia, employers may not discriminate against a person on the grounds of race, sex, marital status, sexuality, pregnancy and physical impairment.

In 1986 the *Affirmative Action Act (Equal Employment Opportunity for Women)* was proclaimed by the federal government. It covers all organisations in the private sector employing more than 100 people. Affirmative action is described in the Policy Discussion Paper as 'a systematic means, determined by the employer in consultation with senior management, employees and unions, of achieving equal employment opportunity for women. Affirmative action is compatible with appointment and promotion on the basis of merit, skills and qualifications'. (AGPS, Canberra, 1984)

You need to check what information your own company has on the current legislation, both federal and for each state where you operate. If there is not sufficient up-to-date information, contact the Anti-discrimination Board in your state.

Discrimination is considered to occur when someone or a group of people is treated in an unfavourable way compared to another person in similar circumstances.

Note that discrimination does not have to be conscious or calculated; it is the act of discriminating which matters. You may be ignorant of the fact that you are being discriminatory in asking a certain question. You may not have even given it a thought. You may not have intended any discrimination. However, if what you ask or say or do is covered by law, you and your company could be in serious trouble. There is no alternative to knowing what the law says.

What does it mean?

It means that you must vet your application forms and only request information that is relevant to the job.

It also means that you have to be very careful in your questioning during interview. You must ask questions in such a way that they relate to the particular task or issue, rather than any assumptions about the individual's personal circumstances.

For example, you could ask candidates, 'You may be required to lift articles up to 15 kg in weight and load them in and out of the car boot. Would that cause a problem?' You should not ask if they have any back problems or a heart condition.

You could ask, 'You may be required to spend two or three nights a month interstate, would that cause a problem?' You should not ask who would look after the children or if the applicant's spouse would mind.

A final observation

There is no doubt that recruiting staff is a costly and time-consuming exercise. Once the new person has joined, there is another period of anything from six months to two years, depending on the position, before the new person becomes fully productive. We will never be in a position of complete stability and neither should we aim for it. However, there is a clear case for arguing that in many cases prevention is better than cure. If only we had managed him better, maybe he wouldn't have left. If only we had been prepared to pay him a bit more last year, we could have saved him, and we have had to pay more than he wanted to get a new person anyway. If only I had taken the time to sit down and talk to him, I might have found out the way he was thinking.

The ability to get the rest of the sales management job done well will cut down on the need for us to through the recruitment process as often as many of us do.

The employee profile

(This is an example, you must construct your own.)

Can-do factors	Essential	Preferred	Undesirable
Primary education			
Secondary education			
Technical qualifications			
Communication skills			
Selling skills			
Planning skills			
Industry knowledge			
Customer knowledge			
Driving record			
Will-do factors			
Characteristics			
Drive			
Ambition			
Ability to get on			
Stability			
Loyalty			
Social maturity			
Self-reliance			
Perfection			
Perseverance			
Responsibility for actions			
Self-discipline			
Initiative			
Creativity			
Motivation			
Money			
Security			
Status			
Power			
Service			
Competitive			
Cooperative			
Recognition			

Example of a telephone screening form

Date: Position applied for:

1 May I have your name?

2 Telephone numbers where you can be contacted?
Evenings:
Day-time:

3 The address where you can be contacted?

4 What sort of a job are you looking for?

5 What job are you doing now?
Who do you work for?
How long have you been there?

Which products?

Which customers?

6 What was your job before that?
Who for?
How long did you do that job?

Which products?

Which customers?

7 How much are you earning now?

8 What are your academic qualifications?

9 How many nights a month are you prepared to spend away from home?

10 When would you be available?

Resumé requested:
Application form sent:
Rejected:

Typical interview questions

- What did you learn from that course?
- Why did you choose a sales career?
- Why did you take that job?
- What did you enjoy about that job?
- What was your most significant achievement in that job?
- What did you not enjoy about that job?
- Why did you leave?
- What did you learn while you were there?
- What were the rest of the sales force like?
- What sales planning did you do?
- Describe the most creative work project you have undertaken. How did you go about it?
- Can you give an example of when you successfully defended existing business under price threat from a competitor? How did you go about it?
- Is there an example of when you initiated actions which brought about change in your own sales department? Why did you do it? How did you argue your case?
- Can you describe a time when you successfully introduced a new product? How did you go about it?
- Have you managed to create new business? What? How?
- Have you prospected for new customers? How do you go about it?
- Did you manage any of these large accounts in a systematic way? What was it? What do you think were the important factors in making it work? Can you give me some examples?
- Can you give me an example of when you sold a total package?
- Tell me what you understand by customer service?
- Why have you applied for this job?
- What do you know about this company?
- What are your career expectations?
- What are your salary expectations?
- Would you be prepared to live in another state?

Telephone reference check

Name of applicant:

Contact: Position:
Company: Phone:

I am Pat Wilson from Australian Polyplastics. We have received an application from Chris Jones, who used to work for your company. Would you mind answering a few questions on a strictly confidential basis? It is important both for Chris and for us that we make the right decision. We manufacture a range of plastic mouldings which we sell into the food packaging industry. The job Chris has applied for is .... with key duties and accountabilities of ....

1. When did he work for your company? From .... to ....
2. What was his job when he started?
   And when he left?
3. Chris has given his leaving salary as $ ....
   Is that correct?
4. How did Chris's results compare to other sales people?
5. How hard did Chris work?
6. What was Chris's attendance like?
7. How did Chris get on with customers?
   And with people within the company?
8. How was Chris's planning?
9. What sort of a person do you think Chris is?
10. What are Chris's strong points?
11. What are Chris's weak points?
12. Why did Chris leave ?
13. How well do you think Chris would perform in the job
    I have described?
14. Would you re-hire Chris?
15. Is there anything else you think I should know?

Checked by: Date:

5

Induction training

The importance of induction training

Do you remember the first day at your last job as a salesperson? Were you sent a package of documents to look at before the day you started, including a formal agenda for the induction program? Did you undergo a well structured program, with everyone available to spend time with you? So that at the end of the program you felt confident and were prepared to go out and start being productive for your new company?

Or was it more like this: 'Oh, er, Pat, yes of course. Umm. I had forgotten ... look, I'm a bit tied up this morning. My secretary isn't in yet, but er yes, here's one of our product manuals you can browse through, and then when Thelma gets here, I'll get her to introduce you to everyone. All right?'

The initial training and familiarisation a new sales person receives has a powerful influence on the way that he sees the company, his attitude to his job and the way he sells the company's products. It determines how productive new people become, and most importantly, it determines how quickly they become productive.

First impressions last. Bad habits can be picked up just as easily as, and sometimes more easily than good ones. It is therefore important that right from the start you establish a pattern of the good habits before the bad ones set in!

The new salesperson who embarks on his new job through a well planned and executed induction program will be more positive and motivated and will see his new employer as a well run and professional company.

We have already talked about sales productivity and the high cost of sales people to the company. We also know that the effectiveness of external sales people is what provides the money to support the whole organisation. If the sales people do not sell anything, the managing director will not get paid. Sales people are therefore one of the company's most valuable assets, and we need to make sure they are as productive as possible, as quickly as possible. The sooner they are productive, the sooner you as the sales manager can afford to relax a bit. Induction programs are great because everyone gains from them.

Why then do many companies not structure an induction training program? Partly because such items fall into the 'important but not urgent' basket, and as we have seen, such items usually quite wrongly get displaced by the 'urgent but not important' category as we all react to the squeaky wheel. Another reason is that the payback from the investment in the induction program comes later for many people. When the technical people are doing product training, they only see the time they are spending now. They never see the time that will be saved later on by the new person not having to keep coming back and asking questions or, even worse, stuffing something up which someone else then has to sort out.

The main part of the workload in implementing an effective induction program will fall on the shoulders of the sales manager, and so it should! It represents a considerable investment of his time and is a very important activity. It pays enormous dividends to both the sales manager and to the company in producing productive, effective and motivated employees. The advantages of that last much longer than the period of the induction program.

Objectives of an induction program

There are four main objectives which the sales manager should achieve at the completion of the induction program.

1 *Impart knowledge about the company, the market, the products and services the company offers, and the customers.*

The salesperson will be expected to know some or all of the following:

- The company—its history, ownership, operations, structure, culture and goals.
- The product range.
- Product features and benefits, compared to the competition.

- How the products are used.
- The added value services we provide.
- The market place, size, shares, trends.
- Our sales goals and strategies.
- How to sell.
- How the territory is organised.
- Systems and procedures.

2 *Establish selling techniques and customer management in the style we require.*

3 *Establish good work habits.*

These include items such as the following:

- Territory planning.
- Weekly time planning.
- Call planning.
- Account planning.
- Customer records.
- Reporting.
- Administration.

4 *Create a positive, motivated and self-confident employee with the right attitudes towards the company and the job.*

Who should undergo the induction program?

The full program is designed for people joining the company from outside. These new employees should start the induction program on their first day. They should also complete the whole program even if they have previous industry or selling experience. This is because you never know whether their understanding of the market, the relative standing of competitors, and the product features and benefits, is the same as yours. Equally, a person may have had several years of selling experience, and this can be very positive. It can also mean they have picked up bad habits. Not all companies have the same approach to selling. There are different styles, and these will depend on the market position of the company, the strategies and the 'culture'. You need to establish quickly the style you want your sales people to adopt, and the only way you can do that is to spend time with them out in the field in the induction period, ensuring they understand the requirements.

Sometimes it is actually easier to take an inexperienced salesperson and train him from scratch to do things your way, than take an experienced person and try and get him to change. The longer people have been selling in one way, the harder it is to get them to change. That is why you are often better off to define in your employee profile that you want someone who would be used to selling in a similar situation and culture to your own rather than someone who has market and product knowledge, but has traditionally sold in a different way.

If a person is joining your department from another part of the organisation, or even from within your department, there will still be many parts of the program which you should cover. The areas which should not need to be covered will be the company and some of the systems and procedures.

Who owns the induction program?

You do! The sales manager owns it entirely. It is the sales manager's job to produce results through people, and it is therefore his responsibility and accountability to induct new sales people. It is the sales manager's job to put the program together and to ensure that it runs smoothly. You must ensure that such very important issues as work habits and selling skills are handled correctly and professionally. Other important tasks will crop up which threaten to derail the program. You may be snowed under with work. As a result you will be tempted to:

- miss bits out
- send the new salesperson out with Pat, the best salesperson you have
- let him go out on his own, even though you were due to accompany him on that day
- sit him in a corner for a few hours while you go to an important meeting.

My advice is, don't! This program is an investment you are making for the future, and if you get it right you will have a far easier life later on. Pat may be the best salesperson you have got, but does he do everything he should when you are not there—especially with a new person whom he can easily impress? Even more importantly, does he have the specialised skills necessary to train people on the job?

Of course, there will be parts of the program that are conducted by other people. The personnel department may be involved in explaining things such as the superannuation scheme etc. The technical people will be covering the products and their applications. The product managers will be talking about the market. You must make sure they all understand exactly what it is you want them to do. In product training it is more important to talk about what the products do and how they are used, than to go into details of their vital statistics or even too much detail on how they are made. Force a discipline on the technical people to focus the content of their sessions on how to sell the products technically. It is a good exercise for your technical people to go through too!

The new salesperson has an enormous amount of information to assimilate in a short period, and there is no point in cluttering up his mind with things that are not in the first instance going to help him perform his job. Make sure that the salesperson receives some written material to which he can refer later. Encourage the new person to take notes. It helps concentration and leaves a reference for later. Check with the individuals involved in delivering this program that they are going to be available, set firm dates, remind them a couple of days beforehand and don't let them off the hook. (Especially the marketing people, they are the worst of all at wriggling out of these things.)

How long should an induction program be?

One could justifiably say it lasts until the person is competent to perform the job. However, that begs the question. In most situations, a reasonable time for the formal induction period will be about one month. To a large extent it will depend on the person's previous experience and the technical complexity of the products and the job. In many companies, there are product training courses that are run from time to time to accommodate the people who have joined since the last one. That is fine, but if it means waiting for five months until the next one, you are going to have to make some sort of alternative arrangements.

The fact is that a new plan is going to need to be written for each new person. By all means have a menu of items that need to be covered, and some time indications for that part of the program. The way you fit it all together and the components you choose, will vary. People may not be available when you would ideally like them to be. You may have certain appointments you need to work around. The name of the game is flexibility in the way you put the

		Week 1	Week 2	Week 3	Week 4
Day 1	a.m.	Organisation structure Introduction to new colleagues Job description	Product training	Product training	Day 7 field program
	p.m.	Personnel issues Introduce the induction program			
Day 2	a.m.	Company information Our market	Product training	Product training	Day 8 field program
	p.m.	Measures of performance and appraisal			
Day 3	a.m.	Work habits Introduce customer lists and territory management	Product training debrief	Product training	Day 9 field program
	p.m.	Explain in-field details	Behaviour to customer		
Day 4		Day 1 field program	Day 3 field program	Product training debrief Day 5 field program	Day 10 field program
Day 5		Day 2 field program	Day 4 field program	Day 6 field program	Day 11 field program
			Late p.m. sales meeting		
		Weekly review	Weekly review	Weekly review	Weekly review

*Hollow boxes indicate field program, shaded boxes indicate product training.

Figure 5.1 Outline of a possible induction program

plan together on each occasion. Once you have put it together and obtained everyone's commitment, make sure you stick to it.

A possible induction program outline for a month is shown in Figure 5.1. This would be suitable for a person joining from outside the company and with relatively little sales experience.

Weekly review

Sales managers should set time aside on a regular basis to review with each salesperson how things are going. It is even more critical to do this during the induction period. It may only take an hour, but it should be done strictly every week. It serves to make sure that the program is proceeding according to plan and that any queries the individual might have are addressed. It also allows the sales manager to assess how much of the material the new salesperson is managing to absorb.

A weekly induction review checklist

- Put aside one hour at the end of the week.
- Make it Friday afternoon if you can.
- Ask the new person to summarise the key learning points from the week.
- Reinforce with your own summary, and correct any misunderstandings.
- Invite questions from that week's activities.
- Encourage the new employee.
- Agree on any areas where more work is needed.
- Discuss the next week's activities.
- Suggest any preparation the individual should do.

First thing on the first day

Before the new person starts, a lot of the work on the induction program should already have been completed. The program itself will have been designed, commitments from others received. Ideally, the program should be sent to new staff a few days before they start so that they can prepare themselves. It also reduces the fear of the unknown and gives them more confidence.

If you have a person who is totally new to sales, you may decide to send him on an external introductory course on selling. You will need to have booked this well before the starting date.

Prepare all the documents you will need the week before.

Things to prepare for the induction program

- Job description
- Standards of performance
- Product manual
- Visit schedules by category
- Customer lists
- Customer record cards
- Account plans
- Organisation chart
- Any papers to be signed
- The car
- Business cards.

On the first day, make sure you arrive early—you must be there before the newcomer. Make sure that you have told him when and where to arrive.

When he arrives, welcome him and take him into your office. Put him at ease.

Either hand him the induction schedule or check that he has brought with him the copy you sent him. Explain the program, what it is and what it seeks to achieve. Stress that it is designed to help new people learn as quickly as they can about their new job and company and therefore make them successful that much quicker.

Introduction to new colleagues

Although the new person will hardly remember a name to start off with, you should still formally introduce him to the other members of the team, and to any other people with whom he will have some initial contact or need to know. Try to explain when you make the introduction where people fit into the organisation and what they do.

It is also an opportunity to show the new person around the offices and explain where everything is. Start with the sales office and immediate colleagues, and show the new incumbent where he will be located.

Some people are bound not to be there and you should make a note to catch up with them later. Give the employee the opportunity to ask any questions about the organisation and who is who, when you return to the office.

Organisation structure

This is the best time to introduce the organisation structure. Ensure that you have an up-to-date chart, stating people's names, job titles and reporting relationships. You should be able to show the structure of the sales department, the rest of the division or the whole company, and if appropriate, how your company fits in with a larger corporate entity.

Explain the company, its history, what its operations are and the culture of the company.

In the sales department, explain how your area is organised and what the key responsibilities are of the various jobs.

Avoid the temptation to spice up your explanations with your own assessment of the individuals who occupy the various positions.

Be positive about the company and supportive of all company policies.

Personnel issues

There will be a number of documents and administrative issues of a personnel nature that are best handled by a personnel department, if you have one.

Items best handled by personnel

- Signing of any papers accepting employment and the rules and conditions of the company. This might include clauses about use or disclosure of business confidential material.
- Explanation of the company superannuation scheme.
- Company policy on sick days.
- Company policy on vacations.
- Setting up the mechanism for salary payment.

Items to be covered by the sales manager

- The company car
  - — keeping maintenance and service schedules
  - — policy on private usage
  - — any insurance conditions, e.g. spouse, and stress no drinking and driving
  - — care of the vehicle
  - — the car policy, i.e. what car entitlement is, how often it is replaced, etc.
  - — any employee buy-out facility (often a good way of making sure employees really do care for their cars and have them serviced regularly)
- Working hours, both official and what convention suggests
- Dress standards
- Company expenses policy.

Introducing the job description

The job description (see Chapter 3) should be introduced on the first day. It is important to cover what it is and why it is important before getting into the detail of the content.

What it is: a statement about why we employ people, in other words, what the overall purpose or role is, followed by a brief description of the critical activities, together with the responsibilities and the accountabilities.

Stress the importance to both the company and the employee. The employee needs to know what he is supposed to be doing and on what basis the company will assess whether he is doing a good job. Coupled with the standards of performance, this will help the individual and the company identify training and development needs, so that the employee can grow and improve in his job. There is then an objective basis on which recognition, reward and advancement can be planned. Present the job description as the basic building block of the sales management system.

The company needs to be sure that employees concentrate their time and effort on those activities that will produce results, rather than carry out less productive tasks. As the individual develops his skill base, the company benefits too.

Stress that the job description is a living document which is to be used and which may change from time to time, reflecting the changing needs of the sales job.

Read through it slowly together, word by word. Pause frequently to make sure there are no points that you need to explain or elaborate. Encourage questions, and introduce any documents mentioned in the job description, as you proceed, such as account plans, call cycles or record cards.

At the end, ask the new employee how he feels about it, adding that this is the essence of his job and it will form the basis on which he is appraised.

Standards of performance

There is a natural lead-in from the job description to standards of performance (see Chapter 3). The key message to get across is that measuring against standards of performance is a positive process. There is a tendency for many sales people to see the whole process as simply 'big brother' giving you a mark, and telling you where you need to lift your game. It is not surprising that such people do see the process as being negative. If you sell the new incumbent on the positive aspects, you will have fewer problems later on, and it makes it easier for you to get the process accepted by the rest of the team.

The following are some of the sales arguments you can use to show sales people how they gain from having standards of performance:

- Clear definition of what their job is, and to what standards they are expected to perform.
- Recognition of what they do well.
- Objectivity—everyone is judged on the same basis.
- Helps define their individual training and development needs, leading to more skills, greater job satisfaction and more success.
- No surprises—they know where they stand.
- Remuneration really can be based on performance.
- Identifies, through the job description of the next position up, what the preparation might be for promotion.

Field training new people

Field training is one of the most important tasks of the sales manager. It should be ongoing for the whole sales team (see

Chapter 6). In the case of a new salesperson it is particularly important, in order to establish the right behaviour from the start.

For someone with no prior sales experience at all—and such people can sometimes be the best to employ—the initial training the salesperson receives can influence the way he sells in the future, more than any other single factor. You have a tremendous responsibility to build up the ability and the self-confidence of the new person. Sending him out with Harry is just not good enough.

Much of the next chapter is devoted to the subject of training and development, and far more will be said there about techniques of training.

Outline of the field training part of the program

If you can find an external course which presents selling technique in a very similar way to the way you structure your calls, then it is a good idea to try to get the new person to complete such a course first. Many sales courses, however, concentrate on styles of selling that may not be appropriate. Check them out. Try to keep a consistent approach through the sales force. The best approach to formal sales training is to get a consultant to design and run a program in-house for your company which exactly meets your needs. If you have done this, then you will probably have a copy of the manual that accompanied the course. Give this to the new salesperson to read before you go out and visit any customers. Discuss it, and reinforce what you see as the key points.

With any new process, it is much easier to understand if there is a structure that can be broken down into steps. The sales process is ideal from this point of view, and you need to make sure that the steps are clearly understood. (Opening the call, identifying needs through questioning technique, selecting features and benefits relating to the customer's specific needs, overcoming objections, and closing, is one example of simple sales structure.)

Once the salesperson has gained some idea of what selling is all about, you should get out in the field. That should really be as soon as possible. It is not generally a good idea to make people spend weeks inside learning about the products or whatever, without finding out what the real world is like outside. Even in the case of very technical products that may require intensive training, you should still get the sales people out in the field so that they know how to relate what they are learning to the selling situation.

Ideally, aim to spend several days out in the field after the first couple of days of the program are completed. Initially, you should conduct the calls to demonstrate how selling techniques are applied and to establish the standards and style you want the salesperson to emulate.

Observation is the best technique at this early stage. However it is important that you explain before each call what you are going to do, and how you are going to do it. Cover aspects such as call planning and, if appropriate, bring in customer records and account planning. This gives the salesperson context and makes it far more likely he will understand and retain.

Points to cover before the call

- Why the call is being made.
- What you plan to achieve.
- On whom you will call in that customer, buyer etc.
- How you will open the call.
- What information you have.
- What you need to find out.
- Some of the benefits you might sell, and the corresponding product features.
- What sort of objections might crop up, and how you will handle them.
- How you will close.
- How you will introduce the new person, and what role he will be expected to play.

During the call, the new salesperson should listen and watch.

Then, after the call, you should ask him to tell you what happened, and you should review that call. Summarise the key learning points as you see them.

Depending on the technical nature of the products, the salesperson should be encouraged to take over running a part of the calls so that he masters the techniques. This should start to happen after a few days out with the manager. The manager will still of course be accompanying the new salesperson. After five or six days out in the field together, the new salesperson should be handling most of the calls.

After that it will be possible to let the salesperson start to make some calls on the more straightforward accounts on his own. At the end of the first week, when the salesperson is out on his own, the sales manager should go along and do the first assessment on the salesperson, and give him feedback on how he is going.

Field training more experienced people

In the case of more experienced people, the process will be similar, but faster and less detailed. The manager should explain how the firm sells. Then, for the first two days out in the field, he should do all of the selling. Then the new salesperson should take over the selling for the next two days, but still with the sales manager present. Then, as in the previous case, the new salesperson should go out and do the selling on his own, with the manager accompanying him on the last day of the week to do the first assessment.

One final word. Going round and introducing a new person to the customers in his territory is not the same thing at all as the process just described. This process is about acquiring selling skills, not about getting to know people.

6

Training and developing the sales team

The training role of managers

If the prime role of a sales manager is to produce results through other people, it follows that one of his critical accountabilities is the level of performance of the people who report to him. Inevitably that means that unless the sales manager inherits an ideal world, the perfect team, he will have to devote time to developing the skills and knowledge of his people.

Most sales managers would agree that good training will:

- improve sales results
- help overcome competition
- improve the attitude of the entire sales force
- reduce staff turnover
- make new sales people effective faster
- translate the manager's sales skills to all the activities of the sales force rather than just his own.

Even the government agrees; there is a section on the *Training and Guarantee Act 1990* at the end of this chapter.

Unfortunately there are still far too many companies which have either no training program for their sales departments, or only an ad hoc rather than an integrated approach.

Here are some of the commonly held fallacious viewpoints:

- My people are all experienced sales people; many of them have been in sales for over twenty years. They know everything there is to know about selling.

These managers are the ones who either never get out to observe their people in the field, or those who don't actually know enough about selling, themselves. It is terribly sad that companies which have this approach actually ruin the career chances for their own people. The sales job is very different from what it was ten, let alone twenty years ago. If they have not through training helped their more mature people keep up to date with the changes, they have forced them into a position where they are ineffective in their own jobs and of little use to anyone else. Such victims often get retrenched or are made to take an early retirement. They are especially vulnerable if there is a takeover. Never neglect your more experienced people; they need training too.

- Sales people are born and not made. All you have to do is pick the right ones to start off with, and then you are right. Either you can sell or you can't.

  Only if you are talking about those remarkable people at the markets of Petty Coat Lane in London on a Sunday. However, that has nothing to do with selling as we mean it in business today. Research does not bear out this viewpoint at all.

- My sales people have been on nearly every course there is, and the only thing they need training on is product. They need to know the product from the ground up. You can't sell anything until you have worked on the factory floor where it is made.

  Training courses serve a very useful purpose. However, that is only a beginning, not an end. The sales manager must ensure that whatever is covered in training courses, is then implemented and developed. With respect to product training, yes, it is important. However, lengthy factory visits, or getting involved with processing paper work for several weeks, is not at all necessary to successfully sell a product. What you need to know is what it will do for the customer, relative to the purchasing options he has.

- Watch and learn. I let them come out with me and that is how they learn the right way of doing things. Watch a professional, that's how to learn.

  As we discussed, that technique is useful for people with no prior experience. However, the best way to acquire skills is to do it yourself. If you do not believe me, ask yourself why it is that your children have been watching you drive for years, yet they still need practical lessons when they start driving.

The point is that the sales manager must be involved in the training and development process. There must be an integrated training and development program for both the team and for individuals, which takes training needs into account and ensures development of skills over time.

The company's need

At the beginning of this book I asserted that the most valuable asset a company has is its people, rather than its products or its image. After all, they were created by people in the first place. The company must look after and add value to its people assets.

We talked about sales productivity with respect to call rates. That is certainly important. However, far more important is the quality of what people *do* in the calls they make. Furthermore, the company needs to develop people to be promoted through the ranks of the company, eventually to provide the senior group who will run it at some point in the future.

The individual's need

Most employees have a desire to perform well. It is doubtful that we want on board those who do not. Individuals have greater self-esteem and confidence when they know they are performing well. One of the real motivators is job satisfaction. At the same time, sales people want to achieve their financial and career objectives.

There is no single person in the organisation who has nothing more to learn. Everyone can benefit from training. As we have mentioned, there is the need to keep up to date with changes in the sales job.

Training responsibility

This chapter is purposely titled 'Training and Developing the Sales Team'. Some managers who work for companies large enough to have their own training department, see that the training department is responsible for training. That is not quite right. The department is responsible for providing one aspect of training, usually the more formal workshop style training. The fundamental responsibility for training and developing the staff remains the sales manager's and it cannot be abrogated.

Certainly, some training can be delegated to others, such as product training, or computer skills. Some training will be done by external consultants, or at public seminars. However, the responsibility for training is still yours.

The sales manager's training responsibility is to:

- identify the training needs of individuals and the group
- develop an overall program to meet those needs in a logically agreed order
- set the training objectives
- select the best training methods
- carry out the training or arrange for someone else to do it
- monitor the results
- reinforce training programs on an ongoing basis.

The sales manager is the only person who has the knowledge of the team and the individuals, based on observation of them in the workplace, and the authority over them, to make training work effectively.

Ultimately it is your responsibility to decide what is done, when, how and by whom, within certain budgetary constraints. You will be judged how effectively you do it by the sales results you achieve.

Barriers to training

If training and development are so important, why is it that sales managers do not in general perform the training role they should? There is a variety of explanations, including the following:

- *They are not convinced it is necessary.* If you fell into this category, hopefully I have convinced you by now.
- *They do not see it as their role.* Again, I hope you are convinced now that it is.
- *It is not in their job description, so they don't get judged on it and therefore spend their time on the things which are, and on which they will be judged.* Change the job description immediately.
- *They do not know how to train.* This book will give you some ideas, but training is a skill and you may find it useful to do a 'Train the Trainer' course.
- *They do not know enough about the subject matter.* You don't have to be the best salesperson on the team to be able to train, but you must know enough about it to be able to help people improve. If you really do not know the subject matter, delegate it if it is not a critical area (how to use the VDU), but if it is, start worrying, you are probably in the wrong job!

- *It is hard when you have been one of the team to suddenly take on the role of trainer.* You would presumably not have been promoted if you were not up to it. Training is part of your job. Being one of the boys isn't. Grow up and get on with it.
- *Most managers are busy doing other things which either seem more important or urgent.* We already know this important/urgent bind. Unless you break the cycle and start training your people, you will always have more important and urgent things to do. You are going to have to be more assertive in your time management and the way you set priorities. Life wasn't meant to be easy.
- *Australia is an egalitarian society based upon mateship, and there is no place for one person placing themselves above another in one sales team.* Wake up and smell the coffee. Firstly, the boss isn't necessarily a superior being, but he is in a supervisory capacity in the workplace. Secondly, business or any other organisation for that matter, can only work with some kind of structure. Even the highly egalitarian kibbutz has structure.
- *They have tried it before and it didn't work too well.* Hopefully, at the end of the chapter you will have got some ideas which will help make it more successful next time.

Subjects for training

There are a number of subjects in which sales managers will be called upon to train their people. They can be divided into the three categories of knowledge, skills and attitudes. *Knowledge* incorporates things you 'know'. Once you know it, you know it. For example, the type of business a customer is involved in. *Skills* on the other hand are practical activities, and the more you do them the better you become, for example, selling or negotiating. *Attitudes* are about developing a philosophy and value system in your sales people which will lead to a more mature, professional and effective approach to their jobs.

The subjects you will need to cover in training will be some of the following, depending on what industry you are in:

Knowledge

- product range, specifications, packaging, pricing
- product applications
- how the customers use the products
- margins a retailer makes on them

- the market, size, shares, trends
- product features and benefits, relative to competition
- the customers, and everything about them
- customers' systems and procedures
- our systems and procedures
- our marketing strategies
- our promotional program
- our company and its goals.

Skills

- basic selling
- presentation
- negotiation
- organising events
- merchandising
- planning
- analysis
- problem solving
- reporting
- time management
- interpersonal skills
- communication
- training others how to sell or use our products
- account management.

Attitudes

- aiming high
- cost effectiveness
- customer service
- leadership
- contribution or profit.

Assessing training needs—training needs analysis

Out of the large range of subjects that we could include for training, we need to decide on the critical ones that are really going to make a difference to the results. This will depend on the type of selling your company does, and the marketing priorities. This, in turn, will depend on the current challenges. For example, if you are suffering import competition at this time, you may need to direct the training you do towards overcoming import competition.

The key issue will be what the deficiencies are for the team as a whole and for individuals. The only way you are going to determine that is by your own observation. Since most of the skills that really matter are those used at the customer interface, you have to get out in the field and watch what they do. There is no alternative. Any other method is gut feel or hearsay, and they are not reliable enough for you to act upon.

Training, when conducted correctly, is very motivating—but not if the people undergoing training really do not need that particular training. This is why sales forces resist training sometimes. They believe that the training they are doing is not appropriate. They are not adding to their skill or knowledge base. They are not learning anything. This is another reason for you to get out in the field and make sure you have correctly assessed the training needs.

Training methods available

Once you have determined the training needs for both the team as a whole and for individuals, then you can start putting together a program. There are many training methods available to you.

Which one you select will depend on a number of factors, such as whether it is an individual or a group need, what the training subject is, how much money there is in the budget, the time frame required and the availability of some of the options at the time you want them.

Here is a list of the most common methods and the type of training they are most suited to:

On-the-job demonstration

- Skills for totally inexperienced people, particularly for selling in the induction period for new sales people with no sales experience.

On-the-job coaching

- Skills across the whole range of activities at the customer interface, mainly selling, negotiation, presentation. Appropriate for use with all sales people.

External formal courses

- For one-off situations, such as individual needs to catch up to the rest of the team, or as preparation for the next career step. Useful to impart specialised knowledge, generate ideas for incorporation into our own system, introduction to a new skill base.

Formal internal courses and workshops

- Similar to above, except that it is possible to cater for group needs and have courses specifically designed to meet our needs. Also useful in achieving group attitude change.

Non-directive techniques

- Part of the correct technique in on-the-job coaching. Used in the office, a powerful tool in problem solving, analysis and planning.

Role plays

- Any skill base, especially selling, negotiation and presentation skills.

Specialist tuition

- Usually one-on-one. Good for technical skills, such as product technology or computer skills.

Sales meetings

- Knowledge and skills related to specific current issues. Will incorporate some of the other techniques, such as role plays or workshop style sessions.

Sales conferences

- Can be used to include workshop style sessions. Effective way of relaying knowledge to a large number of people. Can be powerful in bringing about attitude change.

Delegation

- An effective development tool, although frequently not seen as such. Ideal for planning, organising and analysis.

This list is not 'black and white'; it suggests what each method is most suited to, but not necessarily exclusively.

Let us now examine these training methods in more detail.

External formal courses

External courses are usually not very specific to your business. They are more useful to more senior people who have the experience to relate course content to their own jobs. They are also usually the most expensive form of training. However, if there is an individual need, and no internal course, this is your only option. External courses can be used effectively to explore ideas to assess whether they could be of value to your organisation. In many cases it is the sales manager who benefits most from external courses.

You should always check the course content very carefully. Speaking from the personal experience of running public seminars, a terrifyingly high percentage of people attending are on the wrong course. In many cases they were 'sent' by their boss, who clearly had not understood what the course was about. If you are in any doubt, ring the course presenter (don't settle for anyone else) and ask about both the course content and what sort of other attendees will be there.

One of the good things about external courses is the other people you meet there, and the chance to hear about their experiences and opinions. Good presenters at such events manage to catalyse very valuable discussion. It can sometimes be the ideas you pick up from another attendee rather that the presenter, which makes the exercise worthwhile.

The success of formal courses and workshops is very dependent on the presenter. It is not just the content that matters. I have heard of the same course run by two different people with incredibly different results. You need to keep a list not only of good external courses, but also of the good, and maybe the bad, presenters.

After both internal and external formal courses and workshops, you should formally debrief the person who attended.

Ask the attendee what the course covered and what he thought about it. Then ask him what were the three most important things that he learned from the course, and then ask him how he proposes to use what he has learned in his own job. You may set him a project based on some aspect of the course.

Internal formal courses and workshops

These may be run either by your own personnel and training department, by an external consultant, or by yourself. Formal courses run by your own people are the least expensive. Whether they represent good value for money or not depends on the applicability of the training to your group, and how good the internal trainer is.

To have your own training department, you will be working for a large company. The trainers will be generalists. They may be able to train in selling, but the course would have to be general enough to cover the product ranges of the whole company. This may or may not be a problem, depending on the diversity of your company. Food and beverage companies tend to do it well. The more diverse industrial based companies have found it doesn't work, and in some cases have disbanded their training departments in favour of using external consultants.

If your training department is running courses on subjects such as time management and speed reading, or computer familiarisation or stress management, fine. When it comes to more specialised and business specific areas such as account management or presentation and negotiation skills, there is good reason to investigate using an outside consultant to design and run the course.

Such training is usually very cost effective. You get the sales group together, which has enormous benefits in communication, team building and motivation. You have a course that is designed to meet your own needs exactly, with your own jargon and sales situations, at a per head investment lower than external courses. The only problem is that to make it cost effective you will normally have to have around ten people or more. Fewer than six or seven people is not viable.

In choosing your training consultant, consider the following factors:

- The consultant should not just pull a program off the shelf and run it; it should be tailored to your specific needs.
- The first time you use a consultant, you should be prepared to invest some money in him, familiarising him with your business, your company and your people. Let him get out in the field and watch and talk to your people. It is well worth the investment.
- Make sure he demonstrates a clear grasp of what the training need is, and is suggesting an appropriate course content to address it.

- Remember that the presenter makes an enormous difference to the result. Check who the presenter will be. Try to use consultants and presenters you have used before, or who have been recommended by others whose judgement you trust. If the presenter is unknown, ask for references and check them out thoroughly.

Effectiveness of formal courses and workshops

It is quite hard to measure the effectiveness of training. At the end of a course, delegates may say that it was great, that they learned a lot and that they enjoyed it. However, the real measure of success is what happens as a result of the course. Sadly, much of the money invested in first class programs is wasted. All too often, after three months people may remember the presenter and what the course was about, but little of the content, and after a year most people can not even remember accurately any of the content and only have a vague recollection of what the course was about. Is this because the training was not good? No. It is because with any formal training, unless the following criteria are met, the effect will decay rapidly, even if it is the best course ever run.

Golden rules for success with formal training courses

- Be quite sure in your own mind what the training need is.
- Brief the consultant fully, openly and honestly.
- Be prepared to listen to any suggestions the consultant makes—he may have more insight into the problems and more experience with the remedies.
- Line management must be involved from the start and be supportive of the goals and the program. The higher the level at which there is support, the more the chance of lasting change.
- The managers supervising those undergoing the training, should also attend the program, even if they do not participate in all the role plays etc.
- The key items the company wishes to integrate into the job must be written into the job description.

- The immediate supervising managers must have a plan of how they are going to reinforce the content of the program through both reminder sessions at sales or other meetings, and on an ongoing basis on the job.
- If the supervising managers are not skilled in training and developing their staff, they should undergo training to help them. This is best done immediately after the main training program, so that the content can be used in the 'Train the Trainer' session.
- The first part of the process, as we referred to before, is a debriefing of the group or of individuals to see what they got out of the program and what they are going to do about it.

Specialist tuition

If there are any courses or one-on-one training sessions run by company internal specialists on subjects such as product knowledge, market knowledge, financial skills, computers etc., be sure that you brief the person providing the training, so that they are quite clear what you want the attendees to get out of it. This is most important when it happens as part of the induction program.

As with other training, hold a debriefing session afterwards with the person or persons who have undergone the training.

Non-directive techniques

The basis of non-directive techniques is simply this: helping individuals, through a series of focused questions, to solve their own problems and come up with their own solutions, and hence learn.

This technique is used frequently in on-the-job coaching (see pages 93–102). It is also used in 'quality time' (see Chapter 9), but it has some of its strongest application in its own right in helping people learn problem solving, analysis and planning. It is also a good technique for developing the attitudes of aim high, 'return on investment' thinking, customer service and leadership.

When someone comes to you with a problem, it seems expedient to just tell him what he should do. Or if a salesperson has done something wrong, to tell him what he did wrong, and what he should have done. These are wasted opportunities since no one learns from being told what to do. Not only that, it does not encourage people to think for themselves, but rather to rely on you. People will tend to behave according to the way that you treat them.

The next time that a salesperson, external or internal, or anyone who reports to you, comes into your office with a problem, you have a chance to use the opportunity to develop their skills and attitudes. You will not have time to do it every time, but you should do it frequently.

To see how the technique works, it will be helpful to understand the structure of how to solve problems. (See Figure 6.1 on page 88 for a complete approach.)

Adopt the following procedure for solving sales problems:

- Probe for all the facts.
- Decide what constitutes the successful resolution of the problem.
- Identify all the possible actions, without qualifying them as you go.
- Look at the pros and cons of each action.
- Decide on the best approach.
- Plan how you will implement it.
- Plan a fall-back position.

Focusing the questions

The technique involves asking questions in such a way as to elicit the right answer. The technique is called non-directive because you are not directing the individual either by telling him or by leading him too much through the questioning.

You should start by asking the questions in the broadest possible way. If you are not getting the right responses or all of the responses, then you can start focusing the questions down more. Start asking questions designed to get respondents thinking in a certain way, or opening up an area which had not been considered.

If, in the final event, you are still not getting sufficient response, then you will have to focus more, even to the point of saying, 'Do you think this would be a way of handling it?' That is tantamount to telling, and should only be used when the more broad questioning has failed. However, it is still softer than straight out telling, 'this is what you do'.

1 Define the problem

—not just the symptoms

2 State the objective

—what constitutes the solution of the problem

3 Find out the facts

—define what you *need* to know
—opinion or fact?
—question assumptions
—recognise gaps in your knowledge *and assess how critical they are*
—if necessary, stop and find out

4 List all the possible actions

—be *complete*
—include apparent non-starters

5 For each action:

- list all the consequences—positive and negative
- assess the likelihood of success
- determine the relative costs
- define any downside risk

6 Select the best alternative

—based on *logic* and *rationality*,
—and *intuition* and *experience*

7 Plan implementation of the solution

—logical, step by step

8 Plan for any contingencies

—'what if's'

9 Communicate the plan

—to those who need to know

10 Monitor success

—learn from the experience

Figure 6.1 Problem-solving flow chart

The degree to which you will need to guide the salesperson will be a function of his 'maturity towards this task' (see 'Situational leadership', Chapter 11). Very mature people may be able to go through the whole problem without you needing to add anything to their thought processes. However, that is rare. In most cases there are learning points to be made.

Let us look at the sort of questions you might ask for each of the steps.

1 *Probe for all the information.* Often when people come to you with a problem they either do not have all of the information necessary to make a decision, or they present it in a haphazard way. Part of the training process is to get sales people to come to you with all of the information organised in a logical and coherent manner. If the issue were to be a cancelled order, you would need to know:

- the customer
- the product
- the size of the order
- at what stage they cancelled it
- why they cancelled it
- whether they could take it later
- whether there is any formal agreement covering cancellations
- what costs we might incur
- whether it can be sold elsewhere
- what else they buy
- who cancelled the order
- if we accept cancellation, whether there is something else they could buy from us
- etc.

Clearly you need to have a logical and analytical mind, too. In fact, many managers find that they learn a lot from this procedure as well. They even find that as a result of the process, they often come up with a better solution than the one that came to mind at the start.

If there are facts which you need but which the salesperson does not have, then time should be taken to find out before proceeding to the next step.

2 *Agree on what constitutes the satisfactory resolution of the problem.* This will generally take into account the needs of all parties, typically both us and the customer. In the case of conflict, it may not be possible to completely satisfy both parties, so you may have to agree on certain essential elements. Satisfactory resolution of the

problem might include the necessary actions to prevent it from recurring.

3 *List the possible options.* The first question is easy. 'What are the possible options?' If he comes up with all the ones you can think of, then go onto the next step. Do not qualify them as you go through because it detracts from the logical flow of all the things we could do. This logical approach is the way to ensure that we have really considered all the angles and are not jumping to solutions. It is an excellent mental discipline, which will serve you both as sales manager and in subsequent positions.

If, on the other hand, you get a few options but not all, then you may have to start focusing the questions. For example:

- 'Is delivery the only issue?'
- 'Are there any other variables?'
- 'What do you think the customer will be thinking?'
- 'What else but price is important to them?'
- 'Is there a way we can protect our profit?'

These questions are not to be used indiscriminately. You will be asking them with a specific intention or idea in mind, and you will be trying to lead the salesperson to the point where he says: 'Aha, I hadn't thought about that. What he really is worried about is ... which means that one of the things we could do is ...' It is his idea, he has come up with a solution, and you have acted only as a facilitator. As a way of learning, it is powerful.

If you are still not getting the right responses you may have to focus more:

- 'Are there any options in the delivery area?'
- 'Is there a way you could give a little more in this area and maybe seek a concession here?'
- 'How good are his sales people, is there a possibility there?'

If you still are drawing a blank stare, tell by asking him:

- 'Would it solve the problem if we ...?'
- 'How would you feel about ...?'
- 'Is there an option of ...?'

4 Once you have the complete list you can start to *qualify the possible actions*. 'What are the pros and cons?' Again, if the whole picture is not appearing, you may have to prompt:

- 'What about the effect on us?'
- 'How do you think he would feel about that?'
- 'What would it do to inventory?'

- 'And extra costs?'
- 'Who would provide the labour?'

You are constantly reinforcing the discipline of thinking things through—cause and effect.

5 *Decide on the best approach.* Ask for a recommendation and why. This should be fairly straightforward, since the pros and cons have been identified. However, better ideas may emerge, or as often happens, some hybrids—do options three and five at the same time, or option three but with part of option two. In this case, you might ask: 'Is there any combination of the options which you think has merit?' or 'Is option three on its own the best we can do?'

6 *Agree on how to implement it.* The less experienced the salesperson, the more important this step is. It is really an exercise in call planning. The questions might be:

- 'How will you go about it?'
- 'How will you sell it to them?'
- 'Why should they be enthusiastic?'
- 'What benefits are there in it for him?'
- 'Do you anticipate any problems? How will you handle them?'
- 'What offsets can you seek?'

7 *Contingency planning.* Have a fallback position. This is where you might consider the 'what ifs' and agree on some alternative plan.

Tips on non-directive technique

Keep the training need of the individual in mind as you proceed. Also keep in mind the maturity of the individual with respect to the task and adopt the appropriate leadership style (see Chapter 11).

Depending on the maturity of the person, you can work at different levels:

- The overall idea or concept.
- The key elements of the plan.
- The plan in detail, including selling techniques.

Don't be afraid to probe:

- 'What if?'
- 'Are there any other facts I need to know?'

- 'Is there any danger in that?'
- 'Is there a more cost effective way of doing it?'
- 'What objections might they raise?'
- 'How would you overcome that?'

Keep stretching your people mentally.

Are you being directive?

You are being directive if you start a sentence with a verb or specifically, an imperative such as 'tell ...', 'phone ...' or 'check ...'.

Using an auxiliary does not change anything, so that 'you could phone ...' or 'you should ...' is also being totally directive.

Equally, closed questions starting with 'Can you ...?' or 'Will you ...?' fall into the same category.

You are being non-directive if you start off with an open question such as 'How?', 'What?', 'Why?', or if you use words such as 'recommend', 'options', 'possibilities'.

Non-directive techniques require practice. These techniques are a skill and require experience before managers feel completely comfortable using them, but those managers who do use them find that they develop the skill required fairly quickly and have found the technique very successful.

To develop good non-directive training skills:

- listen intently to what the other person is saying
- be alert to the problem and the possible solution
- while keeping your mind on the issue, also keep thinking about this individual's training need, and his 'maturity' on the task
- show empathy and patience
- be genuine
- be receptive to his ideas—he may actually come up with some better ones than yours
- build on what he says
- show respect and consideration
- give praise where it is warranted.

In using non-directive techniques avoid:

- overreacting
- jumping in too soon
- interrupting
- taking a contrary position before all the facts are out
- being condescending
- being patronising
- asking too many questions. The technique is based on asking questions, but you must make sure the interview does not degenerate into Gestapo-like questioning.

On-the-job coaching

The philosophy

This is the training the manager does with his people while they are performing their jobs. In the case of external sales people, it means while they are out visiting customers. This is the most important activity in developing the critical skill areas of selling, negotiating and making presentations.

It is designed to reinforce existing skills and then to build on them by developing new skills, often drawing on the content of formal training courses that have been undertaken.

Sales forces selling to the retail trade, supermarkets and grocery stores, and pharmacies, and those doing medical detailing, seem to understand the need for this activity far better than sales forces operating in the industrial area. There is often in large consumer products companies a position of field manager or supervisor whose specific job it is to train people on the job.

In the industrial area, if sales managers do get out in the field with their staff, it is on joint selling missions. Many will claim this as a training role by saying that after the call, the content is often discussed. However, this is not what on-the-job training is all about. To start with, when there are joint selling missions, usually the senior salesperson tends to take the lead. Certainly the salesperson does not plan and run the call as he would do in the course of a normal day.

The other issue is that as we have already discussed, observation is a very limited training technique which should be used for individuals who have no previous experience.

The purpose of field coaching is to address the skills that sales people use on a regular basis. Of course, that means running the whole call.

This is where the real crunch comes, and where I have tremendous fights with sales managers. Interestingly, I encounter less disagreement with sales people, who often have a better insight into how training works than their bosses.

It is assumed that an on-the-job coaching day would not include customers where there was a serious problem, or where we are in the middle of negotiating a major contract. It would be to the sort of everyday accounts which we visit on a regular basis. Therefore, the sales manager should not participate in the call at all, even if it means losing the sale. It is this question of losing the sale that upsets sales managers. This suggests that they still have not really understood their role, which is t*o produce results through other people*. There is a training film where a salesperson, after such a training call where he lost the order, says to his sales manager: 'Why didn't you save the order?' The sales manager quite correctly answers: 'I don't want one order got by me, I want hundreds of orders got by you'. So it is sometimes necessary for the salesperson to lose an order, to learn how to avoid the same mistake the next time. Learning from our own mistakes is much more powerful than learning from watching others pull us out of the fire.

When the sales manager swoops down from on high and saves an order that he thinks the salesperson is about to lose, what other damage is he doing? He may just have been wrong in his judgement. The salesperson may very well have got himself out of trouble and gained the order. Your interference may well annoy him, sap his confidence and make him look stupid in front of the customer.

If the salesperson does look as if he really will lose the order, let him. Chances are that it is not the first time, and unless we do something about it, it won't be the last. It is much better to go through the whole disaster and then let the salesperson really learn from the experience so that it does not happen again. In most cases, it is not too late to go back and get the order in any case.

The need to check performance

There is another reason for going out with the sales people to see how they are performing. If we have a pay for performance policy, and we have standards of performance, we need to be able to make an objective assessment of how they are performing so that the company can decide what salary increase they should get. Unless you go out and see for yourself, the whole exercise will be based on gut feel and becomes a farce.

It is interesting that many sales managers feel that the sales people will resent both on-the-job coaching and assessments of their progress as an input to their formal appraisals and eventually their salary review. Yet my experience is that they don't. It is all in the sales manager's imagination. There was one particular case I recollect, where the sales force was expected to resist the implementation of this system. After it was presented to them the reaction was, 'Why haven't we had this before?—this is exactly what we need'.

The smart salesperson realises only too well that he gains from being able to learn more skills and do his job more effectively. It increases his self-esteem and confidence. It improves his results and his chances for promotion, and it makes him better able to command a good salary, either within the company or outside! If he is performing well, he wants the recognition.

The customer's reaction

We have discussed already some of the main reasons why sales managers do not fulfil the obligations of their training and development role. These are the reasons too why they don't go out and coach their people on-the-job. However, there is another reason: they believe that the customer would not be comfortable, or would expect the sales manager to run the call (careful, your ego is showing again) or that the customer would play up to the game. It is true that some customers will realise exactly what you are there for. So what? They will figure that it is a good thing anyway. The odd one may play up—but only the first time. However, in general there is no problem. Is it worth shelving the most important activity of the sales manager because of the isolated problem? This would simply be to throw out the baby with the bath water.

It means, however, that you should agree on the role the sales manager is to play before each call. There may under certain circumstances be the odd call where the sales manager does not shut up. More importantly, you need to agree on how the sales manager's presence is to be explained. This can be as simple as: 'Pat is out with me for the day to find out what is happening in the real world' or 'You know Pat, of course, he's spending some time with each of the sales guys to get an understanding of what is happening out here'.

If the sales manager knows the customer, there will be some pleasantries exchanged. Then it is up to the salesperson to take the lead and say: 'Well, let's get down to business. The reason I wanted to see you today is ...' If the customer directs a question to the sales manager, he should field it back to the salesperson. 'Fred, Chris is the one who knows your account, especially now that I have been in the ivory tower the last two years, and I think it is better if he answers that.' If the customer asks a question which only the sales manager can answer, and there are not too many that should fall in that category if the sales manager is communicating effectively, then the sales manager should say: 'Fred, I would like to discuss that with you. Would it be possible to come back to it at the end of Pat's presentation? I don't want to interrupt his flow.'

Last tips for on-the-job coaching

One last piece of advice before we have a look at the steps to follow. Don't spring it on them at the last minute. Make a date well in advance and try to make a day of it; it is a much better use of time. If you feel you are being taken to only the tame accounts, then the next time you make a date with the salesperson, nominate the customers you want him to include on that day.

On-the-job coaching is something that managers recognise they need to do with the junior members of the team. When it comes to the salespersons with several years of experience, the sales manager would prefer not to do it. The rationale goes along the lines that the senior people do not need it, they have been selling for years and they would resent the sales manager going out on a coaching day with them. It is true that there is not much use in you going out to coach people if you cannot add anything to the call. However, you are the sales manager and you should be able to add something even to the most accomplished sales people. Added to which, the fact that sales people have been selling for years does not mean they are good, and as we have discussed, the sales job keeps changing anyway.

You do not have to be the best salesperson to be able to coach. You do have to understand the steps in selling. Beyond that, there is a large element of analysis involved. I will readily accept that there are many sales people far more skilled in selling than I am. However, if I listen carefully to any call these super sales people might make, I should be able to find some item where there is a learning point. That is because human relationships are very complex, and the selling process is equally complex.

You may not go out as often with the more senior people, but you should go out on coaching days with them.

The twelve-step technique for on-the-job coaching

There is a twelve-step sequence which should be followed in on-the-job coaching. It covers three phases of the process: before the call, during the call and after the call. This is it:

Before the call

Step 1 Check the customer records, account plans etc.

Step 2 Question the objectives of the call.
'Anything else?' 'Can we aim higher?'

Step 3 Review the call/ sales presentation plan
Key sales techniques.
Likely objections and solutions.
Any problem areas and recommendations.
Role play important points if necessary.

Step 4 Agree on your role. Usually shut up and observe the call!

Step 5 Summarise and encourage.

During the call

Step 6 Watch and listen.
How the call goes versus the plan.
Strengths.
Weaknesses.
Improvements from last time.

After the call

Step 7 Decide on the key learning points.
Two or three, no more.
Identify some good points, there are bound to be some.

Step 8 Overview the call.
What happened versus the plan?
Let the salesperson lead: 'How did you go against your plan?'
'What did you achieve compared to what your objectives were?'
Don't get into the detail of the call at this stage.

Step 9 Analysis of the strengths.
'What did you do well?'
Let the salesperson take the lead. Add your own comments.

Step 10 Analysis of weaknesses.
'What would you have done differently?'
Let the salesperson lead.
Use non-directive questioning techniques to let the salesperson solve his own problems. Avoid telling, but rather focus the questions to the areas where the key learning points are.
'Why did it go wrong?'
'What should you have done?' 'Why?'
Role play it if necessary.

Step 11 Agree on any action to address the learning points.

Step 12 Agree on the next action with the customer.
Let the salesperson lead.
Use non-directive techniques if necessary.

Notes on the twelve-step technique

The behaviour you adopt is important. Take the whole exercise seriously, otherwise the sales people won't. However hard, once you have agreed on a date to go out, do not cancel it, otherwise the sales people will get the impression that the activity is not as important as other things that displace it.

Do not be patronising or overbearing. Be as natural as you can. Use a normal tone of voice. It is as important to recognise their strengths as it is to help them overcome their weaknesses. When it comes to giving credit for the good things, be careful to not go overboard, otherwise it lacks credibility. It is fine to just say: 'I thought you handled that objection on delivery well, and you certainly got his attention when you brought out the benefits he would get from the new technology'.

You will find that the pre-call phase is the easiest. The degree to which you probe will depend on the maturity of the individual and his experience. The whole point of the pre-call phase is to reinforce the importance of having records and plans up to date, and using them in the planning of the call. It is to be hoped that eventually sales people will consistently plan their calls in advance—more than giving it some cursory thought between the car door and the receptionist!

If there are elements of the planning that you believe are missing, don't tell, use non-directive techniques. 'Is that the only thing he is interested in?' 'Is there anything which could go wrong with that approach?' 'Is there another angle? ... Maybe in the delivery area?'

We have discussed your suggested role in the call. Shut up and listen. Many sales people laugh heartily at the suggestion that their garrulous sales managers might be capable of doing this. It is hard, but that is what you must do. This does not mean that if the customer speaks to you that you sit there silently, pretending you have not heard him. You will of course exchange pleasantries. It means simply that you do not get involved with the running of the call. Once the salesperson gets into the call proper, that is when you fall silent. If the customer tries to drag you in, field it back to the salesperson as we discussed before.

Even harder is the fact that you have to listen intently, decide what is going right and what is going wrong, what the key learning points are, and remember the call well enough to be able to draw on what happened to make your point. This requires practice. It is made harder because you cannot sit there and take notes. You must not let your attention wander. While you are thinking about what has just happened, you might miss the next part of the call. If you feel you need some practice, each sales manager can make a video of a role play done inside the office, and then pass them around among the other sales managers, and play them back using them as practice for this technique.

One way to avoid getting dragged into the call is positioning yourself physically out of the limelight. Try sitting a bit behind the salesperson and off to one side, and let the salesperson take the seat right opposite or in front of the customer.

In the period from the end of the call to when you get into the car you should have made up your mind what the key learning points are which you want to cover. Do not try to cover too much. Otherwise the salesperson will lose focus on the priority issues, get confused and probably depressed. If there are other points which you need to bring up at some stage, but not now, make a note in your notebook.

At step 8 make sure that the overview is just that. The salesperson will tend to get straight into the detail, but force through the discipline of looking at what happened compared to what you planned, especially in terms of the outcome of the call. It is quite possible that the outcome could have been on plan, but there were some important learning points in the call which need to be addressed. The salesperson might have got lucky! Equally well, the call could have been handled really well from a technique point of view, but still not achieved its objective for some unforeseen reason. Remember that these coaching days are more about technique, knowledge and skills than they are about results.

The most important steps are therefore 9 and 10. When you ask what the salesperson saw as his strengths, you may find that all he wants to do is tell you how he stuffed it up. Make sure that you do bring out a few positive points from the call before you move on to the weaknesses. If the salesperson volunteers a strength which you believe was a weakness, you might say: 'Well, we need to talk about that in a minute or two. A couple of things I thought you handled well were ...' Never say you agree if you do not.

In identifying the weaknesses, try to call them that. Avoid saying: 'Well, what did you do wrong?' It is much more pleasant to say: 'How could it have been improved?' 'What would you have done differently?'

At the end of the interview, in step 11, you might ask the salesperson to list the benefits for various different customer needs and then discuss it in 'quality time'. Or to make a point of trying some alternative closes over the next week, make a note of how they went, and to talk about it on the Friday. Try some simple exercises to reinforce the learning points, if it is appropriate.

Assessment

The main purpose of the day and the whole focus is training. However, it is also reasonable to provide some feedback on how the salesperson is going. There is also a need to record progress so that there is an objective basis for the less frequent appraisal (see Chapter 7). Appraisals are a company-wide activity and happen either once or twice a year in most organisations. They generally have to conform to a company standard form, and this often is too general to be able to include specific items relating to the sales job. However, you as sales manager can introduce a more frequent assessment based on the standards of performance flowing out of the job description, say once every three months. Then use those as the input to the annual appraisal. Or you could do assessments at the end of an on-the-job coaching day. The latter is more immediate; the former gives a more global view. If you opt for the former idea of doing it every three months, you must make notes at the end of the coaching day. It is a good idea to keep a secret book, where you make a note of things as they happen, to be referred to in appraisals or 'quality time' later on. You might keep one for each member of the sales team. Keep them under lock and key.

How to handle assessments and appraisals will be covered in Chapter 7. At this stage, suffice it to say that even if you are not going to do a formal assessment at the end of the day, you should have with you the job description and the standards of performance, to refer to with the salesperson, and to remind you both what the key results areas are.

You should also summarise the main issues to arise from the day, encourage the salesperson and set the next on-the-job coaching date.

FIELD ASSESSMENT FORM

	E	AA	BA	U	Comments
Pre-call					
Record cards					
Objective setting					
Call planning					
Customer knowledge					
The call					
Opening the call					
Needs identification					
Benefit selling					
Questioning technique					
Overcoming objections					
Closing					
General					
Use of sales material					
Product knowledge					

E: excellent AA: above acceptable BA: below acceptable U: unsatisfactory

Key development actions:

1
2
3

Signed: Sales representative ________________

Sales manager ________________

Date:

Figure 6.1 Example of field coaching day assessment form.

How often?

It will vary, depending on the needs, how large the sales force is, the time available and the territory. You might set two or three category standards. New people once a month for the first year, after the initial one-month induction program is over. Those with one to three years of experience, every six weeks. Those with three to five years, every eight weeks, and more experienced people once every three months. You need to set your own program. Make sure you do it, and do it well, consistently and frequently.

Role plays

It seems that role plays provoke either a very favourable reaction or a very unfavourable one. There are few people in the middle. Role plays are undoubtedly artificial, but they are a good way to help people develop skills in a safe and controlled environment. Those who do not believe in role plays possibly do not understand what they are all about.

There are two reasons for doing a role play. One is to develop skills alone. In such cases, it is purely technique we are looking at. Therefore you can break the company rules, make up facts, whatever. It does not matter because it is only the techniques we are looking at.

The other reason for doing a role play is to debug and practise an upcoming event, such as an important negotiation. In this case, we have to stick to the facts as closely as we can. We should ensure that the person playing the buyer is completely briefed and, if possible, knows the buyer personally. Such role plays are not foolproof, but they allow you to see what the presentation sounds like, and may raise some issues you have overlooked. Sometimes they can give the salesperson more confidence when it comes to the real thing. At the same time they are also about practising and developing skills.

There are some rules for running role plays which will help.

A good way of controlling the situation is to role play against case studies or pre-prepared briefs.

Give people plenty of time to prepare.

Tell them before the session if they will need to bring any material with them to use in the role plays.

Make it clear whether we are just developing skills or whether we are debugging presentations.

State quite categorically that the purpose of role plays is to learn and not to judge. Avoid any senior people being present if you can. Role plays are not an indication of how people perform in the field. Role plays are often about starting to develop new skills and everyone is on a learning curve. Individuals should be encouraged to try things out which they would not do first in front of a customer. The result of a role play is irrelevant. It is what the participants mainly, and those observing secondarily, learn from the role play that matters.

Brief the observers about the scenario and, if necessary, ask the buyer to leave the room while you do it.

During the role play, demand silence from the rest. Observers tend to get restless and lose concentration. For this reason, it is not a good idea to have a group of, say, twelve sales people spending all day observing, say, five role plays and only participating in one. You are better advised to break it up into two groups and do half a day with each group. One way of forcing concentration is to pick on one person after the role play to participate in the debriefing.

Allow the participants to stop when they want to, call 'time out'.

Try to make the whole exercise as non-threatening as you can. Once you have run a few role play sessions with the team, they will be more relaxed about it.

School the buyers beforehand. Anyone can play the role of the vile buyer. It might be amusing once, marginally. However, it is unrepresentative of most selling situations and must be discouraged. Tell the buyers to react like a reasonable person in the situation. The buyer should not make the role play useless in terms of learning experience by being an unrealistically soft push-over.

Set time limits if you have a number of role plays to get through or are debugging a presentation which will be limited. If the role play gets bogged down, be prepared to stop it at any time, but do not interrupt to give the salesperson advice. If you feel they are going to run short of time, tell them how the time is going.

The best way to debrief is to use exactly the same technique as in on-the-job coaching, that is, ask them how it went versus plan, what they did well, what they would have done differently, using non-directive techniques, etc. You should run this yourself, but to keep the attention of others, you can always ask a particular person: 'Pat, what did you think were the strong points of Tim's presentation?' If you keep picking, they will tend to pay attention out of fear of you embarrassing them.

Do not let the pack of critics get stuck into the poor salesperson doing the role play; that can be very destructive. You must let the salesperson comment first on what happened, and then maybe the buyer.

At the end of each role play, summarise and encourage the individual. If someone really makes a mess of a role play, try to let him down gently. Tell him that the whole point about role plays is to learn something. 'We all know that you do it quite differently in the field. That is not the point. The key issue is, have you learned something you think you can use?'

The video option

It can be useful to videotape role plays. This then allows you to go back and look at some of the points in more detail. When a salesperson can go back and watch what happened, it becomes a much more powerful learning tool. I once saw a salesperson call the buyer a liar in a role play. When this emerged in the debriefing, he denied it. Then when he saw the tape and realised what he had said, he was mortified. He could not believe he was capable of saying what he said and vowed to be far more careful in the way that he expressed himself in the future.

The technique also allows you to look at some of the more subtle aspects to sales presentations, like the tone of voice, facial expressions and body language.

Hints on using video

Promise the team that the tapes will not be shown to management—and mean it. To prove it, you can always give the tape to the most adventurous performer to take away and keep for private use.

Choose a room which is large enough, and watch the light. Many modern cameras work better in totally artificial light rather than partial light from a window.

If possible, set the 'office' up behind a screen to give privacy to those who are doing the role play, rather than in front of a group of people staring at them. Then the rest of you can watch through a video monitor.

With respect to equipment, if you have to hire it in, get all the equipment from the same place—don't mix and match because inevitably you will have different jacks etc. Use monitors, not TV's, so that you can watch at the same time as you are recording. With some TV's that facility is not available.

Get the rental people to set it all up, preferably the night before, so that if there is a problem you will have time to put it right. Make sure they show you how to use it, and have a go. Trying to pore over the manual with a room full of people waiting to do role plays is not too impressive.

Don't forget to get tapes. Check that all the connections and extension cords you might need are there.

Position the microphone close to the actors. Those on the new cameras are better, but sound on the camera microphones of the older models can be poor. If you have one of these older models, you may need a separate microphone.

Avoid using video lights, they are hot, noisy and quite distracting. Modern cameras do not need them, in any case.

Operate from the VCR rather than the camera, if you can.

Always reset the counter to zero before you start.

Let the actors tell you when they are ready to start. Allow them to pause, cut, go back, whatever.

During the role play, you should sit by the VCR so that you can see the counter. This is not necessary if there is a readout of the counter on the screen. Listen intently and make notes as you go along, jotting down the counter number for reference. Mark the things he did well with a tick. Mark the things where he could have done it better with a cross. Items which are not clear, mark with a question mark. That way, when you come to summarise, it is easy for you to make some order from your notes.

At the end, thank the actors. Only congratulate them if it is warranted, even though their colleagues might see fit to applaud. (They may be applauding their courage rather than their skill.) When you debrief, run the tape to show only those critical points, unless you have got heaps of time on your hands. For the majority of people, to watch the whole thing again will be boring and not very productive.

You will find that the counters are rarely totally accurate. Start with a number two or three less than the one you noted down and then you should be either about on cue, or at least not further ahead than you want to be.

The cost of hiring is not great. For an afternoon, you should be able to get by with $60. Even so, for most companies it will be more expedient and more cost effective to buy a camera.

Sales meetings

Do you ever get the feeling that your sales meetings are becoming tired and lifeless? If so, it is probably because you spend far too much time just kicking over the last month's sales figures. Chapter 14 is devoted to holding more effective sales meetings. In this chapter, let it be said that one of the things you should be doing when you get your people together is to devote more time to the future, and to build in a training component. The sorts of subjects which lend themselves to training in sales meetings are problem solving, product knowledge and role plays of specific challenges.

Reinforcement meetings

The sales manager may from time to time choose to do some formal training himself. This could be at a 'reinforcement session' or as part of a sales meeting or even a conference. He is performing a similar role to that of a designer and a presenter of a formal workshop.

Select subjects that are pertinent to current priorities.

It is easier to handle reinforcement of subjects already covered in formal training than to design a whole new course from scratch.

Choose topics that are consistent with group training needs as you have assessed them during field visits.

The session could be anything from a couple of hours to two days.

You could also run it in parts, two hours after the monthly sales meeting for a four- or six-month period, as an example.

One-off sessions are more cohesive and complete, and allow participants to settle into it. The serialised ones maintain interest over a longer period of time.

Decide what the objectives of the training are, what it is that you want participants to know or to do better as a result of the training.

Break down the subject into relevant sections with a logical flow. Make sure that the subject has structure, break it down into components so that it can be easily understood.

Plan participation through the questions you will be asking. Have a mental list of the possible answers and particularly the ones you are looking for. Set some exercises for people to work on in groups of two or three. That way you get everyone involved, and sales people prefer to do things rather than listen. Design some role plays.

Prepare your props. Decide what are the key learning points you want to leave them with, and have these typed up and put on an overhead acetate slide. You can make copies of the slides to give to each attendee so that they have something to take away and refer to. Prepare any pre-course briefs, including any work they need to do before the session and anything they need to bring. Put together any handouts and prepare the exercises and have them typed up.

Running notes

Write your running notes. Break the session down into sections and put an approximate time for the session. Put down in a logical order all the things you want to cover in the correct chronological sequence. If you are detailed, these notes can then be passed to other managers who can then literally run a program from your notes. And of course, vice versa. If you have five state sales managers and each one designs a session and puts running notes together in detail, each manager ends up with five sessions he can run. It is very cost-effective training.

In the notes, on the left hand side write down the instructions of what you are going to do. For example, **State**: means that you are going to make a statement. **Ask**: clearly a question. Put in the body of the notes some of the responses you want. **Show V1**: put on the overhead slide. **Exercise 3**: In the body of the notes say what you expect the answers to be. The notes might look something like the example in Figure 6.3.

25 minutes	**Selling skills**
Section 4	**Identifying needs**
Ask	Why do people buy things? *Possible responses:* *—they want them;* *—they need them;* *—the person next door has one.*
State	Wants and needs are fundamental to the buying process. If we can understand people's wants and needs, it will be the key to how we sell to them.
Exercise 3	What needs do our customers have? Work in twos or threes. Allow ten minutes. Take feedback. Note items on flipchart.
Show V2	Summarise the basic needs.
Ask	Do our customers always know they have these needs? *Answer: Usually yes, but not always.*
Ask	What does this suggest to us for those who do not know? Possible responses: *—they may not buy;* *—we must show them they have needs.*
State	We can also demonstrate to customers they have needs.
Ask	How would we do that? *Wait for one or two responses. Then*
Show V3	Go through and explain how we can create the recognition of needs.
Video Clip 2	Explain that the clip is about creating needs. Tell them to watch the technique. Show the clip.
Ask	What techniques did the salesperson use? *Wait until you get the response:* *'Asking focused questions to show that the buyer could have a problem.'*

Figure 6.3 An example of running notes for a training session.

Getting the logistics right

Whenever you are holding a training session with all your people together, whether it is run by you, your own people or an external consultant, the same rules about the venue apply. If the budget will allow it, get off site. Otherwise there will be interruptions, the sales people will scatter at the breaks and you will never manage to start a session on time. Outside venues do cost a little, but the investment usually pays off. If you have people coming from out of town, try to arrange a package deal at the motel where they are staying to keep the costs down. Venues have been known to cut or waive the room hire if you stay in the place and eat in it. Use your negotiation skills!

The room should be large enough to accommodate the group comfortably. Squarish rooms work better than oblong ones. The best set-up is to have the attendees sit on three sides of a square and the presenter on the fourth. Lighter rooms and ones with fresh air and windows that open are best. If there is a window, face it yourself so that they do not have to squint at your profile against the light. Agree on timings and catering with the venue. Check that the equipment you might need is there and working.

A list of possible equipment needs

- Flipchart for things you might want to refer to later.
- Bring 'Blu-tac' to stick paper on the wall.
- Overhead projector—make sure there are spare bulbs. Some of the very slim models which work on reflection can be tiring on the eyes of the presenter.
- Don't forget the screen.
- Whiteboard and pens. Use black or blue, they are easier to see. Watch you don't write on the board with a permanent pen. If you do, you can go over it with a whiteboard pen and rub it out, especially if you are quick!
- Video cassette recorder for any films you might want to hire. (There are some great films around for hire. Go and see some, the main suppliers often have open days where you can see their selection free of charge. In choosing a film, make it pertinent and decide how you are going to use it. It is always a good idea to set some sort of exercise

around it.) Make sure you have the right system, VHS, super VHS or Beta.

- Video camera and monitor (see the previous section).
- Blank acetates and pens, and paper and pencils.

Brief participants beforehand by memo and verbally. Cover the session outline and objectives, and send out any pre-course briefs. Give advice on timings, dress code and any details such as parking and how attendees are to pay for any expense items. Make sure they know where to code training to, especially as there is a need to log expenses on training separately for the Training Guarantee Act requirements. Set a policy on smoking.

Issue instructions on phone calls, both incoming and outgoing, and arrange for messages to be handled through the venue's staff.

Some hints on training technique

Training in formal sessions is a skill just like any other, The more you do it the more comfortable you will become and the better you will be. The following are a few tricks of the trade:

Prepare well. The best way of doing this is to prepare the style of running notes referred to above.

Make sure you know the subject well yourself.

Follow the principle, 'Tell them what you are going to tell them. Tell them. Tell them what you have told them'. As an example, give them the session structure and content. Run the session section by section, according to your notes. At the end of each section, summarise the key points.

Be confident. False modesty along the lines of 'This is my first time ...' are inappropriate. Do not apologise for your acetates (get them right, if possible use a laser printer and a desk top publishing program, and check the spelling of your slides carefully). Do not apologise for getting things out of order, no one but you will notice. Don't apologise for not knowing the answer.

You need to encourage all of the people present to participate. Watch the group carefully. You will always be able to tell the ones who want to speak. However, you should also encourage the quiet ones, too. Hold the hoggers. 'Just a second, Pat, let the others have a go too.' Talk to the group, not to your acetates or the whiteboard. Make eye contact and spread it throughout the group. Stand to the side of the flip chart as you speak.

Try to keep to your timings, but at the same time, if there are important matters that are relevant to the topic, which the group wants to talk about, invest the extra time in doing so. You will find that sessions often take longer than you expect them to. It will depend on the discussion you generate. The sign of a successful session is that there will be discussion, and you should plan on that when you set your timings.

At the same time if they are straying from the point, be prepared to bring them back. You can always make a note to cover particular issues outside the training session. If contentious issues arise, address them, but be prepared to defer resolution.

In terms of style, be yourself, relax into it. Remember that people learn and remember more if they have a bit of fun too. If you haven't managed to get a laugh out of them, you are probably being too uptight. There are some trainers who use pressure and confrontation. They like to put someone on the spot in front of the rest of the group. Personally, I find it counterproductive. If you do that early on in a workshop you can get the whole group offside and they will all clam up. Try to draw the quiet ones out, sure. However, do not make them even more timid by terrifying them. Try to let the sensitive ones down gently if they make an inept response. 'I think there's another way of looking at that ...' If someone is being a real pain in the proverbial, then you might have to take them down a peg, but choose your moment and how you do it.

Questioning technique

Questions are very important in training technique. There are 'overhead' questions. These are where you ask a question but do not direct it at any person in particular. 'How will we handle that?' This is a non-threatening question, but in the early stages, if the group is not very confident, you may end up with little response. If you use that type of question all the time, you will find the conversation dominated by a few people only, and some will not participate at all. The 'Overhead Direct' allows a little time for thought before you nominate a person to answer. 'How will we handle that ... Chris?' You can turn an overhead into an overhead direct if you are getting no response after a few seconds, simply by adding a name.

Putting the pressure on a bit more is the 'direct'. 'Chris, how will we handle that?' You can also redirect, perhaps while you are still looking for the response you really want. 'Good point Pat. What do the rest of you think? ... David?' or 'Perhaps, Fiona. Do the rest of you agree? What does Ed think?'

If you are asked a question and don't know how to respond, a sneaky thing to do is this. Say: 'That's an interesting question, Thelma. What do you think? John? Anyone?' If someone comes up with a good answer, you say: 'Right, Rick, that's the way to approach it.' No one will ever know that you did not know the answer yourself. If no one comes up with an answer, then you can admit that you do not have a solution either.

The Training Guarantee Act 1990

The Federal Government has recognised the important role training plays in the development of Australian industry. The above act was passed in 1990 and is binding on all companies operating in Australia. In essence, what it says is that every company with a payroll of more than a certain threshold amount will be subject to Training Guarantee legislation. In the year commencing 1 July 1990, that amount was fixed at $200 000, and in subsequent years the threshold amount will be indexed by a factor which will depend on the changes in the average adult weekly earnings. The Act imposes a levy, a training guarantee charge, on employers covered by the legislation who spend less than a certain percentage of their payroll on training. For the years 1990–91 and 1991–92 that percentage is 1 per cent and for the year 1992–93 and for subsequent years the percentage will be 1.5 per cent. If the companies covered by the legislation invest more than the required percentage in training, they pay no levy. Those companies that do not invest the 1 per cent or the 1.5 per cent will have to pay the levy. Money that is invested in training is allowable as a tax deduction for the company, but the levy is not. There is a very real incentive, therefore, for companies to invest their money in training.

The Act also defines what is meant by training, and what can be considered as justifiable expenses. This means that all companies will now have to keep records to show their compliance. The records will have to show the training undertaken and a record of all the associated expenses. Claimable expenses include not only the direct cost of training, for example, course or consultant fees, but travel to the venue and in the case of in-house workshops, all the venue charges, hire of equipment, refreshments etc. Also claimable are the salary component of the individuals undergoing training for the time spent in training. The expenditure must be totally or principally for eligible training programs.

Eligible training programs are those which meet the following criteria:

- The training program is structured.
- The principal purpose is to develop, maintain or improve employment-related skills.
- There is no other significant objective of the program which is not job related, such as recreation.
- The meaning of a 'structured' program is such that the following elements are included:
  — Design of the program by a person with a working knowledge of the subject. This person should have either completed a train the trainer program of two or three days, or have had experience of designing such programs of more than three years.
  — Identification of the skills to be acquired, before the program begins.
  — Identification of the training methods to be used.
  — Expected outcomes are to be formulated.

An excellent little book which tells you exactly what you really need to know without spending hours sifting through the Act, is *Understanding the New Training Levy*, published by the Business Library and written by Keith James and Judy Balding of KPMG Peat Marwick.

Most would agree that the concept of the *Training Guarantee Act* is excellent. Many will say that it is an administrative nightmare. However, it encourages training, and you need to make sure that you keep the necessary records to show that expenditure meets the percentage requirement. Otherwise you will end up paying a levy, which is, of course, not tax deductible.

7

Appraising your people

'Appraisal' for many is a word with a sinister ring. Many people have the feeling that it is when the company has the opportunity to tell them what their failings are, to bring them out in a highly critical environment and to have them recorded in the secret files of the personnel department for ever. People fear the appraisal or see it as an inevitable ordeal whose only significance is that it will haunt them when it comes time for a salary review.

Yet appraisals should be positive, constructive, and motivating events. It is logical that for a person who is performing well against the job he knows he is supposed to be doing, the appraisal is a formal recognition. For those who are keen to advance it is the chance to talk about what development they should be concentrating on in the next period, in order to perform their current job better, and to prepare themselves for the next step.

The problem would seem to be that most people think that the appraisals they undergo are not handled well. They are not objective; the supervisor makes judgements based on gut feel; they are not constructive and they are not fair. In many cases that is absolutely true. When appraisals are handled well, they are very useful tools, but when they are handled badly they become very demoralising and even destructive.

The successful appraisal will incorporate the following elements:

- Each individual will have a clear and up-to-date job description so that he knows exactly what he is supposed to do and what his priorities are.
- There will be standards of performance so that individuals know what constitutes acceptable or good performance.
- The standards are as clear and objective as possible so that there can be no difference of opinion as to whether the standard is being met.

- The supervisor has spent time out in the field with the salesperson and is making judgements based on observation over a number of days.
- The supervisor knows how to conduct appraisal interviews, understands their purpose, takes them seriously and prepares well for them.

The need for appraisals

As part of understanding the reasons for appraisals, it is worthwhile to just list the reasons why both the company and the individual need appraisals.

The company's need for appraisals

- To take stock of the skills, knowledge and attitudes of all employees.
- To define both group and individual training needs.
- As a basis for payment for performance.
- For individual development as a step in career path development.
- To ensure that employees focus their efforts on the critical tasks as defined by the job description.
- As a means of providing formal recognition to those who are performing.
- As a motivational tool.

Why individuals need an appraisal system

- Confirmation that they are indeed spending their time on the things the company wants them to focus on.
- Feedback on what the company thinks of them.
- Knowing that the system for comparing them with their peers is fair and objective.
- Recognition for the things they do well.
- Help in improving their performance, which in turn leads to:
  — better prospects for promotion

  - higher earning capacity
  - more job satisfaction
  - higher self-esteem
  - respect from others.
- It provides a fair basis for remuneration, leading to better motivation through the avoidance of the creation of 'hygiene factors' (see Chapter 8 on motivation).
- A chance to discuss their jobs and open some formal two-way communication.
- A chance to discuss their careers and agree on the development priorities for the next step.

How appraisal and assessment fits in with field coaching

The two are very much allied. However, the focus and the scope are different. Field coaching is really the first step in the chain. Unless the sales manager goes out and spends time in the field observing how the sales people perform, he has no objective basis for appraising, especially in the critical results area of face-to-face selling and all the planning which goes into that. Furthermore, if there is no development and training as a result of the time spent in the field, the chances are that there will be less performance increase, and possibly none at all. If you do assessments either at the end of each field coaching day or every three months, when the formal appraisal comes up once a year, there will be few surprises at all, and you will have had a year to work together with your salesperson to improve his performance.

Field coaching is primarily a training activity, as indeed the name suggests. There is a degree of assessment because the standard to which the salesperson is expected to perform has to be referred to in order to identify the key training needs and agree on a program to address them.

The appraisal is more formal, and locks into the total company structure, and is primarily about how people are doing. However, at the same time there is a component in there of identifying training needs.

The field coaching days gradually mould performance to achieve the best possible appraisal.

Handling assessments is very much the same as the appraisal in terms of conducting the interview. If you do assessments at the end of the field coaching day, the criteria you use will be almost exclusively about what the salesperson does in front of the customer, together with some call planning. In selling where such activities represent the major results areas for the job, you are better advised to do the assessments at the end of the coaching days. With selling where there are other important components, such as account management and account planning, you are better off doing assessments every three months, using the field coaching days as one input, and then, say, the quality of account plans, the account profiles, review meetings, forecasting etc. as other input.

The content of these assessments will be far more specific to the sales job than the overall company appraisal done once a year. You will find that having done the assessments first, it is then easier to use the content to refer to the more general format of a company appraisal form.

Appraising staff

The first thing to remember is that you are not God handing down a personal judgement from on high. You are discussing another aspect of business life. There will be two (hopefully) mature people discussing and reviewing performance. One way of looking at it is to compare it to the periodic check on your car, or a check-up at the doctor. Do as you would be done by. In the same way that you should be performing assessments with your people, so should your boss be doing the same thing with you.

A large part of the efficacy of appraisals and assessments is the preparation you put into it and the thought you give it.

Preparing for appraisals or quarterly assessments

You should agree on a date well in advance. Do not leave them until the last moment. The last minute appraisal suggests to everyone involved that you do not take it very seriously. Once you have set the date, do not change it. Allow enough time for the interview. Do not arrange other appointments for straight after the interview just in case you need the extra time. The chances are, if you have been using quality time and doing regular field visits, there will be no surprises that will prolong the interview. However, these appraisals are so important that you should not risk having to terminate them because you have run out of time. Typically, most appraisals will be over in an hour, though they can take longer. Allow half an hour more in your schedule than you normally need.

During the period since the previous appraisal, keep notes in a special book. These might be comments from field visits, or observations you make during quality time, or sales meetings or whatever. Our memories play tricks on us, and if we want to make a point, it is most important to be able to refer to an instance. It is not very convincing to suggest that the salesperson does such and such, and then, when he asks for an example, you can't think of any. It is important to note down both positive and negative factors. Make sure you take great care of these books, keeping them under lock and key.

Prepare well. Collect all the information you might want to refer to. The list could include:

- account plans
- call rate analysis
- field coaching assessments or notes
- previous appraisals
- job description and standards of performance
- sales results.

Whether you are using your more specific assessment sheet or your company appraisal form, decide how you will rate the salesperson on the basis of the information you have collected. It is important to use the information as the reference rather than forming generalised gut feel opinions about the person. This is the point where you must be as objective as you possibly can be. For each rating you decide upon, ask yourself the reason for that rating and how you would substantiate it if you were to be cross-questioned on it. Not that you expect to be, but only as a matter of discipline.

Give the salesperson time to prepare and encourage him to do so. Remind him of the date for the interview a few days beforehand. Make sure he has a copy of the empty ratings format. The salesperson should actually fill out an empty form before the meeting. You should also ensure he has a copy of his job description and the standards of performance.

The most important areas to spend time on in the interview will be the variations from plan, both positive and negative. If things are working better than we expected, let's find out why and build on it. Maybe the same approach can be used successfully elsewhere. At the same time, both the sales manager and the salesperson should give some thought to the reasons for any below-par ratings. In particular, it will be important to come up with some actions that will improve performance.

The appraisal interview

Conduct the appraisal or assessment interview in a quiet area and ensure there is no chance of interruption whatever. A meeting room may well be better than your office, as long as you take with you all the information you might need to refer to.

Start on time!

Your style should be businesslike and relaxed. Adoption of the right style for many managers seems to be a bit of a problem. They can often slip into either being overbearing or over-conciliatory. Try to be as natural as you can, but not overly intimate or matey. You must remember that reviews are a natural part of business life. You will be dealing with facts and there is no need to treat the matter as being much different from looking at any results versus plan. The only problem is that people's feelings might be involved. That is why as long as you can be objective and stick to the facts, these interviews work much better.

In introducing the interview, restate the reasons for it and what the employee gets out of it. (Refer to the list on pages 114–15.) Ensure you put it in a positive light. 'An opportunity for both you and the company to review progress, to help you build on the strengths and for us to agree on any actions to help improve your performance further.' If it is appropriate to do so, you might add, 'and a chance to explore your career development'. End the introduction with a set of words like: 'The key word is consensus, and agreement on priorities for the next period.'

Handling the ratings

Either the sales manager or the salesperson can start with their suggested ratings. What you do will depend on the circumstances. If the sales manager suspects he will have a hard time, either because the ratings are not looking too good, or because there are some ratings which the sales manager will want to rate lower than the salesperson, then the manager will probably state all the ratings. If the appraisal is likely to be quite good and the salesperson a reasonable and mature individual, it would be more appropriate for you to handle half each. This obviously works much better if the salesperson has already filled out what he thinks the ratings should be.

Providing the ratings are clear and the standards are clear there should not be much disagreement. You will sometimes find that sales people will tend to be harder on themselves than you would be.

This can be a function of their personality, and you will normally be able to pick people with that tendency. For them, the appraisal is a very motivating experience. They are usually a little low in assertiveness and confidence, and the interview can be used to build them up. You will generally not have any problems trying to talk a salesperson into a higher rating than the one they suggested.

The problem comes the other way around—when the salesperson claims for himself a higher rating than the one you believe appropriate. That is when you both will need to refer to evidence to decide the rating.

In most organisations, at the end of the day the manager will have the last word. It may be escalated to the sales manager's immediate supervisor, but usually it will be the sales manager's view which is upheld. As long as he has been doing all the things we have discussed so far, that is the way it should be. However, that may not really be the point. One of the key things about appraisals is that we want not just to take a snapshot of where performance is every now and again, but to see it continue to improve. We hope that it is a dynamic system. If the salesperson does not really agree with your rating, deep down inside, for whatever reason, then he will not be motivated to do anything about it. It is for this reason that it is very important indeed to reach real agreement on the rating. Real agreement, rather than the salesperson giving in to get the whole thing over with.

If the sales manager proposes a lower rating than that of the salesperson, you may well be addressing the need for attitude change, and you should tread carefully. The salesperson may not have understood the standard required or even the need for that part of his job to be done at all. A classic example is the salesperson of action who believes his job is to go out and sell, and all planning and reporting just gets in the way of what his job is all about. In such cases you will need to go back to the job description and review it with the salesperson. You may need to explain why the job description contains the elements it does and why they are important. You can see from this the importance of underlining the job description with new people from the very start.

Once having talked about the job description, you may then refer to the standards of performance. You may then need to refer to your notes to give specific reasons why you have rated the individual how you have. Once you have gone through this process, you should ask the salesperson if he wants to reconsider his viewpoint. Aim for genuine acceptance of what you have said. If you fail to get genuine agreement, then the chances are you will end up with problems in the future.

Introductory comments to set the scene

It is a good idea for the sales manager to set the scene with some overall comments before discussing the individual ratings. This alerts the salesperson to the overall tenor of the interview. It avoids the salesperson launching into his idea of the ratings thinking he has done very well, when in fact you have an alternative view.

Such introductory comments might be:

- 'Overall a good appraisal, some improvements in key areas and only a few issues we need to address.'
- 'Overall a bit of a mixed bag. You certainly have some strong points we need to build on. At the same time there are some areas, and quite important ones, where we must agree on a plan of action to help you lift your overall performance.'
- 'An excellent appraisal as I am sure you expect. Well done.'
- 'A disappointing appraisal, and I am sure that will come as no surprise to you. However, let's see what we can do about ensuring that we can turn it around for the next time.'

This opening statement should encapsulate the overall flavour and end on a positive note.

Some tips on handling the interview

It is as important to spend time recognising the strong areas as it is talking about the weak ones. Explore to find out if there are any lessons to be learnt which can be used elsewhere.

If you need to criticise, be sure you criticise the behaviour and not the person. If it sounds as if you are making a personal attack on the individual, you will build up resentment and a lack of cooperation. If you depersonalise your criticisms there is more of a chance the conversation will remain objective and not emotional. Say: 'Call planning is poor', not 'You do not know how to plan your calls'. Say: 'Interpersonal relationships are capable of considerable improvement', not 'You do not get on with other people very well'.

It sounds less confrontational and less threatening.

Do not try to change someone's nature. It is quite useless to say to someone, 'Your problem is that you are too shy, you are just going to have to overcome it'. Help them to understand their own personalities, and help them minimise any adverse effects on the business. It is in cases like this where industrial psychologists such as Chandler and Macleod can be helpful. If people realise they are shy, or that they tend to get depressed and see everything as negative, then they can almost stand behind themselves and prevent certain behaviour occurring. A great way to help people overcome shyness and difficulty in expressing themselves is to go to Toastmasters. The key issue is to not change the basic personality of the person; you never will. Rather, you try to provide them with a way of controlling their behaviour.

Listen to what they say about how they perform, and why. You may get some insight into your own management style, or you may get ideas on how the functioning of the department could be improved or the sales job made easier.

Gain agreement on action priorities once you have completed the ratings assessment, and agree on a program with the salesperson.

Concentrate on the two or three key issues, don't try to do everything all in one go.

Resist the temptation to generalise. Do not be tempted to say, 'You always ...' or 'You never ...' in a negative way.

Be prepared to talk frankly about career prospects. Ask them what they want to do, and be honest about your own views. Be realistic about time frames. At the same time, if they are people you want to keep and develop on a career path, be sure they know. You stand a better chance of keeping them if there is not a position right now. Try to build some development training into the program for the next step. This might be formal internal or external courses. However, it might also be delegating specific tasks to them.

Give them the opportunity to broaden out the topics of discussion by asking if there are any other issues affecting their performance or to do with the appraisal which they would like to discuss.

You might even ask if there any things you as a manager could be doing to assist them more. This is close to asking them to give you feedback on how they perceive you as a manager. It is quite reasonable for you to get such feedback. However, the appraisal is not the ideal time to do that, because it de-emphasises the focus on the salesperson's performance. In the worst case it could give the salesperson the idea that the reason for a poor appraisal was that it was all the boss's fault, and finally he got the chance to say so! The appropriate time for you to get feedback is in the quality time you spend with your people. It requires establishing the right environment to do it effectively.

At the end of the interview, summarise and stress the positive points, even if it has been a bad appraisal, and the action points you have agreed to.

Encourage the salesperson and be constructive.

Finally, make a note in your action priorities of anything which you need to do as a result of the interview. Make a note in your book of any discussion points you may need to refer back to in case of questions later on.

Account plans and appraisals

An excellent vehicle for appraising people selling in the industrial or at consumer retail head office level, is the account management process. The concept is that significant accounts should be managed in a structured way. There is a cycle of activities which keeps repeating itself. The main components of the first phase are the account profile, the account SWOT (strengths, weaknesses, opportunities and threats for us at the account), and a search for value added opportunities. The planning cycle starts with setting of account objectives (including sales budget figures, volume, dollars or contribution), strategies and activities. Elements such as relationship building and filling gaps in the account profile are included. The plan is then implemented and periodically there is a formal review with the customer of how the mutual business is progressing (see Chapter 13).

If it is the salesperson who is running the account—including proposing the account plans, getting them signed off with the manager and then implementing them—there is no better way of deciding whether he has been doing the job or not than those plans. They reflect his ability to plan based on the quality of the information he collects. They include both sales results and some other objectives. The activities defined are the most likely actions to get to the result we want. We can see immediately if the account manager has been doing the job, and if the plans are going wrong, we can correct them before it is too late. Clearly there will be other factors to be taken into account, such as the account manager's skills in selling, negotiating and presentation skills, which we will determine on field visits. As one of the key criteria for appraisals, the account management system works very well.

Some general points about appraisals

Dismissal legislation is becoming tighter and tighter. If you need to dismiss someone you must log all the discussions you have, and particularly appraisals. You may even have to present them in court! If you need to you can put a salesperson on monthly appraisal. If you are considering dismissing someone, it is suggested that you advise your own immediate supervisor and that you take advice either from your own legal department and personnel office or from the organisation which is your legal representative (see Chapter 12).

Appraisals should be signed as correct by both parties. If agreement cannot be reached in an appraisal interview, there should be a path to escalate the matter to the next higher level of supervision.

Salary reviews depend on the content of appraisals. In a payment for performance system, and most companies claim to have one, the appraisal will be the major input into remuneration decisions. However, the salary review should not be held at the same time as the appraisal. It should be held as a separate meeting.

When the sales manager has been promoted from the ranks, he is faced with having to appraise his former peers. Many find this an intimidating experience. Both the sales manager and the salesperson are going to feel a bit more tense than usual. It is perhaps more important than ever in these cases to dwell for a few moments on the introductory statements about the need for the appraisal from both the company's and the individual's points of view. The sales manager should stress the objective nature of the process and try to make the interview as neutral as possible. The sad fact of life for mateship, is that when one of the members of a team is promoted to the position of a manager of that team, they simply are no longer one of the 'boys'. If they are not prepared to accept that, then they were not the right choice.

Avoid the stereotype traps

Because of their own personalities there is a tendency for managers to fall into one of the three main types of inappropriate behaviour in appraising. Try to avoid them.

The tyrant. His mind is made up and he does not want to be confused with the facts. Overly assertive and often aggressive, he has made up his mind what is wrong with this person, and uses the appraisal as the ideal time to tell him. He tends not to listen to what the salesperson says and will dominate the whole interview. He often criticises personality traits and leaves the salesperson at the end of the interview totally demoralised and in a shaking state of frustration and emotion.

The unprepared. He usually does not take appraisals seriously and does not understand why they are important. He will leave them until the last possible moment, and then will treat them as a form-filling exercise to keep the personnel department in a job. He does not prepare, has rarely if ever been out in the field to observe how his people operate, and makes his ratings decisions by the seat of the pants. He will rush the interview, not want to take the time to talk about any of the issues, and will leave the salesperson with the feeling that the whole exercise was a complete waste of time.

The manager who wants to be loved. He is terrified of offending anyone and wants very much to be liked by the sales people. If questioned or challenged he will back down and can let himself be manipulated into changing his rating for a higher one. In general he tends to be 'soft' on the ratings, giving people the benefit of the doubt so that they end up with higher ratings than other managers would give. This can create some real prima donnas, especially with people who are reasonably good. The problem is that they develop unreasonable expectations from their careers which eventually are disappointed. The poor performer is the one who gains from such managers while the good ones will resent it that the manager has not got the guts to give them the recognition they deserve relative to the others.

Designing your own assessment form

There will be no degrees of freedom on the company-wide annual appraisal form. The items to be rated will be defined as well as the ratings system. Most systems, including the widely used Hay scheme, have an uneven number of rating levels. Typically they will use ratings such as: Excellent, Above Average, Average, Below Average and Unacceptable. There is an enormous tendency to put people in the 'average' band because it is not contentious. However, that means that there is no differentiation in salary review at the end of the day between those who are doing quite well and those who are not. For this reason there is a good case to be made for the assessment forms that you will be using on field coaching days or once a quarter, and which you can design yourself because they are outside the company system, to use only four rating levels. They would be: Excellent or Outstanding, Above Acceptable, Below Acceptable and Unsatisfactory.

Acceptable is a better word than average in the sense that we don't want to encourage people to be average. Having no middle category to put everyone into will force the discipline of differentiating between the good performers and the poor performers.

You should look at the job description to decide what are the key items to include in your assessment form. It is easier to divide the form into groups such as Knowledge, Planning, Skills and Reporting, and then to put the few key items down under each heading. Resist the temptation to put more items down. Keep it as simple as you can.

Do not forget to leave enough space to address agreed action priorities.

If you want to, you can have two forms, one for field coaching day assessments, which addresses the customer interface skills in detail, and then another form to be used for your quarterly assessments, which would include broader issues such as account planning or

QUARTERLY ASSESSMENT FORM

	Ratings				
	E	AA	BA	U	Comments
Planning					
Call plans					
Account plans					
Territory planning					
Time management					
Knowledge					
Customers					
Market					
Products					
Systems & procedures					
Skills					
Needs identification					
Benefit selling					
Handling objections					
Closing					
Presentation skills					
Negotiation skills					
Reporting					
Attitude					
Aim high					
Profit orientation					
Cooperation					

E: excellent AA: above acceptable BA: below acceptable U: unsatisfactory

Priority development activities

1
2
3
4

Signed: Sales representative ______________

Sales manager ______________

Date:

Figure 7.1 Example of quarterly assessment form.

reporting. Make forms accountable; in other words, both the sales manager and the salesperson sign them.

Management by objectives

Many companies have a management by objectives system, also known as MBO. This simply means that there is agreement between the sales manager and the salesperson at the start of any period as to what the salesperson is to be judged on for that period. The idea is that it allows focus on the key challenges of the period. The extent to which MBO works well as a stand-alone system depends on the type of job. If the job is very project centred, it works very well. The manager and the subordinate can agree what are the main projects for the period and agree on what exactly is to be achieved. It may work better than just basing appraisal on a job description, because the actual content of the job will vary with the projects being undertaken. There are not too many jobs which would fall into this category. Perhaps some of the research and development jobs, but certainly no sales jobs. In sales jobs there will always be a large component of managing day-to-day activities. For this reason there are some who feel that MBO is too limited. It focuses on a few items but ignores the management of the day-to-day business which might make up 80 per cent or more of the results areas of the job.

In this case, the best solution is to combine the two systems. Have the standard appraisal or assessment forms as we have discussed them based on the job description, and then add to the form any specific results which we agree with the salesperson they should achieve. You add on an MBO component at the end. That component will change for every appraisal period, and will be agreed between the sales manager and the salesperson at the end of every period for the next period.

8

Motivation

Introduction

One of the most common responses I receive from sales managers when I ask them what their current priorities are, is motivation. It seems every sales manager has at least one motivational problem on his hands at any given time. Managers find motivation hard to deal with. Maybe that is why when sales managers write their employee profiles, the word 'self-motivated' often creeps in.

We all talk about motivation; it is, after all, a common everyday word. While we all know what it means, it is hard to come up with a clear definition for motivation as we mean it in a business sense. Since motivation is fundamental to us achieving the best results from our team, it is a critical activity of managers. Before we start talking about how we might practise it, let us try to agree on a definition.

Motivation is 'creating the environment in which the individual consistently performs to the best of his abilities'. In fact, motivation is a subject matter for psychology. Again, the psychologists have difficulty defining it, because they tend to do so in terms of the particular theory which they subscribe to. The behaviourists talk about 'energising' and 'activity levels'. There will be aspects of all of these definitions which will have some meaning to us, but the lay person is always left with the feeling that none of them really says it all. This is partly because there are also many theories of motivation, and the same can be said of the theories; there are many elements which we can relate to, but no single one which we can say encapsulates the whole subject.

The best thing the sales manager can do is to know a bit about the major theories and take from them whatever he finds appropriate to a particular situation. This is in fact exactly what a good psychologist or psychiatrist does. They pick therapies based on the different theories of personality, and then use whichever one is right under the circumstances.

If for the time being we can agree on the definition above, we then have to decide how to 'create the environment' referred to. It must be remembered that we are here talking about the deepest part of our involvement in human behaviour. Human behaviour is very complex, and many of the elements of motivation are not on the individual's list for open discussion. Many of us find it hard to be open and honest about motivational issues. There are some which are socially accepted as being valid motivators, such as money, promotion, job satisfaction or maybe not liking your boss. The degree to which these are acceptable depends on the culture or society. They may not be acceptable in Asian societies, for example. Equally, there are powerful motivational issues which people feel it is not acceptable to talk about. These include factors such as pride, status, the need to be appreciated or liked, security or the need for power.

That is one of the reasons why 'exit interviews' will often not reveal the real reason a person is leaving. Especially so late in the day, when you have decided to leave a company, why would you get involved in some painful revelations about your secret feelings? Even if the reason you left was that you felt that you didn't fit in, you had a different background from your colleagues, and would find it hard to manage them and didn't particularly get on with them, at an

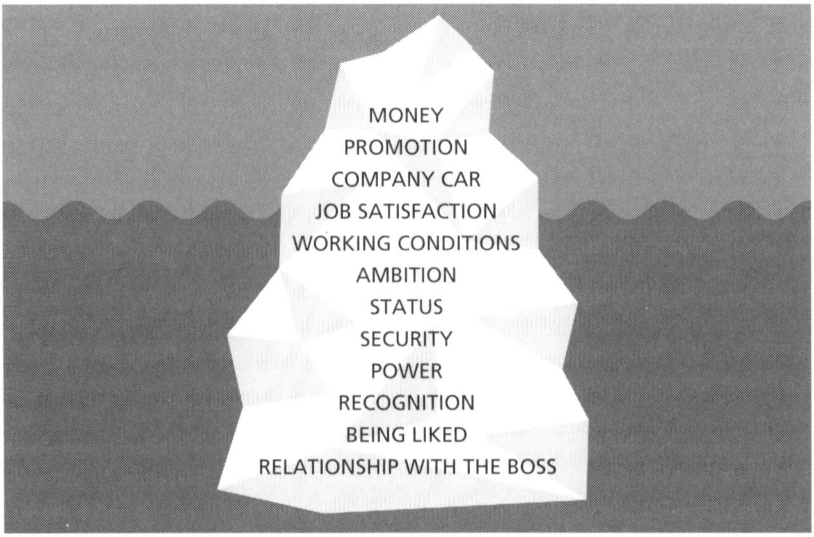

Figure 8.1 The motivational iceberg.

exit interview you would probably say that you were leaving for more money or better career prospects. It's just easier and doesn't rock the boat. Don't put too much store by exit interviews.

Asking the question of a salesperson, such as 'You don't seem as motivated as you were, what is wrong?', is just as likely to give you the wrong answers for the same reasons. When it comes to motivation, you have to delve a bit deeper and do more consistent work in getting to know your people.

Look at the motivational iceberg on page 128. The concept is that some motivational issues will be visible above the surface, but the most important ones may very well be lurking dangerously below the surface. Ask yourselves honestly which ones are motivational issues for you. Then ask yourself whether you think your line manager knows. Would it make life easier for you if he did know? Would you tell him? Under what circumstances would you tell him? Now you will be beginning to get some insight as to how difficult motivation can be. For most managers, it is like trying to solve a puzzle with no clues.

Some facts about motivation

Before we review some of the approaches to motivation by the various theorists, let us make some statements where there is common ground.

Everyone has needs. When these needs are being satisfied, people are more likely to work productively. When needs are not being satisfied, the degree of commitment is greatly reduced. Every individual is different and has different needs. You cannot project what you yourself feel about something and then expect others to feel the same way. Because they are not you. There may be similarities because needs, or at least perceived needs, are to a large extent formed by society. Recognise that Australian society is different from American, Greek, British, Italian or Japanese society. It is these common needs that companies try to address in the way they structure remuneration packages and working conditions. We should recognise that the values of society are changing. One of the challenges of the future will be to structure the employee–employer relationship in such a way that the needs of both can be satisfied. The chances are that as the younger generation becomes disillusioned with consumerism, quality of life will become a more important issue.

A person's needs will change over time. Many needs will depend upon a person's personal circumstances. Others will depend on personality make-up and will tend to be more durable. It is inconceivable that a person's needs satisfaction in their personal and social lives would not affect the motivation in their business life, and vice versa. We all understand that the person whose partner has left him is going to be depressed and demoralised in his work too. However, we also need to appreciate that the person who has been president of the local tennis club, and who is suddenly dumped, will also be demoralised.

All of this means that you can never take anything for granted, and unless you really know your people, it is going to be hard to understand their motivations.

Review of motivational theories

Theories of personality and of other aspects of psychology follow the current thinking of the times. This is a well known phenomenon called *Zeitgeist*, literally meaning 'time ghost'.

As psychology branched away from philosophy at the end of the nineteenth century, it was predictable that the early theories of motivation would follow very similar lines to the main approach at that time, namely behaviourism. This remained the case for a number of years.

Rewards and punishments

It is hard to ascribe the principle to one theorist because there were so many at the time. The idea simply was this: to motivate someone all you had to do was to reward them when they did the job right and to punish them when they did not. The reward encourages the person to repeat the behaviour and the punishment discourages them from repeating it. In a simplistic way, behaviour can be modified in this way. In the very early stages of life, we know that such a strategy can produce results. We use it with our children when they are young. However, we also know it does not work as well as the children develop.

In the workplace it has some serious limitations. The appearance of unions and alternatives of employment made the principle of punishments non-viable. An employer who tried this method of motivation today would end up with strikes and no employees.

Mechanistic motivation

Frederick W. Taylor studied the way workers in a steel mill performed their jobs. He separated jobs into their component parts and trained people to specialise. In the industrial area it created a revolution, identifying the optimum work practices and lifting productivity. However, the approach was geared almost entirely to the work itself, and in the course of time, limits were reached and apathy set in. The moral seems to be that machinery and processes will run only as well as people want to operate them. Taylor's approach to motivation may have some value in lifting productivity and, concerning sales, has implications for getting our systems and structures right if we want to get the best out of people. However, his approach did not take into account the individual, and the things which drive him.

Human relations movement

It was Douglas McGregor who took a large step in this direction with his well known Theory X–Theory Y approach. His Theory X said that most people inherently do not like work and are lazy. They prefer to be directed and are not interested in assuming responsibility. That most people have little capacity for creativity in their jobs and that they have to be coerced into doing their jobs. The way to motivate these Theory X people is to strictly supervise them, provide them with the security of a job and tell them exactly what to do. Control is the key to managing basically unreliable, uncommitted, irresponsible and immature people. By anyone's standards, it is a very depressing view of the work force! Yet as we read it, there will be elements of it we can agree with. One gets the impression that certain government departments fall into this mode and indeed some of the larger banks and utilities. However, such organisations are not inevitable, which suggests that not all people are as McGregor suggests in his Theory X.

Indeed, McGregor proposes an alternative type of person, the Theory Y person. Theory Y says that people in fact do enjoy work as long as the conditions are favourable, and seek it out as a natural part of human activity. People are not inherently lazy and unreliable, but as long as they understand and are committed to the corporate goals, they will direct and apply themselves to these goals. Most people have the ability to be creative, given the right conditions, and will tend to seek responsibility if they are committed to goals. To motivate these people, the manager should provide the right working environment, and a mixture of recognition, satisfaction in their jobs, involvement in the business, as well as the basic security supplied to Theory X people.

This sounds a bit more like the way we would like things to be. In some organisations they probably come close to it. Which would we prefer, Theory X people or Theory Y? Obviously, Theory Y.

McGregor went on to say that the type of people you end up with will to a large extent depend on how you manage them. If you manage people in a Theory X way, treating them as lazy and unwilling to work, and controlling them closely, that is the way they will start to react. Imagine a group of people which has been managed for a long time by a Theory X manager, and suddenly a new boss comes along who has always managed in a Theory Y style and immediately changes the management style of the group. How will they react? I suggest they will be confused, all at sea and very nervous. They will not be used to it and will not know how to behave. They will suddenly feel very insecure. McGregor says that in moving a group of people from Theory X to Theory Y, we must be careful to take it very slowly. There are perhaps some lessons here for what might happen in privatisation. As a manager, look at your own style and the style to which your people have been accustomed to being managed. If you want to move more towards Theory Y, you will get better results, but manage change carefully.

Theory X	**Theory Y**
1 People dislike work and will avoid it if possible	1 Work is necessary to people's psychological growth
2 People must be forced or bribed to make the right effort	2 People want to be interested in their work and, under the right conditions, they can enjoy it
3 People would rather be directed than accept responsibilities, which they avoid	3 People will direct themselves towards an accepted target
	4 People will seek, and accept responsibility under the right conditions
	5 The discipline people impose on themselves is more effective, and can be more severe, than any imposed on them
4 People are motivated mainly by money	6 Under the right conditions, people are motivated by the desire to realise their own potential
5 People are motivated by anxiety about their security	7 Creativity and ingenuity are widely distributed and grossly under-used
6 Most people have little creativity —except when getting round management rules!	

Figure 8.2 McGregor's Theory X and Theory Y

Hierarchical needs

As we move further away from the more scientific approaches towards a real understanding of human behaviour, we come to Abraham Maslow, one of this century's great psychologists. He did most of his work in the 1950s and 1960s, and is most closely identified with the concept of 'self-actualisation'. Maslow writes that each individual has an inner core, an essential nature which is very resistant to change. This inner nature includes instinctive needs, capacities, talents, physiological needs. Each person has some common characteristics with all other humans and some individual ones unique to that person. Healthy growth is growth towards the full expression of one's inner nature. The achievement of this is what is called 'self-actualisation'. It is the actualisation of these latent capacities and potentialities towards the 'full functioning' of the human and personal essence.

Since this is the direction of natural healthy growth, it follows that the practice of motivation is providing the environment for the individual to achieve this growth.

Maslow then expressed the basic needs in a hierarchy, the most well known of his concepts. The hierarchy starts off with physiological needs, and then progresses to safety, social, self-esteem or ego, and then finally to self-actualisation. He says that these needs have to be satisfied in the same particular order, starting off with the most basic physiological needs, like food, drink and sleep. The next level is security and shelter, and then progresses through such basic social needs as the need for love. Eventually one arrives at the higher levels of need such as self-esteem and respect, until the pinnacle, which is 'self-actualisation' or 'self-fulfilment'.

The triangle of hierarchical needs shown in Figure 8.3 on page 134 shows how the needs build up.

In a business sense we could slightly reinterpret some of these needs and put labels on them which help us understand how Maslow could be applied to motivation at work. There is much that most of us can identify with in Maslow's approach. If any of you have been through a take-over or a situation where your company has been sold, you will have seen an enormous change in the levels of motivation. One day you might have been working close to the upper levels on the Maslow scale, and then suddenly it is not clear whether you will even have a job. All the concerns about recognition, job satisfaction, team spirit and so on, go out the window. During the period of uncertainty, and in the case of involvement of the FIRB (the Foreign Investment Review Board) that can be months and months, you will find that the organisation hardly functions. All the energy is diverted into worrying about what is

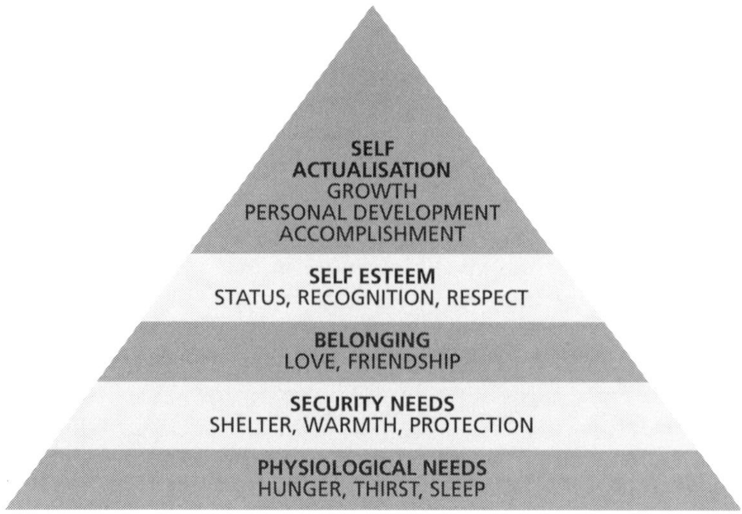

Maslow's hierarchical needs

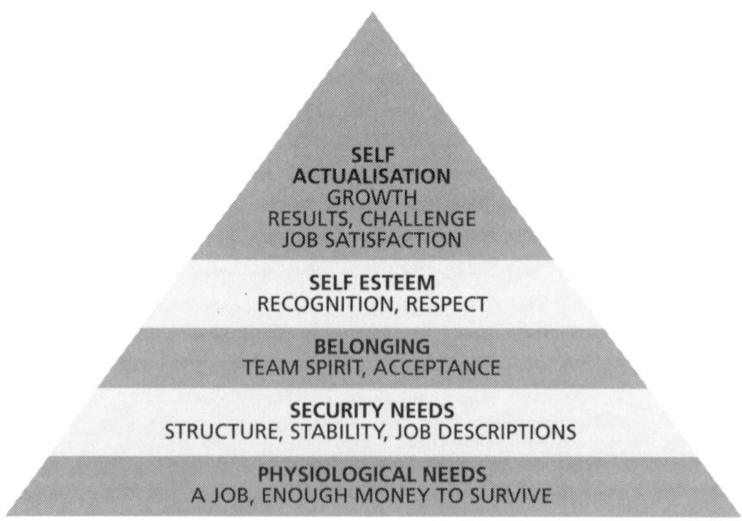

Maslow and employment needs?

Figure 8.3 Hierarchical needs.

going to happen. Who will have a job? Will the sale go through? Will the new owners keep it going or close us down? Will the job be the same? The level of motivation is the lowest one, and that is reflected in the quality of the company's total operation.

This demonstrates the point that once having achieved a certain level of motivation does not necessarily mean that one stays at that level. As soon as one of the lower needs are not being met, you fall back to that level of motivation.

Satisfiers and dissatisfiers

Frederick Herzberg conducted a study of a large number of people in a wide variety of jobs and at different levels of seniority. He asked two basic questions. What are the things which cause you to experience extreme dissatisfaction in your job, and what are the things which cause you extreme satisfaction? He then collated the information in a chart format showing the frequency the various factors occurred, and therefore an order of ranking. See Figure 8.4 on page 136.

Any factors appearing on the left-hand side of the chart show a greater potential for creating dissatisfaction than satisfaction. Either improving those factors or removing them altogether as negative factors, however, will not create a motivational environment, and any satisfaction as a result of your actions will only have a short-lived effect. Herzberg expressed it by saying, 'You just remove unhappiness, you don't make people happy'. He referred to them as 'hygiene factors'.

It is interesting to note that many of the dissatisfiers in the Herzberg model are the same as the basic needs of the lower levels in the Maslow approach. Herzberg is suggesting that things like money and status are demotivators. This means that if they are not right they have the power to destroy motivation, but when they are put right they do not motivate in any long-term sense. These dissatisfiers tend to be about work conditions rather than the job itself.

Two major dissatisfiers worth noting are the company's policies and procedures, and supervision. Although this study was a company-wide one, and this item may have more relevance to other departments, it is still worthwhile recognising the power of policies and procedures to get people down. Make sure yours are right. In a sales sense, the policy which creates the greatest interest is the company car policy. Try not to leave such matters solele in the hands of the accountants. Remember that the company car is the overt sign to a salesperson's mates and neighbours of exactly how well he is doing.

Poor supervision is a key dissatisfier. This means that managers who are not good at their job will not only produce poorer results

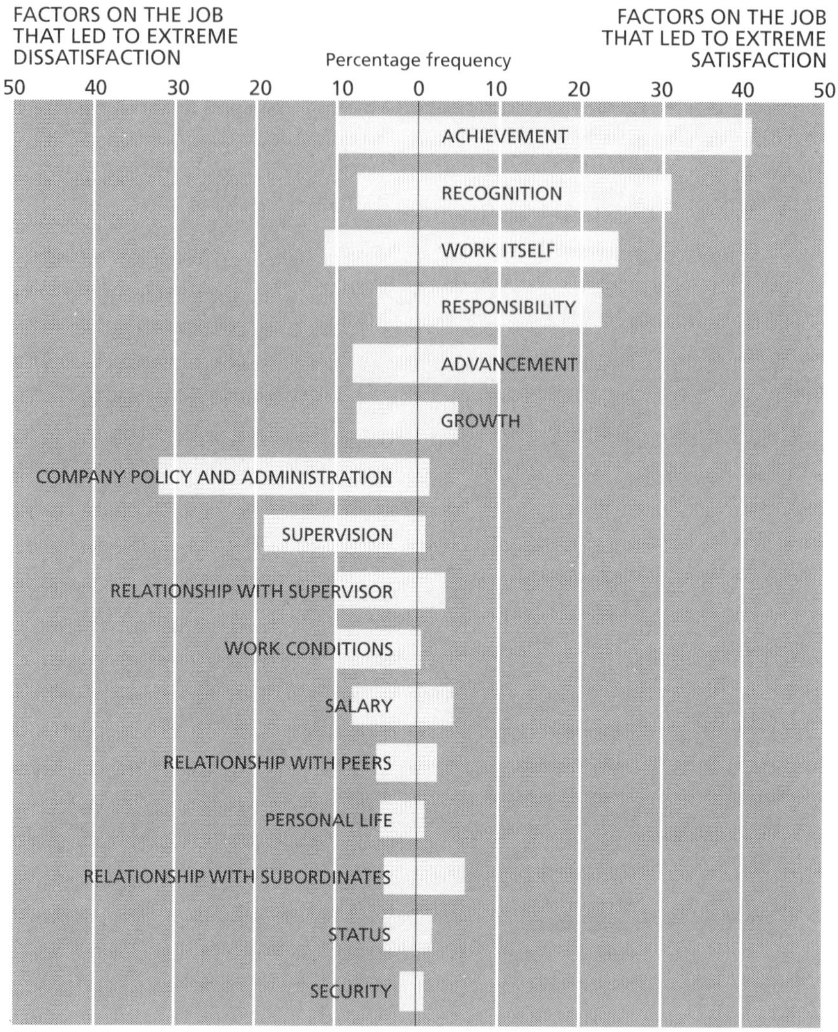

Figure 8.4 Herzberg's factors of satisfaction and dissatisfaction.

directly through their lack of competence, but indirectly too by impairing motivation.

The satisfiers are more about the work itself. Notice the emphasis on achievement, recognition and the work itself—what is sometimes called job satisfaction. These items are much more like the higher levels of Maslow. There is, according to Herzberg, absolutely no point in trying to use any of these satisfiers as motivators if there are still dissatisfiers or 'hygiene' factors present. This is because the presence of the dissatisfiers overrules the satisfiers.

What the sales manager should do is to clean up any 'hygiene' factors first. Get rid of the dissatisfiers. This then leaves people in a state of 'positive neutrality'; they may not be demoralised by anything, but they are not motivated either. Then the sales manager can start to apply the motivators to create real motivation in his team.

It should also be noted that most of the elements considered by Herzberg, do not act exclusively as either dissatisfiers or motivators. There is some overlap. Thus work itself tends to be a motivator, but sometimes it can also be a demotivator, if it is not right. In the same way, advancement is a motivator half of the time, when people feel they are getting the advancement they deserve. However, the other half of the time it is a dissatisfier, when people are not getting the advancement they want.

Achievement, power and affiliation

More recent (1970) is the work of David McClelland, who believes that the three key motivators are the need for three things: achievement, power and affiliation. All of these three needs are present in everyone, but it is the mix of the needs which is the key to that person and his motivation.

Need for achievement

People who have a high achievement need tend to show the following characteristics:

- They get a real kick out of excelling.
- They set realistic goals and will take calculated risks, but they will not gamble or trust to luck.
- They are prepared to take personal responsibility for the consequences of their actions.
- They seek out challenging tasks and take more initiative than most.
- They require quick concrete feedback on how they perform.
- Their primary reason for working is not either for financial reward or for the power over others.

To motivate such people is mainly a question of providing them with a challenge in their jobs, allowing them freedom to achieve results and feedback on how they are performing. There are some similarities with the higher echelons of Maslow and some of the Herzberg motivators.

High need for power

The need for power is the need to influence, coach and get others doing what the individual wants. McClelland did, however, make a distinction between 'personalised' and 'socialised' power. It is the exaggerated form of personalised power which would be seen by others to be a negative thing. Such a person would act for self-aggrandisement and would treat others in a manipulative or demeaning way. On the other hand, socialised power can be for the benefit of the team, especially if it is used to influence the group towards common objectives.

High need for affiliation

The need for affiliation when it is strong will produce a person who has a strong need to be liked and accepted by others. They will work very hard to gain the approval and liking of the team members. One of the most important aspects of their work will be the people they work with. In a manager, this can sometimes be counterproductive. The manager is called upon sometimes to do and say things to his people that they are not going to like. The sales manager with a high need for affiliation will find it very difficult to do this in case it threatens the relationship which he has with them as individuals.

By the same token, a salesperson with a high nAff (as it is rather strangely abbreviated in the trade!), will be so keen on being liked by his customers that he will allow them to take advantage of him and will never be able to sell effectively.

In fact Leonard Chusmer in his book, *Matching Individuals to Jobs*, makes the point that sales people should have a different mix of the three needs from sales managers and sales directors if they are going to succeed. He logs the ideal jobs against the scores out of five on the three needs. He puts the achievement first, then affiliation, and power last. Typically a salesperson will be a 4, 2, 2. In other words, high on achievement and lower on power and affiliation. A manager, on the other hand, will have a profile like 3, 2, 4, lower on achievement and higher on power.

Implications for managing motivation

Having reviewed the ideas of the leading theorists has probably left most readers in a state of uncertainty. There are some things from each of the approaches that will strike a chord, but not one theory that seems to encapsulate everything. Probably the two theorists who offer the most practical applications to motivation on the sales area are Maslow and Herzberg.

In practice, what does it mean? It means that you have to get to know each of your people well.

Create the right kind of environment for them to open up to you so that you obtain insight into their motivational influences. Creating this environment is not easy for everyone. It means that you have to take a genuine interest in each person, and show them that you take an interest. Take time to talk to them, for example in quality time. Take an interest in their interests and whatever they hold important. You do not have to share their interests, just show that you are sufficiently interested in them to ask. Do not judge them, but accept them as the individuals they are. Do not project the way you look at things onto the way you expect them to look at things. Be patient and listen to what they tell you. Be sincere and honest in everything you say to them. Show respect and consideration for their feelings. Whatever they say to you should be treated with discretion and in confidence. Do as you would be done by, and you can expect to be a good way down the road to creating that relationship of trust.

Remember that the motivational influences will change over time and depending on what is happening in that person's social or family life.

Make sure that there are no hygiene factors operating. Know what the major factors are likely to be, and find out how people feel about any areas of possible concern. Be honest in looking at your own behaviour. Be aware the whole time of the possible motivational effect of your actions. It takes a long time to build up trust and credibility, but it can be destroyed in a matter of seconds.

Do not forget the motivational iceberg, the fact that unless you create the right atmosphere of trust and open communication, there will be motivational issues which people will want to keep hidden below the water line.

Make sure that you recognise work well done and give credit for it. How often does a person express surprise to hear from a third party that their parents are proud of them, and the person then remarks, 'Well, why didn't they ever tell me?' The same can be true of managers. The higher up the organisation you are, the less likely it is that anyone will ever give you a pat on the back. Yet everyone likes to be appreciated and to be told that they are doing a good job and that their contribution is valued. This is one of the reasons that well performed appraisals and assessments are so valuable. One of the most powerful ways of giving recognition is to do it publicly, for example in a sales meeting. This can be supplemented by asking the person to explain to the group what they did and how they did it. A formal memo, especially sent to their home address, is another way of giving recognition. In this case, the person's family also gets to know.

Look at how you can make the work more interesting and varied. This is particularly important with either routine sales jobs or internal sales, administrative and secretarial positions. Involve people more, communicate with them. Build in more responsibility, delegate more (see Chapter 10).

Keep the team and individuals informed of goals and standards and the progress towards them. Encourage ideas from the team and, wherever possible, let them implement their own ideas.

Ensure that you have the same rules and standards for everyone, irrespective of the personal preferences you may have for one individual rather than another.

Never take anything for granted and never assume anything. We are dealing with the amazing and beautiful complexity of the human being, which can often drive a sales manager round the bend. It is too easy to try and play the amateur psychologist, drawing on your own personal experience, and therefore jumping to the wrong conclusions. There is no alternative to spending the time to actually find out what your people are thinking and why they are behaving the way they are. Even then they may not tell you the truth, the whole truth and nothing but the truth. Motivation is hardly an exact science. However, if you observe the foregoing comments, you will be much further down the track in motivating your people than you ever have been.

Salary as a motivator

When I assert that salary is not a motivator, I am often accused of acting on behalf of the client company to persuade employees that salary is not important. This is not the case at all. Salary is very important and is a powerful motivational factor. However, it tends to be a dissatisfier rather than a motivator. It comes into play when it is not right, not when it is.

Salary is a powerful disincentive when it is:

- below subsistence level
- below the individual's habitual living standards
- unfair relative to others within the company
- low relative to what a person could earn in a similar position in the industry with another company.

While on the subject of salary, let's look at what the objectives of a remuneration policy are.

In the sales area the remuneration package is designed to:

- attract the right calibre of people into the organisation
- avoid demotivation through the above mentioned hygiene factors
- reward contribution to the company
- encourage current staff to stay
- enable movement across departmental barriers, especially marketing and technical service
- maintain minimum costs.

The Hay Scheme is used by a very large number of Australian companies. It is not the only job rating and remuneration scheme available, but it is the most widely used. The principle is that jobs are rated on a number of dimensions which revolve around dollar responsibility and people responsibility. This provides a job grading. For that particular job grading, there is a mid-point of salary established, and then people fit within a range of that mid-point plus or minus 10 per cent, according to their competence and experience. This allows companies to ensure balance between different parts of the company, and it also allows participating companies to share information in a meaningful way about the relative salaries for mid-points of the various gradings.

One of the problems with this external comparison is that you can never be sure where similar people in different companies may stand relative to the mid-point. For example, you may have Company A, which for a particular grading establishes a salary of $35 000. Company B may establish a mid-point of $38 000. On the face of it, it looks as if Company B pays better. However, if we then find out that while the sales forces of the two companies are identical in competence and experience, in Company B all the people are around 94 per cent of mid-point, or $35 700, but the Company A people are around 104 per cent, or $36 400, you can see that you might well be better off with Company A, even though in principle there is not as much potential for further salary improvement.

Another issue is whether or not the salary gradings and the mid-points should be public knowledge. Many companies will only tell an individual what his own grading, mid-point and percentage are, and those of the people who report to him. They will not tell you what the next level up is. Some companies will not even tell their people that much. Hay would prefer companies to be more open than they are. The reason they are not is because from time to time there is a need to bend the rules. What do you do if the only way you can employ a person from outside is to pay him a salary that is above the maximum allowable for that job under the Hay Scheme? Many companies pay it and then hope like hell that no one spills the beans! Otherwise you run right into a major Herzberg hygiene factor. The real worry in such cases is that the market has moved up to the point that your salary structure is not high enough for the industry where you operate. We all know that when you hire from outside, under all but fairly severe unemployment periods, you will end up paying more than the previous incumbent was being paid. That is often adjusted over the next few years through salary reviews which slow down the new person until the rest catch up. What a vile world this is! The real moral of the story is to manage your people in such a way that they do not leave.

This begs the question of what the right salary strategy might be. If your remuneration level is lower than similar companies are offering in the same industry, you will start to lose your best people. If you pay high salaries then your fixed costs will be greater, and unless you are getting better productivity then your salary strategy is not cost effective. The best way to look at it is to build as much performance-related remuneration into the system as you can. If you are operating the Hay Scheme, and all of your people are within a few percentage points of each other, ask yourself whether in reality their performance is as close as that. If it isn't, you should try to open it out so that there is a real payment for performance approach rather than a Clayton's one. If you give a salary increase of 7 per cent to a person who performs in a mediocre way, and one of 10 per cent to someone who has performed really well, and they were both on $35 000, then after tax the difference is only $11.60 a week. Hardly something to get excited about! The best strategy is to find the best people you can and pay them really well. Then manage them in such a way that you get the best productivity out of them. That will be a mixture of motivation, organisation, systems and training. For the people you employ who are not quite as good, pay them less, but make sure they know what reward is there when they do start performing well. Remember that to make the whole thing work you must operate an effective assessment and appraisal system.

Salary or commission?

Research suggests in general that straight salary plus car and the usual other benefits like superannuation etc. produce the least results but costs the least. The system that gives the highest volumes is pure commission but it also costs the most. Salaried staff are fixed costs, whereas commissions are variable costs and, in a recession, less of a risk to the company. The problem with commission is that everything is geared to whatever the commission is paid on. If you pay it on volume, you will end up with a high volume and possibly poor quality business. It will not be possible to persuade people to do necessary but immediately unproductive tasks, such as reporting, planning, market research etc. In Australia, which is a very security minded country, there will be concern at not having any guaranteed income. Only certain people will take those kind of risks, and such people are probably only ideal for selling in a small number of selling situations. In most selling situations, volumes or contribution are not dependent just on the efforts of the salesperson, and thus a straight commission basis may be judged as being unfair.

There is an alternative, and that is to either do as suggested above, where the salary levels are a lot wider depending on the performance against a number of criteria emanating from the job description, or to look at a salary base plus commission scheme. Which way you go will depend on the type of selling and the culture of the industry (although there is no reason that you should not try to change a culture).

If the selling is to a large extent dependent only on the efforts of the salesperson, there is no price flexibility, and the salesperson's job is relatively straightforward with a large number of fairly small accounts, then a commission component payable on volume will work. If there is price flexibility, the commission should be paid on contribution or gross margin, as in the case of car sales people, whose commission is a percentage of the net gross margin after taking into account the trade-in price.

In selling in a situation where there are complex accounts, or technocommercial issues, a relatively small number of orders involved, significant planning or where the results depend on events outside the control of the salesperson, then go for the payment against performance through assessment based on the job description.

If the remuneration package is conceptually made up of a low base salary and a significant commission component, then it is imperative to calculate and pay the commission over short time periods. Usually this would be a month, but in certain cases of door-to-door sales people, for example, it could even be done on a weekly basis.

Just to repeat one last word of warning, salary is not a motivator, only a demotivator when it is not right. By rewarding your people well, you will get better results, but they still may not give of their best unless you get all the other parts of motivation right too. You will make it harder for them to leave you without taking a drop in remuneration, and people are reluctant to do that. You will have to look at the motivators if you want the best results of all.

Incentives

There are all sorts of sales incentives available. A sales incentive is something which is not ongoing or seen as part of the standard remuneration package. Incentives might include a cash prize, a holiday, a prize, such as electrical goods. Do they work? The whole idea of such schemes is to lift the overall level of performance. Judged against this, some work and some do not. An incentive scheme which is well conceived and implemented works well. However, and here is the real danger, one which does not meet these criteria can cause a lot of damage to motivation.

Incentive schemes are resented:

- if they are seen as not being fair in their concept
- if they are seen as being unfairly administered
- if the reward is provided a long time after the event
- if they are complicated
- if they are hard to understand
- if they are not seen as a reasonable reward for the effort required
- if the results are not directly attributable to the salesperson's efforts, or to the team's efforts if the reward is a team reward
- if there are any significant hygiene factors operating at the same time.

There is nothing more demoralising to the rest of the participants than if an incentive is won by someone whom the majority of people believe did not deserve it, notwithstanding whether the terms of the incentive were met by this individual or not. That is why you have to be very careful in the design of the scheme. The best way to check it out is to consult the sales people first.

In most sales organisations, the best results are obtained with competing teams, such as state sales teams for example. Sometimes a company-wide incentive can work very well. A certain sales result might qualify for a sales conference in Surfers, a better result on the Barrier Reef, an even better result, Fiji, Bali, Honolulu; and failure to meet budget might mean the local businessmen's club down the road from the plant.

Where incentives are provided to individuals or teams, there should be public recognition. That can be the most motivating part of the whole exercise. I once worked for a multinational which had a 'secret' incentive scheme. I only found out about it because someone who worked in my department won it while I was National Sales Manager. Otherwise I would never have heard about it. The salesperson who won it was sworn to secrecy. It was a cash payment added into his salary one month. When he saw how much PAYE the company had to take out that month, he squealed like a stuck pig. It was not a very successful scheme ...

Hints for getting an individual incentive scheme right

- Link the theme to the marketing plan so that it focuses effort in the right direction.
- Research it well with the sales force to ensure acceptability.
- Plan it several weeks ahead.
- To maintain excitement, limit the scheme to three months.
- Make the prize worthwhile, and either make it something that everyone would aspire to, or build in flexibility (not everyone wants golf clubs).
- Ensure that it is easy to understand and simple to operate.
- Link it to results or activities directly attributable to the sales people.
- Identify the scheme with specific and measurable goals.
- Make sure that the assessment of the winner is objective and clearly so.
- Minimise the individual's tax liability by careful choice of the prize. (Overseas business travel is one very good way of doing this, and the company gets something out of it too. If you have overseas affiliates, it is also a good way of providing international recognition to people.)

Job satisfaction

In sales people there is evidence to suggest that job satisfaction is the single most powerful motivator. It is something that is intrinsic to the job. When deciding on the way you are going to organise the sales department, you should take this into account. Try to build as much variety as possible into each position. There is plenty of scope for sales people to apply a wide range of knowledge and skills to the sales job of the 1990s. The acquisition of skills and knowledge is in itself motivating. Encourage your people to develop, both on and off the job.

Try delegating specific tasks (see Chapter 10 on delegation). Sales people in particular like to be consulted. Try to build this process into major issues through sales meetings or quality time. Put challenge into jobs, help the sales people achieve it, and then give them recognition for it. Stress the vital role they play in the company's operation; make them feel that their job is worthwhile.

The external sales people have much more satisfying jobs than many others. There is more scope for how they perform their jobs, heaps of variety and tremendous autonomy and freedom. On the other hand, it can be emotionally and physically demanding, at times stressful.

Job satisfaction for internal sales people

The internal sales job is in many ways just as important, yet a very different type of job. Internal sales people are stuck at the end of a telephone or a computer terminal. They do not have as much variety or freedom or autonomy. Yet the internal job can be just as stressful and emotionally draining. So often the internal sales people are ignored when it comes to managing the team, including motivation. This is where procedures are most likely to be hygiene factors. However, so can be the relationship with the external people. Those external people do not like letting go, and always think their work should be done first.

As a result, there is usually much larger turnover of internal sales staff than external. The lack of continuity in the office will often cause you to pull your external people off the road to do the internal sales job until you have found and trained a replacement. That is no way to run an effective sales department. It is far better to ensure that you build more variety into the internal sales job, and get those people more involved with the business. Have them attend sales meetings and sales conferences. Get them out to visit customers. Let them see visit reports, listen to their ideas. They have more contact with customers than anyone else in the company.

If possible, arrange for internal sales people to work with specific external sales people, usually a ratio of one internal to two external. Again if the system you operate can handle it, have internal sales people work with a specific client base so that they get to know the customers and the business.

Build up the status of the internal sales people. If you call them 'Order Takers', then that is probably what they will turn out to be. Try a name like 'Internal Sales Officer' or 'Customer Service Representative or Advisor'. Include them in training programs and incentive programs. Make sure that they understand that you value what they do.

Force the sales people to let go of the tasks that should be handled by the internal people. Otherwise you will turn them into glorified clerks paid a salesperson's wage. It is hard enough to get some sales people out of the office as it is, don't let them stay in under the pretext of doing someone else's job. If there are problems handling the internal work which causes the external people to bleat that unless they sit and watch over everything themselves the customers will be messed around and it will affect sales and that is what the salesperson is being judge on, then fix it. Once and for all.

Security

Many Australians are security minded. It is part of the national psyche. It is almost in our genes. All of us have some security needs. None of us would feel comfortable in a rapidly changing environment where nobody knows the rules. In some people, the need for security is exaggerated. It is relatively easy to recognise such people. They usually live in a modest house in a suburb they can easily afford. They are well covered with insurance. They do fairly ordinary things on vacation. They tend to stay in the same job for a long time. They do not gamble, drive sensible cars in a sensible way. They worry a lot—about how the company is doing, whether they will have a job in the future, how the new restructuring will affect them. They do not like change and are very conservative.

The way to manage people with a very high security need is to keep them well informed of everything that is happening. Be open and truthful with them. Provide a high degree of structure and direction. Particularly when introducing anything new, spend extra time with these people to make sure they understand the reasons for the change, what is changing and how that affects their jobs. Give them every assistance to develop any new skills they may require to cope with the change.

Status

If he has monogrammed shirts, personalised numberplates, lives in a suburb a bit above his station, belongs to some pretty smart golf club, fancies himself as a wine connoisseur, and knows and talks about important people, he is heavily into status. Status is a need which in Australia is below the water level. It is not the sort of need which people are going to talk openly about. Your ability to satisfy such an exaggerated status need will depend on the type of company you are. If you are a well known and respected professional organisation, you have a chance. If not, then it will be harder, and you should consider whether you should have ever appointed the person in the first place.

Individual status can be recognised in job titles as expressed on cards. I remember a salesperson being moved into an administrative position in head office. His job was Administration Manager. His card, however, had an extra word: National Administration Manager.

The company car is another way of satisfying status needs, especially since it is such a public part of the job. As a manager you will be limited in most cases as to what you can do in these areas if you work for a large company. If you have a highly status-conscious person working for you, try not to say things or do things which conflict with this person's status image, as long as it does not interfere with the rest of the team or the job.

More important than individual status seekers is the status of sales in general. If you ask sales people what their career aspirations are they will often say they want to get into marketing. Ask a marketing person and they will very rarely say they want to get into sales.

Ask a person next to you on a plane what they do. Very few will say, 'I am a salesperson'. They are more likely to be vague, saying 'I'm in sales and marketing' or 'on the commercial side'.

It is improving slowly, but we are a long way behind the United States in accepting sales as a career of status. In the United States it is not unheard of for a salesperson handling large national accounts to earn far more money and have much more status in the organisation than the sales manager to whom he happens to report. We are now seeing the emergence of positions such as national accounts manager of a similar status in the organisation to the national sales manager. This is good. However, we still need to build up the sales role as a profession, and within our companies.

It is up to the sales management to ensure that sales is portrayed in the right way in the company magazine or newsletter, and that other functions understand the complexity and the content of the sales job of the 1990s. One place to start is to let other functional groups have a copy of your job descriptions. Invite other managers to your sales meetings and conferences. Take other managers out on customer visits, and involve them in account planning. Above all, make sure that the CEO understands what you are trying to achieve in this area and is supportive of it in terms of what he says and does. Get him out into the field and along to sales meetings as well.

Managing change

We have referred to the need to manage change particularly carefully with people who are very security minded. Care must be exercised in general when changes are being implemented if demoralisation is to be avoided. The reasons why people resist change in the workplace is that they fear one or more of the following: loss of job, loss of control, loss of earnings, loss of status, not being able to develop the right skills to cope with the change, loss of the team relationships already established and the need to move to unfamiliar surroundings.

With all these potential fears, it is hardly surprising that more damage is done by people talking about what they think might be the changes than the changes themselves. It only requires a rumour to get out which gets slightly twisted, for the whole project to be virtually torpedoed on the wrong grounds before you have even had a chance to announce it.

You should follow the following steps.

Be very clear in your mind what the end result of the change will be. Change is too traumatic to do for its own sake. There must be a desirable and achievable end result.

Decide what exactly has to be changed. Divide it into a number of chronologically sequenced steps if necessary.

Identify who will be affected and in what way. What changes in any of the motivational issues might come into play, either hygiene factors or motivators. This should be both on a team and an individual basis. Identify any new knowledge or skills which may be required and have a plan for how you will address them.

If possible or practicable, consult with those people in the team who are affected. At least this allows them to feel that they have had some input, and they may come up with some specific points you could have overlooked. This needs to be done in such a way that you do not start rumours flowing before you are ready.

Decide how you are going to sell the changes to the sales team and how you will address any motivational issues which may crop up. Plan your presentation well; this is a sales presentation!

Make the presentation to your people, explaining the background, the reasons why the changes are being made and the specific objectives you have. Go through it step by step and explain any training to be provided to assist them.

Encourage questions and leave plenty of time for them.

Do not try to change too much all in one go. Make the time frames reasonable. Keep everyone informed on progress, and be prepared to change the plan for implementation as you go, if necessary. Finally, check that the goals you set yourself are achieved.

Team motivation

One tends to think of motivation as being something that one applies to individuals, and indeed motivation is a very individual thing because we are all different. However, we do worry about what we call 'team morale', which is another word for group motivation. There is a sense in which this concept is important. It a team works well together it will be more productive. It will spend energy in getting results rather than infighting. How can a manager build this team spirit?

One of the ways is to ensure that the team spends time together as a team, even if they are geographically dispersed. Many companies do not consider that the investment in doing this is worthwhile. Those more insightful organisations which do invest money in getting their people together, know that it does. All members of the sales team have some problems in common. It is a sound strategy to work on problems together. Moreover, the team is a very powerful influence in attitude change. I have seen a team manage to persuade a salesperson that he is wrong in ten minutes, when days of discussion with the manager alone has not worked. One of the reasons for this is that people like to belong (the need for affiliation), and to be a full member of a team it helps if you share their values and views. If you are alone out on a limb, you are more likely to change your mind to 'buy' acceptance. The chances are you will not even be aware that you are doing it.

You also need to encourage individuals to learn from the experience of others. There is value in giving them the chance to check each other out. They all compete for the next job up, and will be interested to see what the competition is really like. So get them together, and get them working together. Form small working groups for particular tasks and special projects. Try to arrange training courses so that the whole team gets to do it together. Give them time at these courses or at any other meetings to spend some social time together, getting to know each other, especially for those from out of town. At conferences you should do the same thing. Do not let the technical or marketing people totally dominate the program because they want to communicate a lot of facts. Insist on having some sales activities where groups of people who do not normally work together have a chance to do so. Build in some friendly competition, award some small prizes and include some good consolation prizes too.

Refer to the team, unite it and establish it as a strong entity in the minds of the rest of the company.

Make sure that whenever you do get together as a group, you build in some fun. This is not the same as making sure there is heaps of grog so that they can all get drunk together. It requires a bit more creativity than that. Get them doing things together, whether it is rafting, bowling, horse riding or whatever. This is not goofing off en masse, but team building, and it is very important to the motivation and wellbeing of the sales force.

In summary

You can see that much of your success at motivation will depend on your ability to get the other components of professional sales management right. However, there is no alternative to spending time getting to know your people and creating the right environment for them to open up to you about their individual motivation. You must totally suspend judgement. Your job is to motivate, not to be a psychologist or to play God.

The last word on the subject is this: there are many overseas studies on what motivates people. Australia is different from Europe, Japan or the United States, and we have different emphases of motivational factors. Quality of life is relatively more important to Australians than material items. Do not take overseas studies of key motivators in sales forces and extrapolate them to Australian sales forces.

9

Communication

Communication is the most over-used and under-practised word in business. If there is one quality which good managers are reputed to have, it is the ability to communicate, the ability to create understanding. Managers communicate all the time, and sales managers in particular, since both the task and the management components of their job depend on communication. Virtually every aspect of a sales manager's job must be preceded by, or involve communication. It must also be remembered that communication is two ways, in and out. The sales manager must not only be good at providing communication to his people, he must also open the channels for effective communication back to him.

While there are always two or more people involved in a communication, the prime responsibility of making sure that the message has been correctly received rests with the communicator. It is an affront to say either, 'You misunderstood me' or 'You must have misheard'. They both suggest almost a wilful misinterpretation. It is much better for the communicator to say, 'I'm sorry, I did not make myself clear'.

Barriers to effective communication

Before we look at what the sales manager communicates and how he should do it, let us examine some of the barriers to effective communication. Because the fact of the matter is that in general the quality of communication in business is poor. The reasons may be one or more of the following:

> People often hear what they expect to hear. It is a well known psychological fact that perceptions are very much influenced by expectations.

If the message that has to be relayed is unpleasant, people are frequently not assertive enough in saying it.

Everyone is in a rush, so that they either have no time to communicate or do so in such a rushed way that the message never gets across.

People do not recognise the need to communicate. They either do not see it as a part of their job, or they do not think it is necessary or important.

At times, there are people who think that holding on to a piece of information gives them power. This generally is not true, and in the cases where it might be, the power it gives to the individual is self-aggrandisement power, which is destructive rather than constructive (see Chapter 8, pages 137–8, McClelland on motivation).

Poor listening skills

Listening skills in the community are very poor. We are all subject to verbal and auditory messages all the time. The only way we can cope is to filter out as much as we can. This is one of the reasons that the most successful advertisements are ones that lock into a message that exists already in people's minds. In their book *Positioning: The battle for your mind*, published by Warner Books, Al Ries and Jack Trout refer to the brilliance of 7-Up positioning themselves as the 'uncola', building on the fact that two-thirds of soft drinks consumed in the United States are colas. The consequence of this overload is that we practise not listening more often than we practise listening.

Poor communication skills

Other barriers to effective communication are lazy expression, the incorrect use of words, using ambiguous words or just not being clear and concise.

How can you communicate if you are not sure of the real message you want to communicate?

People may be afraid to communicate to you because you were judgemental and overreacted to previous communications.

Then there are emotional barriers. What people *feel* about things is sometimes much stronger than what they *know* about things. Hence the expression 'my mind is made up, do not confuse me with the facts'. Attitudes can be so entrenched that a person does not take in what the other person is trying to say. In effect, they refuse to listen or even hear. An emotional barrier between two people is also a barrier to communication. For example, if there is a degree of hostility, or a difference in perceived status or when likes and dislikes intervene.

Given the points above, managers need to recognise the importance of communication to their overall effectiveness, and then to concentrate on making time to communicate and improve their communication technique.

Key communications areas for sales managers

Remember that communication is a two-way process.

What the sales manager needs to communicate to others

- The company culture.
- The overall job of the department, including goals and targets.
- How that fits into the overall company strategy.
- What each individual's job is and what standard of performance is expected.
- How the company and the department are going versus plan.
- How each individual is going.
- How you want things done in general.
- What the marketing strategy is and the major sales priorities.
- Any changes in systems, procedures and policies.
- Any information required for individuals to perform their jobs.
- Any business knowledge you have which could help them.
- Directions for specific tasks.
- Changes in product, pricing, packaging, people and their accountabilities.
- Individuals' levels of authority.
- How the departmental costs are going against budget.
- Successes, opportunities and progress.

What the sales manager needs to receive from other people

- The company goals.
- The marketing plan, objectives and strategies.
- Specific marketing programs.
- Changes in product, pricing, packaging, people.
- How the company is going against plan.
- Any events affecting the business.
- How the account plans are progressing.
- How our business at key customers is going.
- What is happening in the market place, competitive activity, buoyancy, opportunities, anything new.
- How individuals feel they are going, how they feel about their jobs.
- What motivational hygiene factors might exist.
- Sales people's ideas on how to do things better.
- What they need to make them more effective.
- Any business or other problems they have—with recommendations.
- How your boss thinks you are doing.

Seven elements of communication

The whole subject of communication can be conveniently split into these seven elements: Asking, listening, deciding, telling, understanding, retaining and non-verbal.

Asking

A lack of information impedes effective communication. Before a sales manager can communicate, he must have all of the information ready, and may need to obtain it from others. This can be a very straightforward exercise in most cases. However, sometimes the information required is more subtle. It is about attitudes and what people really think. Or it may involve sensitive issues, or things that people are reluctant to be open about. This is especially so when it comes to some of the motivational factors discussed in Chapter 8. In this case it is not just a question of thinking through what you need to know and then asking the person. It is a question of creating the right climate of trust and confidence, which allows people to open up in their communication with you.

Asking suggests an active attempt on behalf of the manager to find out. However, the manager also needs to establish an environment where people will come and offer pertinent information without it being specifically solicited.

Listening

We have already said that listening skills are not very good in our community. Although physiologically it is a simple process to understand, psychologically it is complex. Part of the problem is that we talk at about 125 words per minute, yet we have the capacity to assimilate 500 words a minute when we are listening. This means that we have plenty of time to let our minds rattle away thinking other thoughts. Sometimes those thoughts are much more interesting than what we were listening to. This is where the problem comes, because we can still only effectively attend to one thing at a time. We direct our attention according to our own whim. We can afford to think of other things in the 75 per cent of a second which we do not need for listening. Once we devote any of that 25 per cent of the second we do need for listening to any other mental activity, we stop receiving the message. We have directed our attention elsewhere. We will all be able to recall letting our minds wander and then having to pick up the threads of the conversation again. Easiest of all is to do it during telephone conversations, when there are no visual cues to suggest to the other person that you have tuned out. Do not confuse your ability to think of something else and still make the appropriate Hmm and grunting noises which lures the other person into believing that you are still listening attentively, with listening itself. Such subliminal listening is insufficient for you to receive the complete message.

One of the other common times we let our attention get diverted during the 25 per cent of the second which is critical, is when we are planning our response. For this reason alone you should not go on and on. Always pause and let the other person have their say, otherwise their short-term memory will get so overloaded they will forget what they were going to say, or they will divert all their attention into holding their intended response in short-term memory and not listen to what you are saying.

The sad fact is that to listen effectively you just have to apply self-discipline and rigorous control. You can train yourself to listen, and psychologists believe they have shown to their satisfaction that a trained listener can learn twice as much from a conversation as an untrained listener. Listening is a skill, and like all skills it improves with practice. It is an active process, not to be confused with the passive process of hearing. You must learn to direct and hold your attention on the communication.

One technique I have found useful over the years is to make notes. This takes up the other 75 per cent of the second and at the same time keeps your mind on the same subject. It doesn't even matter if you can't read your writing afterwards as long as it helps you listen. Another technique is to mentally repeat what has just been said. Other things you can do to help, are to avoid those things which tend to divert your attention or impede active listening.

Habits worth avoiding

- Stereotyping.
- Preoccupation with other things.
- Letting your mind wander—if it does, just let go of the thoughts and bring your attention back to the communication.
- Trying to interrupt with what you want to say. If you find it hard to get your word in, make a note of what you want to say, and then go back to listening.
- Emotional reactions to what is being said, such as anger or defensiveness.
- Doing something else at the same time. This is particularly a temptation when speaking on the telephone. Just leave that in-tray alone, get the conversation over as fast as possible, and then get on with the in-tray. You will do justice to neither if you try to split your attention.
- Letting your past experience block the message.

One last point is that people seem to be quite well aware of their poor listening skills. A study showed that 85 per cent of listeners rate themselves as average or below average listeners, and fewer than 5 per cent rate themselves as superior or excellent.

Deciding

When you are ready to transmit your message, plan it. Decide exactly what you want to say, and what you are trying to achieve with your message. Make sure that you express it in such a way that you say exactly what you mean. Try it out beforehand if it is complicated or it needs to be handled carefully. Role play it with yourself. Tailor the message to the individual, using the appropriate complexity of language. In fact, you should always use the simplest language you can; you are trying to create understanding, not win a prize for literature.

Provide any necessary background. Psychologists have shown that understanding is vastly improved when the message is given context.

Plan your message in a logical and sequenced way, leading from the past to the future and from one point to the next logical one.

Telling

At this point you are ready to deliver your communication. In most cases it will be spoken. Speak clearly and firmly and loud enough that people do not have to strain to listen to you but not so loudly that they find it uncomfortable. Use simple unambiguous language. Be concise. Communicate in small bites and make sure you have communicated each bite effectively before you continue. If it is a lengthy communication, give listeners the structure of what you are going to cover at the start, and then summarise each section when you get to the end.

Start with facts, not with conclusions you have drawn with regard to the facts. Modulate your voice. Be interesting, paint word pictures. If it is appropriate, build in some humour; people will always listen more attentively if they think they will get a laugh out of it. (How many times at a party have you drifted out of a conversation on something like politics to listen in to the joke or the funny story the person behind you is telling?)

Understanding

One of the definitions of communication is shared understanding. Sometimes, with the best will in the world you can listen to a message and still not understand it. It depends on whether you have sufficient knowledge and experience of the subject matter. Whether you decide to say 'I am sorry, but I don't understand', will depend on a number of things. It will depend on whether you think you are going to look stupid by admitting it. If you are just one in a group, and the others do not say anything, it is hard for you to put your hand up and effectively say that you apparently have less knowledge and experience than the rest and hence do not understand. Apparently, because the others might well be thinking the same thing.

You may also be reluctant in a one-on-one situation to expose your relative ignorance—especially if the demeanour of the other person is such that full comprehension was expected. Even worse if they say 'it will be clear that ...', or 'and as anyone would easily recognise ...', or 'any old fool could see that ...' Avoid using these expressions when you communicate; they are very destructive.

You may also choose not to admit that you do not understand if you think the matter is not important.

If you follow the principles of communication we have discussed above, the chances are that you will have created understanding. However, you had better double check. Recognise too that most messages have two levels of understanding, a logical and an emotional content. Full understanding embraces understanding both the words and the meaning behind the words.

To check understanding, watch the reaction, especially the eyes. Wandering eyes and avoidance of yours is a sign that the message may not have reached its mark. The surest way is to ask questions, and the most powerful one is to get them to tell you what they think you said. If you get a stilted repetition with a flat tone of voice, they haven't understood.

Ask questions about what you have said. Ask them what they think about what you said. Get feedback.

Use the rule of four.

1 Before trying to get an idea across, tell listeners what you are going to say.
2 Say what you have to say.
3 Tell them what you said.
4 Get them to tell you what they understood.

Retention

It is claimed that we forget 25 per cent of what we hear in twenty-four hours and 85 per cent in a week. Whatever the numbers are, the point is that we all tend to forget what we are told, and unless the memory is reinforced, as time passes, we forget more.

It is therefore important for the sales manager to decide which of the items he is communicating need to be retained for a period. He then needs to adopt some method of helping people retain it.

The sales manager can provide written copy of the key points so that people have something to refer to. The other thing he can do is to reinforce the point by referring to it on a regular basis so that it becomes part of the long-term memory of the sales people. If the manager stresses the importance of the message he is communicating, then the listeners are more likely to push it further into long-term memory.

A powerful way of getting retention is to get people to do something about the message. People remember things they have done much better than things they have heard, or listened to. Actions appear to linger longer than words.

Non-verbal

Sometimes the sales manager can communicate more than he wants to or should. This can happen by the tone of voice or the body language. It is very much harder to avoid these messages than the verbal ones because they are more spontaneous; they do not require mental planning and forethought as verbal messages do. Even so, you should be aware of them and try to avoid giving messages you do not want to. These are some of the things you should avoid communicating:

- You are tired.
- You are frustrated.
- You have had an argument with your boss.
- You disagree with an important company policy or directive.
- You dislike an individual in your department or in the company.
- You are in a vile mood because something has gone wrong at home.
- You do not approve of another person's beliefs or value systems outside the business.

Avoid communicating these sort of things; they detract from your position as a leader and they can demotivate the team.

Communication microskills

This is a subject almost in its own right and for those who are interested in the subject there are a number of academic books covering it. We will just refer briefly here to a few of the guidelines designed to make communication easier, especially in your position this time as a listener, to encourage the communicator.

There are four skills areas to cover.

1 Contacting

To demonstrate that you are available to listen, that you have made contact, the following behaviours may help:

- Relax physically.
- Adopt a comfortable posture.
- Consider the space needs of the other person.
- Demonstrate interest through facial expression and eye contact.
- Lend your attention to the other person rather than your own needs or agenda.
- Look for the things that are important to the other person and follow them.

2 Following

To assist in the communication and demonstrate that you are following the other person you can use the following non-evaluative or judgemental behaviours:

- Minimal encouragers, such as a nod, a smile, leaning forward, or words like: yes, I see, go on, that's interesting, what then?, tell me more.
- Verbal followers, such as picking up the key words or phrases and feeding them back.
- Expanders, such as: I can hardly believe it, that figures, that's not right, you mean that ...

3 Questioning

Use open questions, those which start with How?, Why?, Where?, When? Make the questioning an open invitation to talk:

- 'What are your thoughts on ...?'
- 'How do you feel about ...?'

  Or an invitation to go on:
- 'Could you say a bit more about ...?'
- 'Tell me more.'

  Or an open invitation to elaborate or clarify:
- 'Could you give me an example of what you mean?'
- 'Could you go into that in more detail?'
- 'Why do you think that happened?'

Try to avoid those questions inviting a yes or no answer, closed questions, and avoid leading questions of any sort.

4 Checking and clarifying for understanding

The key phrases to use are:

- 'So, as I understand it ...'
- 'Let me see if I have got this right ...'
- 'It seems then that ...'
- 'If I hear you correctly ...'

Methods of communication

Sales meetings

An ideal forum for communicating with the whole team is the sales meeting. Make a list between meetings, as they come up, of the things which you need to communicate at the next meeting. Allow some time for the team to communicate the things they want to as well. (See Chapter 14 on effective sales meetings.)

Sales conferences

Apart from the motivational value in team building, conferences are very effective as communication tools. The ideal subjects are those which would not normally be covered on a day-to-day basis. They might include corporate strategy, marketing programs, the R & D program, materials management, including distribution costs and methods and packaging. The value in talking about ideas for the future is that you can get an assessment from the whole sales force as to whether from a sales point of view it is going to be viable. Marketing, technology and distribution ignore the views of the sales force at its peril. They are the ones out there at the coal face and have a better idea whether things will work or not. They may also come up with other good ideas and may find flaws in the plan which no one else had thought of. Sales conferences are a massive communications exercise.

Quality time

(See page 166.) The ideal forum to communicate on a one-on-one basis with your people, specifically about matters which affect them as individuals. That includes both work-related items such as customer issues, and also performance-related topics.

Telephone

If you are sales manager with most of your sales people in a metropolitan area, and doing other than very routine sales work, the car phone for your sales people, and probably for you, is not a luxury; it is a necessity. It saves them coming into the office and wasting hours a day driving round congested cities.

Whether you are talking to your own people on the phone or others, make the calls brief and concise. How often do we hear people telling others on the phone the content of the fax they have just sent them? They say more goodbyes than Dame Nellie Melba. Talk about garrulous sales people! As a rule of thumb, imagine you were paying for all the calls yourself—and treat local calls as if they were STD.

Since the pilots' strike in 1989, many companies have found that conference phone hook-ups and video conference facilities can be very effective and cheaper than getting on a plane.

Fax

It has the advantage of providing a permanent record of the message, of being instantaneous and relatively inexpensive. Use it rather than the telephone whenever you can.

Memos

For formal communications when you want people to have a record of the content, memos are great. If the message is complicated or it is to be referred to later, you will need to commit the message to paper. If the same message has to be sent to a number of people in different locations the memo is useful. There is already enough paper floating around companies. Try to avoid adding yours to it unless it is really warranted.

Walls

Yes, walls! A good way of communicating sales results or costs against budget, and to inject some friendly competition is to put graphs up on the wall.

Notice boards

Marginally useful for very few types of communication. Perhaps an invitation to the sales department's barbecue ...

Company newsletter

If you work for a large company it is always a good idea to get as much coverage in the company newsletter as you can. It can raise the status of the sales department, as long as you have significant input as to the story line and how it is written.

Video newsletter

If you have a sales force which is geographically dispersed reporting to you, either a national sales force or a country-located sales force, communication on a regular basis is a headache. There is no doubt that those people in the far-flung corners of the nation have a need to know what is going on, both in a business sense and a personal or social sense. They can be the most isolated people in the whole company and really suffer as a result. A newsletter from the sales manager, recorded on video, and put out every couple of months is usually very well received. Communicate the same sort of business items you would in a sales meeting, but also include some of the social anecdotes to give it a more human and informal flavour. For variety get others to talk from time to time. Invite individuals from marketing, technical department or materials handling or even general management. Make one tape and then have copies made and sent to the various locations.

The grapevine

Many will claim that this is the most efficient communication channel of all. It is a fact of life for all organisations and it certainly has a role to play. When Union Carbide built their radical new head office in the late 1970s at Danbury, Connecticut, the corridors were very narrow and it was very hard to stop and talk. As a result it seems that the informal communications channels declined, which was seen in hindsight as a loss for the company.

The thing about the grapevine is that although it may be fast and wide ranging, it is not always accurate, and is very often uncharitable. The main message might get through, but the reasons for it and the implications will be distorted. Make sure when you are announcing something important that you get the message to the team the way you want it to be told, before it gets promulgated and embellished by the grapevine.

Communication with a sales force which is geographically spread out

There are companies in the primary industries, such as rural or mining, whose sales force is located in very isolated areas. Communication with those people is very hard and at the same time very important. If your sales force is one of these, here is a checklist of ideas to help.

- Use the phone and the fax.
- Make a regular time to call each week, if necessary in the evening.
- Keep a list of the things you want to communicate, and keep adding to it during the week.
- Also make a note of things you want to hear back from them.
- Be prepared to invest money in these calls; they are the prime way for you to motivate people as well as communicate with them.
- Include bits of gossip, but not rumour.
- Get out to see them as often as you can.

- When you make visits, do not fill up your time making joint calls, but build in time to cover the interpersonal things you would cover with metropolitan sales people.
- Ensure that you put time aside to have your quality time.
- Try to be available when they call you.
- Let them call you after hours at home, with time or day restrictions if you want to.
- Consider preparing a brief newsletter or, better still, a video such as was described above.

Quality time

One often hears people say about their boss, 'We never sit down and talk about me' or 'We only communicate when he wants something done, or when the fan is turned on full' or 'He is always too busy, I have tried talking to him, but the phone rings or he has a meeting to go to, and ...'

The concept of quality time is aimed to avoid this common breakdown in communication between the sales manager and the individual sales people. In essence it could not be simpler. It is just a question of regularly putting aside time to talk to each of your people on an individual basis about them and their jobs. It is a way of forcing a pathway for communication. This section might have easily been included in the chapter on motivation or on training, because those are two of a number of activities which might take place in quality time. However, the chapter on communication was chosen, as quality time is primarily about communicating.

Golden rules of quality time

The following golden rules apply to quality time:

1 It is sacred

Part of the effect of quality time is its motivational aspect. It is a time for recognition where it is due, for showing the sales people that they are important enough for you to spend time with them. It provides the sales people with a feeling of worth and belonging. Through non-directional training techniques they will be developing skills. If you cancel out, or are late, or take phone calls during the meeting, you will undo most of the good which comes from quality time. It can happen that urgent and important things crop up occasionally. If so, then give the sales person as much notice as you can of a change in the appointment, and make sure you adhere to the postponed date. Do not allow any interruptions at all.

2 Have an agenda

Both the sales manager and the salesperson can offer suggestions for the agenda, but more often than not it will be the salesperson who has accrued things he wants to talk to you about. There should be no barriers as to what is allowed on the agenda. Most of the items will probably be about the business, though there may be items about motivational issues, grievances, personal problems, whatever. Encourage each person to keep a notebook where agenda items can be listed as they occur to the salesperson. The sales manager should do the same, preferably using the same book that he uses for notes which may be required in assessments or appraisals.

3 Set aside time on a regular basis

For most sales people this should be once a week or once a fortnight. You will probably need an hour or so. Try to make it a regular time if you can so that the sales people can plan their agendas around it.

4 Use non-directional training techniques

This training method is ideal for problem solving (see Chapter 6 on training), and that is often the sort of thing that arises in quality time. When they ask for your advice, do not necessarily give it to them. Use some of the insight from situational leadership, and ask them for suggestions and recommendations.

5 Nominate key training and development needs

In nominating items for the meeting from your side, take into account what you see as their key training and development needs. Do not include items which you are going to cover in the sales meeting with everyone there. Keep it very much on an individual basis.

6 Cover all the important ground

This is the meeting where you do most of your one-on-one work, apart from when you do on-the-job coaching. It is critical that you cover all the important items. If there are still some agenda items at the end of the time allotted, either continue the meeting if you can, or if they can be left until the next meeting put them on the agenda, but otherwise schedule another extra meeting. If you have completed the agenda before the allocated time limit, close the meeting.

7 Keep notes

There is no need to have them typed up under most circumstances, but it is a good idea to keep a record of any pertinent issues. This will be particularly important if there are any action items which will need to be followed up.

Subjects for discussion in quality time

- Not the golf, the match, the TV or the concert!
- Recent customer visits and any significant issues. (Don't spend time going over the things that are on target, only bother with the problems.)
- Important customer calls for the next period. Any information required or difficult situations and how they could be handled.
- Review of account plans (for those operating an account management system).
- Progress on any specific projects.
- Any problem areas.
- Actions on items from the previous meeting.
- Any other business.

These meetings should be relaxed, non-stressful and highly productive. Make sure that you do not allow them to degenerate into a chat because they are relaxed. Keep to an agenda, probe where you feel there are learning points to be made. Be businesslike, yet friendly and supportive. This is your best ongoing communication channel with your individual sales people. Make sure you get the best out of it, for them and for you.

A last word on communication

Communication is one of your most valuable tools. Reserve it for yourself. Every extra link in the communication chain is likely to cause the message to get distorted. Communicate directly yourself with the people you need to communicate with.

10

Delegation

What is delegation? If delegation is correctly handled it is a very powerful motivator and an excellent way of developing skills.

Delegation is the activity of a manager when he entrusts responsibility and authority for a task for which he has accountability.

By this definition, all the work which the sales force does is delegated by the sales manager to the people who work for him. The sales manager is ultimately accountable for the selling job to the customers in his area of control. However, he clearly entrusts this task to his sales people, giving them both the responsibility and the authority to do it.

If you like, these are elements of the manager's job which he permanently delegates to his staff.

What we normally call delegation is when the manager entrusts a task which he normally reserves for himself, to a person who reports to him. In principle there is no fundamental reason why anything for which the sales manager is accountable could not be delegated to one of the sales people. In reality of course there will be things which the sales manager will always reserve for himself and which should not be delegated. These are in the interpersonal area and include appraisals and assessments, recruitment and selection, counselling and on-the-job coaching (unless of course we are talking about a national sales manager delegating those tasks to a state sales manager or a field supervisor).

There is in fact no real difference between the two situations, permanent or specific delegations, with respect to the principles of delegation. In the case of permanently delegated tasks, such as selling, the good principles of delegation are embodied in the job description, standards of performance and assessment approach we have already discussed. When it comes to how we delegate tasks we normally reserve for ourselves, which is really the core subject of this chapter, we follow the same principles.

Before we start, let us see if we can agree on a couple of definitions.

Responsibility is the act of making the person responsible for completing the task as defined. He may come to you for further advice, but you have transferred to him the job of completing that task. You are putting the person in charge and giving him the credit for performing that job.

Authority goes along with the responsibility. It is the power and right to act which may be necessary to get the job done. This may be the right which applies to the position of sales manager, but which to get this job done must be invested in the person to whom the task is delegated.

Accountability is meant here in the sense of ultimate accountability, which still remains the sales manager's. At the end of the day, the sales manager is always answerable for what happens in his department.

There are several benefits in delegating tasks that might ordinarily be considered the role of the sales manager. Some are benefits to the sales manager and some for the salesperson to whom the task is delegated.

Advantages for the sales manager in delegating

- More time is freed up for other important duties.
- The manager gains insight into a person's capabilities.
- It prepares the way for the manager's holiday, retirement, promotion or whatever!
- It provides a more effective distribution of workload.
- It develops skills in the team so that more work can be delegated—which in turn makes the manager look more effective as a manager.
- It eases job pressure on the manager.
- It creates a better motivational atmosphere.
- It is a more effective total use of total time.

Unfortunately, the team sometimes sees such delegation simply as the boss shedding some of his excess workload. In fact, this should not be so at all. A manager who delegates well will be appreciated by his staff.

Why staff appreciate a manager who delegates

- It makes their jobs more interesting and satisfying.
- It makes them feel involved and needed.
- It encourages them to stretch themselves.
- It develops their knowledge and their skills.
- They get more recognition.
- They develop better self-esteem.
- It helps them develop confidence.
- It shows them that the company does have an interest in developing them.
- It breaks the routine.
- It is a motivating experience.

Note that many of the reasons for the sales people to welcome delegation are at the higher levels of Maslow's triangle of hierarchical needs and are in the list of Herzberg's motivators. This suggests that the motivational side of the equation will depend on there not being any hygiene factors present at the same time. This is in fact quite true. If you try delegating to someone who is demotivated because of dissatisfiers, you will find that delegation works far less well. It is again an example of how the whole sales management issue is so interdependent. To get it really right, you have to get it all right.

Why sales managers tend not to delegate

Given all of these advantages of delegation to all parties, why is it that many managers do not delegate enough? There are many reasons, none of which is valid for a professional manager.

- They do not know how to do it properly.
- They think they can do the task better themselves.
- They think one of their subordinates might do it better than they would and show them up.
- They want to take the credit themselves.
- They enjoy doing that particular task themselves.
- It has to be done in a rush and there is no time to explain to anyone else what is required.

- It is easier to do it yourself.
- They have tried delegating before and found that the work was not done properly and the manager ended up doing it himself anyway.
- Doing it yourself is the only way to make sure that it is done right.
- It's easier to keep on doing these tasks rather than getting on with the job of managing.
- They like to be involved in the 'cut and thrust'.

Many sales managers would not even admit to some of the above reasons, but reasons they are all the same. There seems to be an enormous fear of letting go. If any of us wants to advance, even in life in general, there are times where we have to learn to let go. The sales manager who tries to retain too much for himself will be overworked, ineffective and will not be doing the right thing by his own people.

It is true that delegation can go wrong. However, that is not a reason for not delegating. It is a reason for finding out how to delegate properly so that it will not go wrong the next time.

Reducing the risks in delegation

Avoid delegating the wrong type of job. You should not delegate anything which is essential for overall control of the business. Neither should you delegate anything to do with appraising, assessment, discipline, counselling, grievance settlements or matters of a confidential nature. On-the-job coaching is a matter of central importance and should remain the responsibility of the line sales manager or supervisor. Any deviation from policy decisions must be reserved for the sales manager, as should be recruitment and selection, communication with the team and motivation.

The only rider to this is a situation where you are away for an extended period of time when someone is actually standing in for you. This is in a sense a form of delegation, but is more realistically that person assuming your job entirely for the period. Even so, there may be certain matters, such as appraisals, which would be better left until the sales manager returns. The rule of thumb is that the ideal work to delegate is non-managerial work which the manager performs. It is operating work, for example, forecasting, preparing for a sales meeting, preparing a report for marketing, analysing information, administering the budget process. Those aspects of the job that tend to be routine are ideal candidates for delegation.

Choose a suitable person. The choice of individual will be a mix of expediency and the need for personal development. Apart from the individual training and development needs you have assessed for the individual, you need to give thought to whether he has done something similar before. How much knowledge does he have about the job and the situation? How much interest has he shown in that type of work? What training will be needed for him to be able to perform the task? Will he be acceptable to other people who may be involved in the task?

Communicate fully. Communicate directly to the person to whom you are delegating the task, but also to all other people who may be involved or affected, including other members of the sales team, other managers and people in other departments. Your communication to the person to whom you are delegating should include the following:

- Background to the task.
- The reason why the task is important, and how it fits into the overall goals of the department.
- What constitutes the successful completion of the task. In other words, how far the person should take the project, and at what point the job is considered to be completed. This also might include the standard to which the task is to be completed. Be as specific as you need to be, given the knowledge and the experience of the person (see Chapter 11, Situational leadership).
- Explain why you have asked that particular person to do the job.
- If appropriate, given the maturity of the person for that task, provide some guidelines and structure for the person to follow. You might even go so far as to tell them exactly what to do and how to do it. You would only go that far with people who were of very low maturity for that task. Otherwise you would antagonise the person to whom you are delegating.
- Agree on deadlines; give him time to plan creatively.
- Check for understanding; get him to tell you his understanding of what he has to do.
- Encourage the individual and demonstrate that you have confidence in him.
- Make sure that you have given the necessary authority to get the job done.

Monitoring progress

The decision as to how frequently you should involve yourself with what is happening will depend again on the maturity of the individual for that task. If the individual is very mature, you will not normally get involved again until the task is completed. On the other hand, if the individual is of low maturity for that task, you will check at frequent intervals how things are going. This can be done either specifically or during quality time.

When you do check progress, make sure that you follow the principles of non-directive techniques (see Chapter 6 on training) and apply situational leadership (see Chapter 11). It is at the point where you check progress that there is a temptation to interfere or take the project back and do it yourself, especially if progress has been slow and you are running out of time. For this reason, make your checks at a time which allows correction if necessary.

Do not give in to this temptation, otherwise you will have done more harm than good. Remember that if the job is not being done correctly, the fault is most likely yours, either because you did not give specific and clear instructions in the first place or because you overestimated the maturity of the individual for that task. It follows that if things are going wrong, you do not blow your stack, lose your patience or give any indication that the individual has messed up the job.

You sit down with the person very calmly and exercise the necessary damage control. You may assist if necessary, but do not take back the responsibility for the job. You need at a point like this to be very aware of the motivational issues and the need to not destroy, but to continue to build the confidence of the individual.

In most cases, as long as you explained the task correctly in the first place, these checks will be fairly straightforward. If you find that the person has approached the task in a different way from how you would have done it, stop and think before you say anything. It could very well be that they have come up with a better idea than yours. Be adult enough to admit this. Suspend judgement and your initial normal reaction that your way has to be the best. Think about it objectively, and be prepared to accept their ideas. Even if you consider that your approach was better, as long as they get the right end-result, do not cause them to change mid-stream. At the end of the project, you could cover with them, using non-directive techniques, other ways of approaching the task. If there are things which you need to correct at any of these progress checks, again do it using non-directive training techniques wherever possible.

It is clear that this procedure is going to take some of your time. In fact it may very well be that the first time you delegate a task, it would have been quicker for you to have done it yourself. The point about delegation is that it not just a matter of you freeing up more time for yourself, but it is about systematically developing the knowledge and the skills of your own people. You need to look at the time spent in that light, as an investment in your people with a longer term payback than just on this particular project.

Evaluating results

At the end of the process you should be asking yourself the following questions.

- Has something new of potential value to others emerged from this project? If so, what, and what should I do about it?
- Has the subordinate demonstrated a capability such that there are other tasks that might usefully be delegated to him?
- Has the success of this project stimulated a desire in other members of the team to take more responsibility? If so, who, and what could be done about it?
- Did it save any time? If so, how productively did I use the time I saved? (Be honest!)
- As a result of this experience, are there any duties that could be permanently delegated? If they are permanently delegated, they will be transferred to the job description of that person. Note that they may not be part of the position description, in the sense that they depend on that particular person being in the job rather than being a responsibility of every incumbent in that position.
- If the delegation was less than successful, what did I do wrong? If so, have I created any motivational hygiene factors that need to be addressed? Have I caused this person to lose confidence or self-esteem? Have I caused this person to lose the respect of the rest of the team? What am I going to do about it?
- What are the learning points for me out of this experience?

Delegation and accountability

One of the paradoxes of delegation is that even though you entrust the responsibility and the authority for a certain task to a subordinate, you never can abrogate your ultimate accountability. In other words, you are held accountable for someone else's mistakes. However, that is the way the world works. The sales manager can hardly get away with the excuse that sales in his state are down not because of him, but because the people reporting to him are not doing their jobs correctly. The Prime Minister will never win an election on the basis that it was the Treasurer who ruined the economy, but that he had performed well.

Conclusion

The decisions which people carry out with the greatest enthusiasm and motivation are those which they take themselves. Even if there are flaws in the decision, a person may well manage to get it right in the end, because of the commitment which having responsibility creates. Delegation can be a powerful motivator and an excellent training and development method. It may not be easy for a manager to give a person the right to be wrong, but the risks are more than repaid through rewards in terms of:

- your own effectiveness
- better time management
- motivation of your staff
- development of your staff.

Twenty hints for delegation

1 The sales manager remains accountable in an ultimate sense for all the work performed by his department, including those tasks permanently delegated.
2 Whether permanently delegated or just in this instance, define clearly what the task is and what exactly, including standards, constitutes the successful completion of the job.
3 Explain why the task is to be done, its importance and relevance to the overall departmental objectives.
4 Set goals for the project, including times for the various stages. Respect any critical paths, and allow time for slippage and contingencies.
5 Provide whatever guidelines are appropriate for the situation. The more experienced and knowledgeable about the subject the person is, the less guidance and direction you will provide.

6 Check that you have communicated successfully. You may think it is straightforward; they may not. If in any doubt, get them to tell you their understanding.
7 Give the person as much freedom as you can to approach the task in their own way.
8 Build some challenge into the job.
9 At the same time, keep your demands reasonable and the time frame within fair expectations.
10 Ensure that the person feels confident in his ability to do the job. If not, find out why not, and provide the necessary guidance and emotional support.
11 If you feel the need to provide guidance in how to perform the task, do not tell, but use non-directive techniques to elicit the right response.
12 When you assign the responsibility, make sure you also assign the authority.
13 Agree on the appropriate control checks, and then let them get on with the job without looking over their shoulder.
14 Give recognition for good work.
15 Let the individual accept responsibility for poor work as well as good, assuming that the poor work is not as a result of your poor delegation technique.
16 If the job is difficult, recognise that it is, and list the difficulties.
17 Use the team approach. Sometimes two people working together can bring more creativity to the job.
18 Do not rush in and take over if things look as if they are going wrong. Exercise damage control but try not to take back the responsibility for the task. You may have to learn to grit your teeth and make a note that the person needs more training.
19 Don't expect perfection.
20 Analyse how it went and what the learning points are for both you, the sales manager, and for the subordinate.

11

Leadership in management

Much has been written about the subject of leadership. It is the sort of word that finds its way into company mission statements. The trouble with it is that it is a bit too close to 'motherhood' for people to really get a practical handle on how it fits into the sales management job.

There are two points that are worth making initially. Firstly, leadership can mean a number of things.

There is *task leadership*, where a manager plays a leadership role in tasks such as problem solving or idea generating. This can often be a function of the person's creativity, abstract intelligence, ability for lateral thinking and experience.

Then there is *leadership of the team*, of the sales force. It is this leadership that we will be examining in some detail in this chapter.

The second point is that there are two ways of looking at the position of leader of a group of people.

Firstly, there is the position of leadership which is a *property of the job*. A person will command some kind of respect simply because he is in that position. However, that is a very superficial respect; it is really respect for the position rather than the incumbent.

Secondly, there is the leadership that *the individual brings to the position*. That is what creates real respect, and which causes the people who work for that person to want to do so, and to give their allegiance and support to the leader. That is true leadership, and that is what managers should aspire to.

Are leaders made or born? If we are talking of leaders of world stature, one suspects that without a portfolio of personality traits which equip that person particularly well for leadership, they would never have made it. When it comes to the sort of leadership which is required to be an effective manager, there is no doubt that one can do much to hone one's leadership skills. You can learn how to become a credible and respected leader of the sales team.

Skills required of managers

There are of course different levels of management within an organisation. Each of these managers has to be skilled in three main areas: technical, conceptual and interpersonal.

Technical skills

A first line manager cannot be expected to direct the activities of those who work for him unless he knows how to do the tasks himself. As you progress up through the organisation, the need to be able to perform these front-line tasks diminishes. A sales director needs far less product knowledge than a salesperson who is using it every day.

Conceptual skills

Companies are directed by their managers. Successful companies are able to understand what current circumstances require, and often to predict what is going to be required in the future (in fact, this is probably the single most determining factor of a successful company). This requires an ability to absorb information, marshal it in a meaningful way, analyse it, understand the implications, and decide what to do about it. At the same time, the senior managers have to agree on the overall corporate goals and ensure that guidelines are adhered to. The right organisation must be created, and the necessary infrastructure put into place to facilitate implementation. Much of that is what could be described as task leadership.

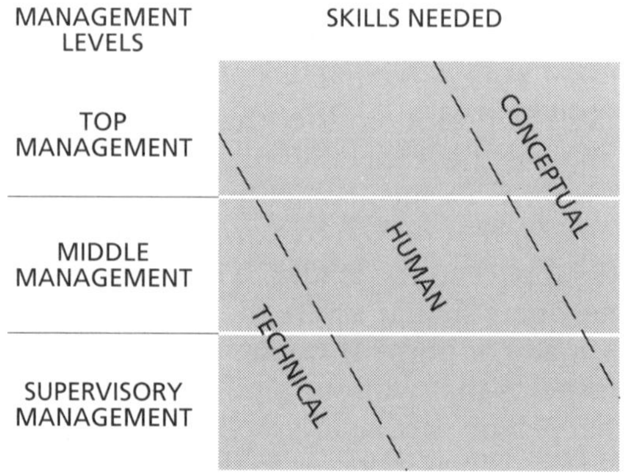

Figure 11.1 Management skills necessary at various levels of an organisation.

Interpersonal skills

Clearly, all managers need to be able to work through people to obtain results. That fundamentally is the manager's job. This requires skills in many of the subjects of this book, such as motivation, communication, leadership etc.

It will be clear that the mix of the three main skills will be different for different levels of management. The relative importance of the three skills at different levels of seniority is shown in Figure 11.1. At the first level, supervisory management, such as state sales manager, the emphasis is on task and interpersonal skills. At the highest level, the emphasis is on conceptual and interpersonal skills.

So, leadership qualities as we have defined them, are important for all managers.

What is leadership?

It is that quality in the sales manager which causes people to make such comments as the following:

- I learnt more from him than any other boss I have had.
- He was prepared to listen.
- He did everything he could to make life easier for the sales people.
- You just have to respect him.
- The word to sum him up is professional.
- He insists on a high level of performance, but he gives every assistance in achieving it and recognition when you do.
- He is an excellent communicator; you always know what is going on and what is expected of you.
- He is prepared to go in and bat for us.
- He is absolutely fair, no favouritism, the same rules apply for everyone.
- He is approachable.
- If you make a mistake he will let you know, but he does not hold it against you.
- He is not at all judgemental; he has his personal interests and beliefs, but he does not expect you to share them.
- He gives me the impression that he genuinely cares about me as a person.
- He has a way of telling you where you are going wrong which still makes you feel good about yourself.

- He has never put anyone down in front of the rest of us.
- He is extremely patient.
- He is just a very wise and mature individual.
- He is the sort of sales manager I would want to be.

Most of these statements are about the way people do their jobs rather than an intrinsic property of the individual. The good leader responds to people's needs for respect, consideration, loyalty, fairness, recognition, involvement and trust. There are some aspects which are akin to being a role model. There is a quality of being part of the team but in a clearly identified leadership role. It is quite possible to be part of the team without being one of the boys.

Note that there are no suggestions of self-aggrandisement or ego-tripping on behalf of the manager.

The quality of leadership seems rather, at least in part, to be the summation of getting right all the things the sales manager is supposed to do. It is all that, together with maturity, and the ability to put the business and the team in front of his own ego. Most good leaders are quietly confident of their own abilities. They do not seem to need to prove anything to anyone. They know themselves and accept themselves for the person they are. This is perhaps what enables them to have the insight into other people's feelings, which allows them to invest all of their energy into the relationship with the other person, by being supportive, rather than investing everything into feeding their own ego. You can learn how to do the sales manager's job, but can you learn this other quality of perceptiveness and suspension of ego, which is what will make a reasonable leader into an outstanding leader? It is more a question of insight and attitude which is available to anyone and everyone at any time. To gain it, take a good, hard and honest look at yourself. Use what you see and learn in your relationships with others.

The new manager

When a manager is appointed to a position from either outside or from within the company, the leadership attitude he adopts in the initial stages will haunt him for a very long time. First impressions last.

If the new manager comes in exhibiting a strong 'nAff' (see Chapter 8 on motivation), and invests too much effort into getting on with the sales people, it will be hard to withdraw to the high ground later. This is particularly likely when a member of the sales team is appointed to the position of sales manager of the same team. There is a great tendency for the new manager to worry about retaining the relationships he had before. This is of course not possible because the previous relationship was a peer relationship, which the current one never can be.

If the new manager goes in 'soft', it will be that much more difficult to establish a harder line on discipline later. Equally well, if the manager presents himself first up as a hard task master and a toughie, then he may erect barriers that will be hard to break down.

If the sales manager is keen to establish his credibility—and this happens especially when he is a little lacking in confidence—he may try too hard to demonstrate his knowledge, to the point where he is seen by the sales people as a 'know it all'.

Neither is the inexperienced manager advised to throw himself at the mercy of the sales people, saying that he is new to all this and he wants them to work together while he is on a learning curve, etc. Whenever there is a new sales manager the team will be on the look out for how they can best manage him. Sales people are very good at manipulating new bosses given half a chance. Signs of weakness are a bad portent for the future.

If there are so many pitfalls, what is the best strategy for the new manager? The best thing is not to rush in during the initial stages. Maintain an air of neutrality until you know how things operate now and how you want to change them. Once you have determined what you want to change, do so without further delay. Initially, all you need to do is explain how you see your role, and espouse any general philosophies you have, as long as they are general enough to not be affected by what you might find out about the sales force and the job later.

Then embark on an information-seeking exercise. Absorb but do not emit at this stage. Find out about the people, how they do their jobs and what they think about them. Spend time with each person. Do not commit to anything at this stage. Imagine you are acting as a consultant, and you are doing the research before you make your recommendations. You must do this quickly and intensively. Decide how you want to run things, and then communicate this clearly to the group, giving them plenty of opportunity to ask you questions. Do not allow yourself to be manipulated, but at the same time do not be inflexible. In these early days, you need to demonstrate sound judgement.

If you are an internal appointment, the information gathering stage will be much shorter, as you will know most of it already. However, you should then follow the other stages as outlined.

Situational leadership

Many theories of how to manage have been advanced over the years. Most of these have been found to lack in applicability. You read the theory but are still faced with the question, 'But what do I actually do?'

There is, however, one theory which was developed by Paul Hersey and Ken Blanchard (*Management of Organisational Behaviour*, Prentice Hall International Editions) which not only provides a sound and logical theory; it also tells the manager what to do under certain situations. It is called 'situational leadership', and it is the only theory we are going to consider in detail, because in my view it represents the best model for sales managers to work with.

The situational leadership model is based on two dimensions which are commonly used to describe management behaviour—task and relationship. By task is meant the degree to which the sales manager defines what is to be done and how it is to be done. By relationship is meant the extent to which the sales manager interacts with the salesperson, or in other words the emotional support or the strokes. The diagram in Figure 11.2 illustrates four basic quadrants, but this is of course a simplification; there are no defined boxes in human behaviour.

The strict definitions of each of these two dimensions is as follows:

- *Task behaviour* is the extent to which leaders are likely to organise and define the roles of the members of their group, to explain the activities each is to do, and where and when the tasks are to be done. It is characterised by trying to establish well defined patterns of organisation, channels of communication and ways of getting the job done.

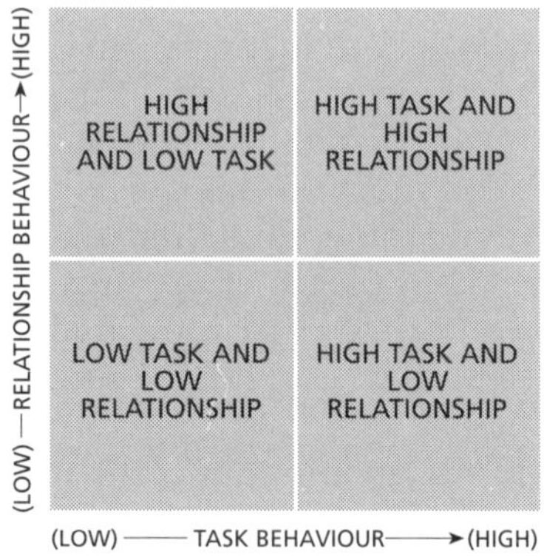

Figure 11.2 Basic leader behaviour styles.

- *Relationship behaviour* is the extent to which the leaders are likely to maintain personal relationships between themselves and members of their groups by opening up channels of communication, providing emotional support, strokes and other facilitating behaviour.

The critical issue raised by Hersey and Blanchard is that there is not just one ideal management style. The best manager is one who can adapt his style to the specific needs of each subordinate according to the task to be done. The best style thus depends on the circumstances, and the circumstances are best described by the maturity of the subordinate with respect to the task.

Style of leader versus maturity of follower

If the basic diagram shown in Figure 11.2 is overlaid by a bell-shaped curve, and an extra dimension, the task relevant maturity of the follower, is added to the bottom axis, we end up with the Hersey diagram. This is shown in Figure 11.3. The curve is prescriptive because it indicates the most appropriate mix of task and relationship behaviour according to the follower's level of maturity on that task.

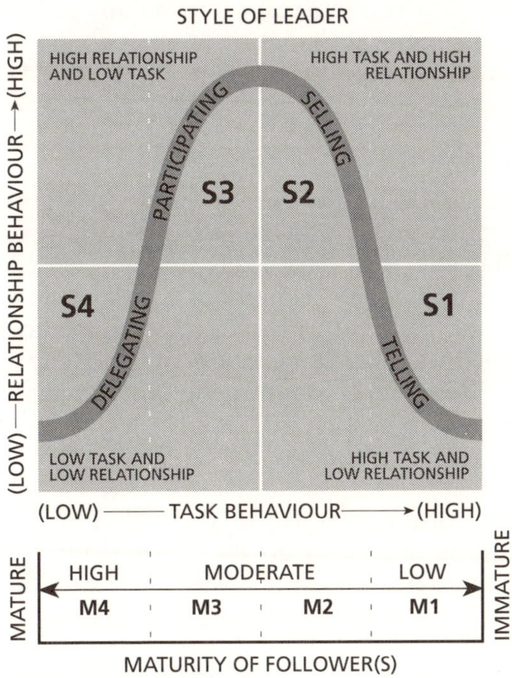

Figure 11.3 Situational leadership.

Each of the four quadrants is given a name: Telling, Selling, Participating and Delegating. You should note that the curve never reaches zero relationship in either the telling or the delegating quadrants. Zero relationship would be a totally inappropriate management style. In the delegating quadrant, this would be equivalent to leave them, and in the telling quadrant it would be something like 'zap them'. One does come across managers who use only these two extreme styles. In fact I had the misfortune to be involved with such a manager and can attest to the fact that neither approach works. He had a turnover in staff which reached over 100 per cent in three years. (The same person would have been a 5, 1, 2 on the McClelland scales, see Chapter 8, and would have been far better advised to stick to selling, which is the only thing he was really good at.)

The four basic styles

Each of the four basic styles is a combination of task and relationship behaviour. Which one is appropriate depends on the maturity of the follower on that particular task. It is not at all correct to see a person in terms of his average maturity. For example, a salesperson may be quite mature with respect to making calls on established customers, but somewhat immature at prospecting or cold calling, especially if he had never done it before and received no training or guidelines.

Maturity
Firstly, let us define what is meant by maturity. Maturity is defined as a combination of 'ability' and 'willingness'. Ability means whether the person has the necessary skills and knowledge to do that particular job. 'Willingness' is perhaps a little misleading. It is not so much a question of whether they want to cooperate or are willing to do the job, but more a question of whether they have the necessary confidence and commitment. Now let us look at the four basic styles.

1 Telling
This is for people low in maturity on this task. Low maturity means that the person is unable to do the job and little confidence or commitment to do it. This is not a very likely situation in the sales department unless you are asking someone to do something which is well outside their normal ambit. Clearly here it is necessary to use a telling style. In the non-business world the telling style is more

common, especially in school. In the army or prison the telling style is also used, but in this case the relationship level would be much lower and close to zero, or the 'zap them' style we referred to earlier.

2 Selling

This style is easy to explain to sales people. Selling is about explaining to people why you want them to do it your way. This is the appropriate style for someone who is often willing (confident or committed) but only partly able to do what you require. Hence they need significant task behaviour as well as relationship behaviour. Typically the followers have low to moderate maturity on the task. The leader remains in control, but provides an opportunity for communication and explanation. Through two-way communication, the leader tries to get the follower to buy into the desired action.

3 Participating

Followers here are moderate to high maturity. Considering the task the leader wishes to manage, the followers believe that they know what to do and how to do it. Typically they are pretty able and mostly willing. At this stage there needs to be an equal partnership between leader and follower. Together they will figure out what to do and how to do it. The follower is as competent to make suggestions as the manager. The degree of task behaviour from the manager is clearly lower than in the previous two styles.

4 Delegating

This is a style of management and should not be confused with the act of delegating as discussed in Chapter 10. You may well use a delegating style in the act of delegating something to someone, but equally well you may use a participating or a selling style in delegating if the situation demands it.

Once a follower is relatively 'expert' at a task, he does not require very much task behaviour. In fact, it would be resented as unwarranted interference. Equally, since there is now less need for communication between the two, the degree of relationship behaviour reduces. Note, however, that it does not drop away altogether. It is never appropriate to have no relationship behaviour at all. That would be equivalent to the previously mentioned 'leave them' behaviour. Even if the manager is not providing direction on how to do the task, he or she still needs feedback about the follower's reactions and progress on the project. The follower is now very able and willing, to the extent that the follower could be considered as expert or more expert than the manager.

The diagram in Figure 11.4 summarises the total situational leadership model.

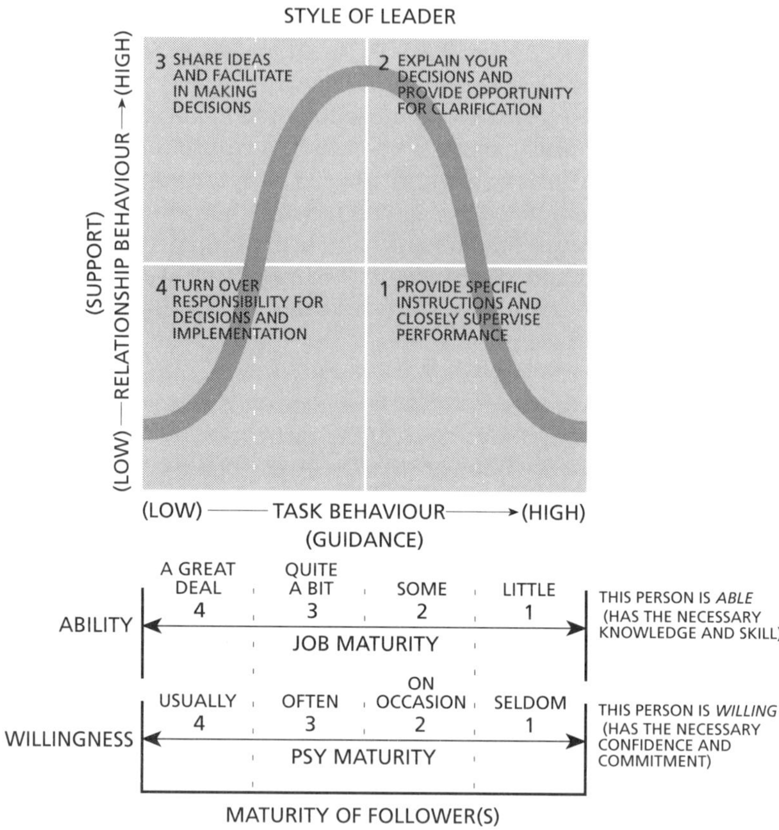

Figure 11.4 Defining maturity and the four basic leadership styles.

Implications for sales managers

There is a situational leadership exercise devised by Hersey and Blanchard which identifies an individual's predominant management style, and the style adaptability. It is recommended that each sales manager does the exercise to find out what his current style range is and what styles he tends to use. From my experience, the most dominant style by far for Australian sales managers is the selling style, followed by the telling style and the participating style, both fairly close together.

A recent study by Bernard Barry and Peter Dowling, described in the Australian Institute of Management publication, *An Australian Management Style?*, has indicated that Australian managers are a fairly homogeneous group, that is, there is not much difference between the way they operate, irrespective of their functional roles. Finance managers operate fairly similarly to sales managers and production managers.

The study also showed some differences among Australian, British and American managers. American managers are extroverted; British managers are more intelligent; Australian managers are more dominating and assertive than either of the others, are more imaginative but less practical!

The most serious finding is that most subordinates, 79 per cent in fact, preferred a consultative or participative management style. Yet the style in which they perceived they were being managed was far more autocratic than they wanted. Indeed, 42 per cent classified their managers as autocratic or persuasive, but only 16 per cent expressed a preference for that style.

Another Australian study, by Sadler and Hofstede, had similar findings. In one Australian organisation, they found that 54 per cent of the managers were seen by their subordinates as autocratic and persuasive.

If this is related back to the situational leadership model, what is happening is that people are being managed mainly in a selling style and that is not what they want. What they want, it seems, is more of the participative style. My own observations support this view.

Each manager should be using a number of different styles, depending on the situation. Most sales managers tend to use the same selling style, regardless of the situation.

As your people become more and more able and willing to perform tasks, as will happen as they grow in experience and knowledge, then the style you use should move along the bell-shaped curve towards participating and delegating. If you continue to use the selling style, it will become increasingly unacceptable to your people.

Caution must be exercised. One of the main hygiene factors in Herzberg's model was supervision. Failure to take the situational leadership model into account could well be causing dissatisfaction in your sales people. You could even find that your most capable and experienced people start to leave because they feel they are being dictated to.

Pay particular attention to the situational leadership model when you are delegating tasks and when you are using non-directive techniques in training and developing your staff.

The bottom line is that Australian sales managers must learn to manage their sales people with more genuine and open participation and delegation.

12

Counselling, discipline and dismissal

This section is concerned with what happens when a person's performance is falling well below standard or when a person does something outside his authority or the company rules, such that it becomes necessary to take up the matter formally with the person.

The goal must always be to correct the situation, for the sake of the company and the individual.

What is the difference between counselling and discipline? The difference is quite subtle and to a large extent one of semantics. The goals of the process and the methods of achieving them are similar in both cases. For the sake of proposing definitions, however, there is in counselling a suggestion of advice. It is more appropriate for a person whose performance is not satisfactory, or a person who does not realise he is in breach of the company rules.

Discipline is about maintaining control or order. It is most likely to be about a more flagrant breach of the company's rules. It is more likely to be as a result of negligence or lack of effort. Even so, discipline is not the same as punishment. Punishment would be called disciplinary action, and in the sales area that is not normally the way things work. In most cases, it is to be hoped that the situation can be remedied through counselling or discipline—in other words, talking about it.

However, it must also be recognised that on occasions the only appropriate course will be to dismiss someone. The sales manager must recognise when that is the case, and follow a certain number of steps if the company is to avoid the threat of being taken to court for unfair dismissal.

Everyone must know the rules

It would be quite inappropriate to counsel or discipline someone who did not know the rules. The first step must be the establishment and acceptance of a clear job description and standards of performance (see Chapter 3). There should also be published policies and procedures. The production of such a document is the responsibility of management, and copies should be made available to all individuals in the company. It should be handed to people during their induction program. Effectively it spells out the rules of the company.

Should there be a special meeting?

If the matter is to do with the way a person does his job, it will probably be more of a counselling matter, which could be handled at the end of a coaching day, if appropriate, or at an assessment interview. If necessary, it could be the subject of a separate interview. In the case of a breach of company rules, which could require counselling or discipline, it should be a separate meeting.

Let us concentrate on the sort of situation, relatively uncommon fortunately, where things have come to the point that they need to be made the subject of a formal meeting. Normally this would be as a result of a significant breach of company rules, or poor performance of a continuing nature which has shown itself to be impervious to frequent attempts by the sales manager to correction through on-the-job coaching. In either event, the procedure for preparing for the interview and conducting it will be the same.

Doing the ground work

Once you are sure that the company rules and the job description and standards of performance are clear, you need to satisfy yourself that there really has been a breach which is worthy of action being taken. In particular, you are ill advised to take action on the evidence of a third party, without thoroughly investigating the matter yourself. You may need to question the salesperson against whom the allegation has been made. However, this would simply be that, questioning. It would not be at that stage in any way a counselling or discipline interview. If after questioning those who may have some input into what happened, it is not at all clear what really happened, make a mental note of it and let the matter drop.

Only if the pattern is repeated a number of times would you consider taking any action without firm evidence.

You will only go to the next stage—of planning an interview—if you have firm evidence.

Preparing for the interview

Set up the meeting clearly, explaining the objective and the purpose of the meeting. (That, of course, must always be correction of the incorrect behaviour.) Avoid any prior discussion with the salesperson about the matter.

Know the point at issue and have the appropriate policy, procedure or standards of performance ready to refer to. Prepare the facts thoroughly and make sure they are relevant to the point at issue. If it is a question of deteriorating performance, make sure that you have the recent assessments and the appraisals available. It will now be more apparent than ever how important it is for these assessments and appraisals to be signed and accepted as correct by both the sales manager and the employee.

Be clear in your own mind what you want as the outcome of the meeting in terms of the necessary commitments to action from the salesperson. Be sure that you know exactly the message which you must get across.

Yet at the same time, do not prejudge the case; there may be aspects of it of which you are not aware.

Structure the interview, deciding how you will gain the agreement of the person that there is indeed a problem that needs to be addressed. You may need to draw upon the content of the notebook you will keep for each person and which should be used in quality time and in preparing for assessments and appraisals.

Have some idea of the type of action plan which would be appropriate to overcome the problem.

Allow plenty of time for the interview and ensure that there are no interruptions under any circumstances. It is essential to have complete privacy, and if you are unfortunate enough to operate in open plan offices, you will need to find an alternative meeting room to ensure privacy.

Conducting the interview

It requires a certain amount of assertiveness on behalf of the sales manager to carry out a successful counselling or discipline interview. Under no circumstances does that mean aggressive. Sometimes, as a nation, we have difficulty in understanding the difference. 'Assertive' means expressing the message clearly and without aggression or emotion. There are no raised voices, but what has to be said is said.

The interview must be direct, factual and totally understood. At the same time, it must be constructive and result in the interviewee accepting what has been said and committing to an action plan to correct the problem.

To achieve this in the interview, you will need to call on your assertiveness skills, be fair and understanding, open minded but firm. You need to be logical and systematic. In the face of emotion, you must control your own emotions.

Hints for counselling and discipline interviews

- Be pleasant and courteous.
- Put the person at ease; there is no point trying to make this a Gestapo style of interview.
- Restate the purpose of the interview, and try to suggest a positive outcome, making it clear that the outcome is to be a plan of action, not some form of disciplinary action or dismissal.
- As quickly as you can, establish the nature of the problem, the offence or shortcomings, as you see it.
- Be specific.
- Be accurate.
- Do not exaggerate, but state the facts clearly without being 'too soft'.
- Be matter of fact and not judgemental.
- Once you have explained the problem, allow the interviewee to state his case, recognising that there may be extenuating circumstances of a motivational nature either on or off the job which could have an effect.
- Listen carefully to what the interviewee says.
- Keep calm, do not get into an emotional argument and do not get drawn into discussing irrelevancies.
- Keep your mind very clearly on the issue at hand and do not be deflected into other issues by a deft interviewee.
- Establish the cause of the problem, whether it is attitude, lack of knowledge or skills, or a motivational issue.

- Be constructive and show that improvements can be achieved.
- Get the interviewee to suggest what he should do, rather than you telling him what he must do.
- Summarise each point so that you both clearly understand what has been agreed.
- You must control the interview.
- There is no need to have anyone else in the interview unless you need to use the testimony of another person directly, and then they should only be involved to the extent that is necessary to establish the facts.
- Record the interview while it is fresh in your mind and confirm in writing any action points agreed to.
- In the initial stages of counselling or discipline, it may not be necessary to have the interviewee sign the notes of what happened, but if there is a need to have more than one such interview, and especially if it is likely eventually to lead to dismissal, it is advisable to have the notes of the meeting typed up and submitted to the interviewee for signature to the effect that the notes are a correct record of the meeting.
- End the meeting on as positive a note as you can, emphasising the action points agreed to.

Handling difficult situations

There are some awkward situations that can arise in counselling and discipline interviews. There may be some genuine reactions and the problem may be at least in part due to misunderstandings, lack of training, lack of experience, domestic problems or ill health. However, there may be some statements that are made purely to evade the issue or put you on the back foot. Usually the sales manager will be able to recognise which one is which. Here are some of the possible situations and some suggestions on how you could handle them.

1 *The interviewee disagrees with your assessment of the facts.* In other words, he denies that he has broken the company rules or that there is a shortcoming in performance. Unless you can back up your assertion with evidence, he will not accept what you say and will not be motivated to do anything about it. He

will also correctly surmise that you could not dismiss him for this misdemeanour without every chance of being successfully taken to court for wrongful dismissal. For this reason, you must be absolutely sure of your facts and have the evidence ready before you embark on the interview. In the case of poor performance, you must have job descriptions and performance standards and assessments of performance on regular checks of the person's work. Anecdotal evidence of customers or other staff from your own company is not likely to be enough.

2 *The interviewee does not accept that the behaviour questioned is outside the guidelines of his job.* The fault in this case may partly be yours, if the interviewee is being genuine. You must make sure that everyone has a copy of their job descriptions and all company policies and procedures and that you as a manager make sure they understand them.

3 *The interviewee accepts that things are going wrong, but blames it onto failure of the company's systems, or onto other people.* The systems issue is easy. Think about it, and if you agree that something needs to be done, then fix it. Blaming it onto others is harder. This is because it comes down to their word against the other person's and unless you are careful, you may get caught in the middle. Prevention is always better than cure, and you should make sure that all the job descriptions for your people fit in with each other, so that everyone understands who should be doing what. In these cases it is better not to get involved with duck shoving. State clearly what you expect of the interviewee, and advise him that if, on a case-by-case basis he is not able to do his job, to raise the issue with you immediately. Then you need to make sure that the other people who may be involved get the same message, and then wait and see what happens. The chances are that whether there was a real problem or not, it will get resolved at this point.

4 *The interviewee explains that there is a motivational hygiene factor operating.* If it is off the job, you need to understand it, be supportive and do anything you can help to resolve the problem. If it is on the job, either it can be fixed or not. If it is a genuine hygiene factor which should be fixed up, take whatever action is necessary to fix it. If it is something which you cannot change, then the bottom line is that either the salesperson is going to have to accept things the way they are and improve his performance/behaviour, or you are going to have to consider saying goodbye. This sort of situation arises when a person has been passed over for a promotion.

The 'wronged' salesperson slacks off because he is disillusioned and annoyed. You may ask yourself whether you handled the issue correctly at the point the appointment was made. However, you cannot afford to have a prima donna pouting because he did not get what he thought he deserved, even if you had not really been assertive enough all the way along about the person's prospects. You are just going to have to tell things the way they are, including what the realistic opportunity for advancement is, and what conditions the salesperson would need to fulfil to qualify. Then either the salesperson accepts the situation, or leaves, or gets dismissed. Don't lead him on with hollow promises, it is not fair to him or to the company.

Following up

After the interview you must make sure that the action plan agreed to is implemented. You have as much responsibility for the future as the other person. Monitor the action plan through quality time, and chart progress through on-the-job assessments and general observation. Ask the salesperson how he feels things are progressing. Encourage him to take responsibility for his own behaviour and give him feedback as to how he is going.

Above all, do not let a single instance get integrated into folklore. There was a very competent marketing person who worked for an organisation where I was the Australian Sales Manager. One customer had mentioned to a senior manager that he found it difficult to communicate with this person. There were in fact many customers who thought he was excellent at his job. However, the sad fact is that it became known that poor Doug did not get on with customers. It was untrue, but it became a piece of folklore such that it ruined his chances of ever getting the top marketing job, which in reality he deserved.

Dismissal

If the recruitment and selection process has been right and if we have managed our staff correctly, it should never become necessary to dismiss anyone. Of course, the real world is different. Often we inherit the recruitment mistakes of our predecessors. Sometimes through faults that we make along the way, we unwittingly create situations that lead to dismissal of a salesperson.

By dismissal is meant dismissing someone from the company for poor conduct. This is not the same as retrenchment, where either the position of that employee is no longer necessary, or where the company can no longer afford to keep all the staff. Under the circumstances of retrenchment the matter is quite different and the conditions applicable to leaving may also be quite different. The employee will usually get some part of the contribution of the company to superannuation and conventionally, if not legally, some compensation such as a week's salary for every year of service. In the case of dismissal, the employee will normally get only the holiday entitlements due and salary for the period of notice. The superannuation payable will depend on the trust deeds of the scheme. There is usually a sliding scale depending on the years of service. For employees of less than five years, and sometimes up to ten years' service, they may be entitled only to their own contributions plus interest. As the years of service increase, there is more likelihood of the employee receiving some of the company's contribution to superannuation. There is often a rider in the deeds which says that in the case of dismissal, at the discretion of the trustees, it may be decided to pay no company contribution at all.

If the problem is that the salesperson is not capable of doing the job, either because of his ability or his attitude (for example, he may find it hard to recommend for purchase a product at a given price when in his view it is not worth that amount of money), an alternative to dismissal might be a transfer to a different job.

However, the time will probably come for each sales manager when he has to dismiss someone. Although it makes little difference in practical terms, people are often given the opportunity to resign, rather than suffer the ignominy of a dismissal. In the case of a dismissal, the company must be sure that the necessary steps have been taken to reduce the likelihood of a successful unfair dismissal case being brought.

Dismissal procedures

Before dismissal, the following steps should have taken place:

- The person's job description must have been provided, and must be clear and up to date.
- The standards of performance necessary to satisfy the requirements of the company must have been communicated in written form.
- The company's policies and procedures must have been provided, with attention drawn to pertinent items.

- In the case of poor performance, there should be a record of a number of interviews where the manager has advised the person of the problem and made every attempt to be of assistance through training and development.

The above-mentioned 'assessment' interviews should be at more regular intervals than the normal frequency. At least three or four such interviews are recommended. As a legal minimum requirement, on the first occasion you should warn the individual and set a standard and time for the standard to be met. This may be a few weeks in the case of poor performance, or it may be immediately in the case of incorrect social behaviour. There should be a review at the time indicated at the first meeting, and at that time a final warning may be issued.

Try to get the person to sign as correct the notes taken at the interview which state what was discussed. There should be evidence which can be presented, such as the notes taken during field coaching days, which shows that there has not been improvement up to the required standard of performance.

In the case of a breach of company rules, unless it is of a major dimension, normally there would not be a dismissal for a first offence. However, full details should be kept of the circumstances of the breach, and notes taken and if possible signed at the end of every discipline interview.

Immediate dismissal is permissible when the issue is one of misconduct, where misconduct can best be defined as an act which could be subject to charge by the police.

The dismissal interview will be a separate one from the counselling and discipline interview. In this case it may be a good idea to have someone else from your company present at the interview, possibly your own boss or someone from the personnel department.

Assuming that the dismissal follows a number of previous interviews, you will have clearly established the facts beyond any doubt. You should have advised your own personnel department and any other person of authority. Have all the financial details worked out beforehand and have all the necessary cheques ready, together with Group Certificate for the year if at all possible. Know what company property you need to account for, including equipment such as car, tools, electronic machines and all company records and files. Make provision for any outstanding expenses to be handled on the spot. For the sake of harmony of the team and to avoid any destruction to the company business or morale, you must ensure that when the interview is over, the person is allowed to clear out his desk, leaving behind everything which is not his personal property, and a taxi called, which you should be kind enough to pay for!

Again, there is no need to be unpleasant. Stick very strictly to the facts. Go over the reasons for the dismissal, including the evidence and notes of previous interviews. Do not be emotional or accusatory. Just state the reasons why you are taking the course of action, and explain the financial details of the final payment. Do not prolong the interview and do not enter into argument or recriminations; it is too late for all of that.

You should also analyse why it became necessary to go as far as dismissing someone. There may very well be some very important learning points from the whole exercise.

The above suggestions are guidelines. Legislation covering dismissal is different in every state, and will continue to change. Therefore you should consult with your own personnel department or the legislative bodies operating in your area to make sure that what you do remains within the law.

13

Sales planning and account management

Sales planning is one of the few activities of a sales manager which is not so much involved with interpersonal relationships. It is more about planning the tasks that the sales department should be performing, and planning the results that should be obtained. In a sense the first planning job the sales manager has to attend to is that of planning the organisation, which is dealt with as a separate subject in Chapter 2.

The items that need to be planned are:

- sales results
- sales activities
- cost control
- cashflow planning.

Sales results

Sales results are a mix of volume sales, dollar revenues and contribution. (Contribution is the amount of gross profit contributed towards paying off fixed costs, and then to profit.) Sales results may be expressed by product and by customer. Most companies will choose to look at their business in both ways.

Sales activities

Once having set targets or budgets for sales results, it will be necessary to plan the sales activities to make the results happen. This will be both a matter of defining customer contact, and planning what happens during the contact. It includes both account planning, which is planning the total business at the account, and planning each individual call.

Cost control

The need to set a cost budget for the sales department, covering all the variables. This does not include just salaries and expenses, but might include other discretionary money for which the sales department is responsible. Such items could include cooperative advertising budgets and other promotional monies. It could include a budget for resources provided by other departments, such as technical service.

Cashflow planning

There are two important aspects of planning that are often either overlooked, or are not addressed with sufficient zeal. They are the provision of credit and the availability of inventory. These two functions are often seen by sales people as something which should be there and which they should not need to dirty their hands with. However, they both have a significant impact on the cashflow of the company and they are both at least influenced by, and more often than not an integral part of sales. The sales actions will be to set standards for average receivables and then keep to them, and to forecast accurately for inventory needs so that the stock can be made available when it is required, at minimum cost.

The classic planning process

In simple terms, the planning process (whatever is being planned) can be summarised in the following five steps:

1. **Where are we now?** An analysis of the current situation, as far as possible expressed quantitatively.
2. **Where are we going?** A forecast of where we will be if we carry on doing the same things as we are doing now.
3. **Where do we want to go?** A set of specific goals or objectives that define the end result we want. They are achievable, quantified wherever possible, and timed.
4. **How will we get there?** The overall strategies or ploys we will use, and the detailed action plans in a sequenced set of steps, stating who will do what by when, and which when all carried out will lead to the end result defined above.
5. **How will we know whether we are getting there?** The control mechanisms that need to be implemented to make sure that the action plans are on target.

Objectives, strategies and activities

Some of the above words are used in different ways. As long as you and your sales people understand what you mean, then the words you use are less important. However here are some commonly accepted definitions of the above words.

Objective. The end result you want, the goal you are striving for. These will as often as possible be quantified, such as the sales budget or the expenses budget, or market share. However, they can also be qualitative, as long as they can clearly be identified as having been achieved or not.

Strategy. This is the overall route you will be taking to reach your objective. It is the same as a ploy or a game plan.

Activities. These are the sequenced actions that are undertaken to satisfy the strategy. They should be sequenced in a clear, logical, and usually chronological order, be specific and state who is to do what by when. This is your detailed route plan, spelling out all the necessary steps. It should be possible to tear off the activities sheet, hand it to someone who should then be able to carry out the plan from that sheet alone.

If you only set objectives and strategies, the chances are that nothing will happen, because it is the activities which themselves cause things to happen. The objectives and the strategies are the necessary preconditions, the thought processes that define the actions. However, it is the activities that make the difference in a practical sense. It is by monitoring the activities that you will know whether you are on plan or not.

Having discussed some of the principles of planning, let us now look at the areas where sales managers need to do most of their planning.

Sales results

Budgets

In most organisations, the sales results are planned on a yearly basis in advance in a document called the sales budget. This process is very important, and the figures at the end of the process will serve to plan production requirements, distribution, profit figures and cashflow projections. They can either be worked out bottom up, or top down. Bottom up means that each sales person should be advancing a budget by product for each of his customers. To do this he may require some overall assumptions on what the business environment is likely to be. He will also need to know of any product changes, and any other factors likely to affect the results, such as tariff changes and import or local competition. This information is often provided as guidelines from marketing. Ideally, the prices for each customer and for each product should also be included, again working within assumptions of what can be achieved in a total sense.

There is a view that if you ask the sales people what they will achieve, they will always call low so that when they exceed budget they will look good. This is a naive view. How they call will depend on a number of things. It will depend on whether they get paid commission on above-budget sales (this will cause them to call low). It may depend on the recent history. If things have been going well they will tend to be overly optimistic, and conversely if things are bad, they will base their views on doom and gloom. It may depend on the culture you have, whether or not you beat sales people over the head for poor performance against budget, and indeed whether you have been performing against budget or not. It also depends on the way you present the whole exercise to them. In any event, it has to be done, and the sales manager must give insightful guidance and go through the figures that are submitted with each salesperson, and agree with the salesperson on any necessary amendments. In fact, many sales managers will tell you that more often than not the sales people will call high, especially the well motivated ones who are generally performing well. They tend to think they can pick up all of the growth at the expense of the competition. It gives rise to the 'paradox of levels'. Each single figure can be justified. However, you know very well that when you put them all together, it just cannot be achieved.

The top down way is a question of starting with what the company needs, either to satisfy shareholders, or the overseas parent company. Sometimes it is a question of playing politics. We know we need an expansion, otherwise we are going to be in real trouble. The only way we can justify the money required for the expansion is to produce certain results this year so that our parent will cough up the ready. So that is what we have to put in. It depends on your culture, but as a sales manager I have always recognised that there may be needs for these sorts of figures, but I have fought hard and long to make sure that my sales department is not held to political numbers in which no one believes. Let there be two sets of figures, one for New York, Tokyo, Frankfurt or London, and another set, against which the sales department will be judged. Otherwise you are condemning the sales department to a demoralising result before they even start. By all means let us build in challenge. However, too often sales managers get themselves locked into numbers which they know they can never ever achieve.

Ideally the top down figures, which will also include the marketing department's global view of the situation, and the bottom up figures, need to be compared and contrasted. They should be brought together wherever possible. If the sales department has been given the right information, is competent and fair dinkum, and most sales departments are, and there is a significant discrepancy between what the sales managers will commit to and what the company says is reasonable, then the company ignores what the sales managers say at its peril. Sales managers are right more often than not.

Once the budget is set, it is set. There may be quarterly reviews, but that will not change the budget. If the company is performing worse than budget for whatever reason, then it is critically important to recognise this, and to analyse the reasons. If it is possible to take corrective action, fine, but if not then we must make amendments in the other side of the equation. If the contribution is not being achieved, then there will be less money available than we thought for the expenses that were budgeted for. That is when there is an argument over what should be cut, and what should not. The golden rule is to not cut any expenses that are likely to lead to increased sales. Do not slash advertising, or put off sales people, or stop your technical support or sales people travelling to customers. Skinny down in other areas which will not have such an immediate effect. We all know that there needs to be a balance between the immediate needs and the future needs of the company, but far too many accountancy minded people cut the very areas that are capable of reducing the sales losses. A large national company took the very strange step of taking away the car telephones of their sales people to save money, and as a result caused the sales productivity to drop considerably as the sales people started diverting one to two hours a day from selling to driving, in order to get into the office. Once in, they found it very hard to get out again!

Sales performance against budget

It is clear that we need to measure our performance against these budget figures on a regular monthly basis. To make it easier, have the information technology department or bureau provide the figures to you in the easiest way to interpret and analyse. Do not spend time on the figures which are on target, but analyse the variances of those which are not.

If you only budget for and measure volume, then that is all the sales people will ever think about. That may be appropriate for a business where the prices are set and do not vary, and where there is not much difference in contribution across the product range. However, in most businesses it is much better to get the sales people looking at the contribution they make at each customer and with each product. You should try to put together an account profitability analysis for key accounts. Not only will it tell you how much you are really making at major accounts (or maybe you are scared to find out?), but it allows comparisons for diagnostic or even negotiation purposes. Include the contribution based on standard cost from the plant, or actuals for imports, and then make an adjustment for freight, credit and if necessary, any special packaging requirements. If there are significant variations in sales or technical support, you can add those in, based upon an average cost per call. However, there is little point in allocating anything further than that. Only measure and control those items which you can manage or influence and which are likely to make a significant difference to the account profitability figures.

Other sales results you may need to consider will be market share or market penetration. You have to decide what are the key elements in your business. Current sales puts the money in the bank for every one, but in some businesses, strategically, market share is much more important. If you are in a seasonal business and your sales are 10 per cent above last year, but everyone else is 20 per cent above, you had better start worrying. (See Figure 13.2, on page 217.)

Sales activities

What is actually required to achieve the sales results will vary from selling situation to selling situation. Where there is a very large number of orders, each of relatively small value, obtained in a routine fashion, such as the 'route trade', the key planning activity is probably how you get round the route. Clearly, the quality of what the salesperson does and says will be extremely important. That was dealt with under training (see Chapter 6). What we are talking about here are the sales planning issues. In many cases, there are sophisticated electronic methods of assisting sales route planning, which accompanied by electronic order entry and reporting, can really streamline the job.

Selling through distributors/retailers

In selling through a distribution network, where the customer is the distributor, dealer, reseller, or retailer, who then sells the product to the end user, you must clearly define at what levels you are going to devote the selling effort. There will be some selling done at the point where the decisions are made on distribution, the head offices of the supermarkets, the distributors or the cooperatives. There will also be some at the retail or outlet level, where the job may include merchandising the product, getting local store commitments, ensuring that agreements with head offices are being implemented, or training the staff of the outlet to sell and support your products. There is often a job to be done with influencers, especially with technical products where either government departments or Quango's or consultants may have a viewpoint which can influence the user.

All of this must be understood and planned. There needs to be a consistent set of plans which flows from the head office plan down to each outlet where there is a sales job to be done. This is, in fact, becoming one of the key issues for the 1990s. The decision on where a supplying company will direct its effort into the distribution network, and how it goes about it, is becoming one of the key determinants of success for such businesses. This is reflected by the gradual change towards allocation of funds to the distribution network rather than just to the consumer. It is a factor which sales forces selling to the grocery trade have been grappling with for a number of years. Those who have not adopted a strong account management discipline have paid the penalty in terms of the amount of money they spend to get distribution and the promotion and positioning in store, which they seek.

Unless you get the distribution right, you may spend a fortune on media advertising only to find that the user cannot buy your product because you cannot get distribution. You may even find that the retailers become so adept at switch selling that you end up advertising for your competitor to pick up the business at the point of sale.

It is such an important issue, and has both a strategic and therefore marketing dimension as well as a tactical sales dimension. For this reason, the sales and marketing departments in such businesses must find a better way to work together, or do what some of the larger consumer goods manufacturers have done and set up a department whose job it is to 'market' to the distribution network as opposed to the user. Such departments are often called trade marketing departments.

The planning cycle for distributors can be a year, split either into quarters or in a seasonal business, into the various seasons. The most successful approach is to gain overall agreement in principle to a modus operandi for a longer period, such as a year, and then to fine tune the details of the plan for each season or each quarter, depending on the needs of the marketplace at the time. The supplier should always seek agreement on the joint business goals and strategies, and a sharing of the investment of time, money and resources to achieve them. A key part of the whole process will be the need to review progress towards these joint goals on an ongoing basis. This is best done in the form of a quarterly Business Review and Development meeting (a BRAD), or a seasonal review.

Key account management

What we are talking about in essence is key account management. The principle is almost the same for those companies selling to a customer who is the consumer, which is the case in most sales. Many companies will find that 80 per cent of their business is locked up in 20 per cent of the accounts. These are then the critical accounts where we must direct most of our selling effort. So there is an element of focus on the 'key' accounts. At the same time, it will be important to ensure that what we do for these customers is really what they want us to do. We need to find ways of adding value to our package of goods and services, such that we can either lock out the competition, gain more volume, get higher prices or longer commitments, or a mixture of all of them. This assumes of course that we do not have a strategy of offering a no frills service at a no frills price. There will always be some market for such businesses, but it will flatten off at a quite low percentage of the total market.

The fact is that most people and most companies will make their decisions on a value for money basis and not just on price. Most companies have a preference for pricing higher but providing added value to their customers in terms of the way that they service them. This is hardly surprising when you think that anyone can use price at any time. However, to learn how to provide service takes time and skill. If you want to lock out your competitors from undermining your whole business at the stroke of a pen, then you have to opt for a strategy of selling on service and not price. This fact has been proved time and time again. It is based on the marketing concept of differentiation.

Key account management and differentiation

Differentiation is the provision of a package of goods and service such that the customer perceives them to be different (superior) to those available from other suppliers. And furthermore, such that he is prepared to reflect that perception in the quality of the arrangements he will make with that supplier (share, volume, price, contract period).

Key account management usually is based upon differentiation. It is a process, a philosophy for managing accounts and a discipline in planning and allocation of resources. It is too complex to go into the details of what is involved in a book on sales management; rather it is a subject deserving of a book in its own right. However, it will be clear to the reader that there are a number of steps that need to be followed.

The account management cycle

Firstly, there must be a very clear understanding of the marketing plans and strategies which will emanate from the strategic marketing plan and the corporate strategic plan. If you do not know what the marketing plans are or do not have a clear idea of the corporate direction, then ask for them. You can hardly run a sales department if you do not know the firm's overall direction.

At an account level you need to know everything about the account which might be helpful in managing the account and which will allow you to identify opportunities for you to add value to your package in the customer's eyes. Generally this means knowing much more over a broader range of your customer's operations than most sales forces know. In fact the average customer knowledge in Australia is pathetic. That is because most sales people only call on a small number of people within the customer's organisation—people like the purchasing manager and, from time to time, the production or development people. They generally have far less to do with marketing, sales or general management. All of these problems must be addressed within the account management framework.

You must also ensure that the information you do keep on your customers is kept in a systematic and secure way. On computer is the best way, especially if you are working for a large company where there is the possibility of networking it through the mainframe. In any event, it needs to be kept in some more public and enduring manner than a salesperson's neurons. Make sure that when the sales people walk out the door they do not take with them in their heads all the information the company had on the customers.

You should also do a SWOT analysis for your major customers, where you identify your strengths and weaknesses at that account as well as the opportunities for you and the threats to your business. It is at this stage where you are including the dimension of what the competition is doing. It is surprising how much planning goes in the comfortable but dangerous ignorance of what your competitors are doing or are likely to do.

Based upon this information, you should now undertake a systematic search for opportunities to add value to your package. You should also record the deficiencies in your information base, for this exercise is bound to expose some. You must also identify the relationship building opportunities between your company and the customer. This will include the need for multi-level selling. Note that we are here suggesting that the sales manager may well have some sales role to play with major customers, which may on the face of it seem to conflict with earlier statements that the sales manager should get on with managing and let the sales people get on with the selling. There is in fact no conflict as long as it is realised that the salesperson, let us call him in this case account manager, is using the sales manager as a resource, but is still retaining the sales responsibility himself. The sales manager will have specific tasks to perform at these major accounts, as indeed might the managing director, but he will not be running day-to-day sales at the account and will not be running the salesperson's calls.

The next step will be the writing of a specific account plan for this account, which will build on the analyses done and will consist of objectives, strategies and activities. Such plans should be proposed by the account manager, accepted by the sales manager, and then implemented by the account manager, including regular monitoring of the plan. Progress of the plan will be reviewed in quality time. Overall, since the plan expresses both the results required at that account as well as the activities most likely to produce them, they make one very good element of assessment and appraisal for account managers.

The cycle comes to an end at the review stage, when more information leading into our information base and the marketing planning may be obtained. In this way the cycle rotates. Periodically there will be some negotiation on the financial arrangements under which we will both do business. They could take place in principle at any time during the cycle. However, the further round the cycle you are, the more differentiation you should have created and the easier the negotiation process should be. It is most important to manage all your key accounts in this fashion, not just the ones where you are currently under threat or where there is a contract coming up for renewal. This is because most business is lost rather than gained. If you really are doing the right thing by your customer, you will not lose the business, or at least not unless you make a decision to walk away from it. If your customer loves you, he will tell you that there are problems and then you can decide whether to meet a competitive situation or not. If he doesn't love you, he will ditch you without telling you. It is easier to keep a customer you have than get a customer you don't have. If you account manage all of your major accounts whether you have just signed a four-year contract or not, you will make it much harder for your competitors to break into them.

Start off with planning at the highest level, the head office account, drawing from what you know of each of the operating sites, subsidiaries or retail outlets. Then flow the planning process down to whatever level is necessary.

A model of the account management cycle is shown in Figure 13.1.

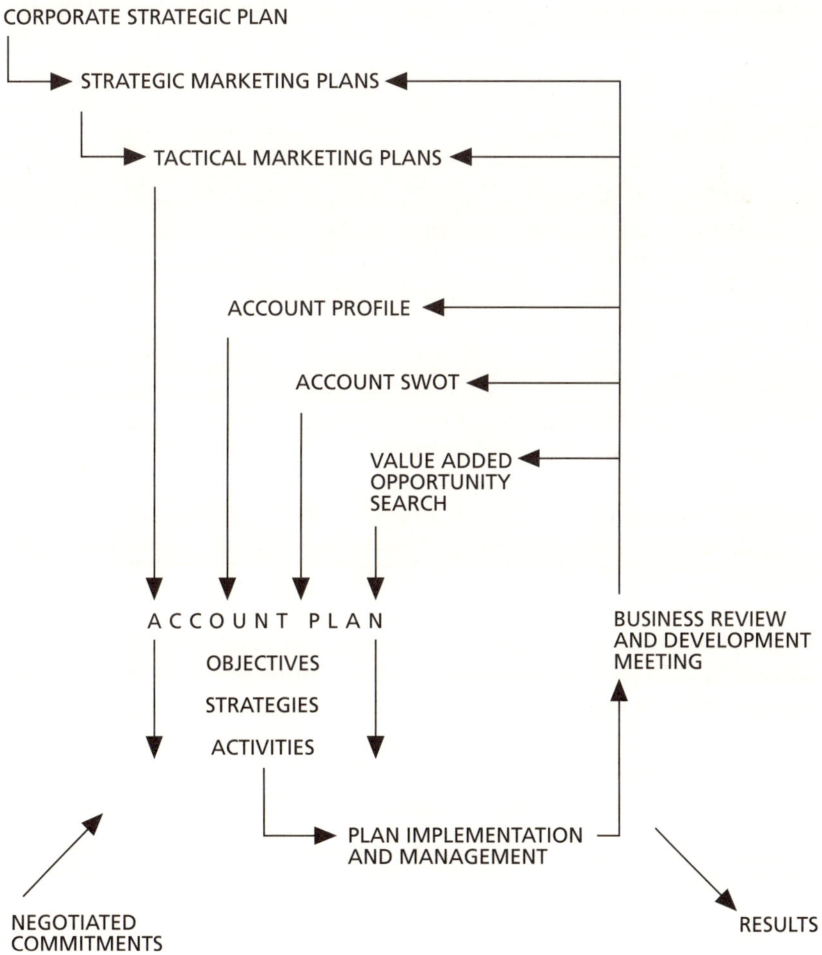

Figure 13.1 Account management cycle.

The account management cycle is appropriate for managing both customers and distributors or retailers. The major difficulty is in the contents of the accounts plans, since the distributor or retailer needs to make margin on volume sales for a given inventory investment, rather than for the product itself.

Other aspects of sales activity planning

We have discussed what are the main things a sales manager will want to plan and control in sales activities. There may be others, depending on the type of business and selling situation.

Other areas for sales planning and control

- Sales call productivity.
- Driving distance.
- Performance against route plan.
- Reporting of sales calls, sales activity, market reports.
- Number of sales promotion events.
- Use of bonus stock.
- Use of promotional funds (see next section).
- Number of complaints.
- Technical support provided.
- Samples.
- Prospecting calls and conversion rate to orders.
- Ratio of new to repeat business.
- Business lost.
- And there may be others appropriate for your particular business.

Just remember that planning is a tool, a means to an end, not an end in itself. Only plan and control those items which you assess are going to have a significant impact on the results. If you get carried away with planning, controlling and reporting on too much detail, you will not have enough time to do the productive things such as selling. Planning exists to be supportive of the productive work.

Cost control

As sales manager, you will usually be accountable for controlling certain costs. The degree of accountability, which should go hand in hand with authority, will depend on your company.

Costs under your control might include:

- salaries for all the staff
- sales incentives and commissions
- company car costs
- telecommunication costs
- printing and stationery costs
- travel and entertainment expenses
- training costs
- sales rebates and promotional dollars
- samples
- costs of settling complaints
- cost of work performed by technical service or other resources.

Some of these items may be set against the marketing budget. In any case, the sales manager should make a budget each year for the cost centres he is responsible for and then should control actuals against budget, concentrating on any areas of variance.

Controlling promotional funds

The largest item after salaries will be promotional funds for those of you who are selling through a distribution network, and particularly those of you selling to the grocery trade.

In that particular case, the budget will be enormous, and a major part of the sales management job will be the management of those funds. Often this will be done with guidance from or in conjunction with either marketing or 'trade marketing'. One might argue that it falls more into sales activities than into cost control. This is irrelevant; the important thing is to plan where you will invest your money and control what happens. In turn, that means knowing the effectiveness of the money you invest as a sales multiplier. Cooperative advertising and case-off deals are designed to increase sales both for you and for the distribution chain. Many might see the exercise as a way of throwing money at the distributors. Such a view will lead to a lack of respect by the distribution chain, and total rape of your bottom line. You must see these promotional monies in the light of an investment on which you need a return through incremental sales.

Each company should set standards for the promotional effectiveness of their products. This will vary according to the promotional needs of the products. Do not get sucked in to spending money promoting a product which does not need it, or promoting it in a way that does not work. Case-offs do not always have the same promotional effect on all products.

You end up with a number of variables, such as the cost of the promotion, the case-off deal, the period of the buy, the amount of margin you are prepared to invest, the incremental sales you make, which all leads to the question of whether you make a profit as a result of the exercise, or not. Trying to play with all of these is an essential part of the planning process. Logging what happens is a critical part of the control, and necessary as input to the next exercise and to be used in negotiations with the trade.

This would normally be very hard to do. However, inexpensive software which operates on IBM-compatible personal computers, and which was developed in Australia for exactly this purpose, is now available. It is designed for use by account managers, sales managers, marketing or trade marketing. There are two versions, Promax and Procalc, developed by and available from the Professional Assignments Group in Sydney.

Cashflow management

Credit

Credit is a bore, but until the goods have been paid for, a sale has not been successfully concluded. (Some would go further and say that the sale has not been successful until the product has been paid for and used with satisfaction.) In most companies, the decision of whether to provide credit or not will be made by the finance department. They may also administer the collection of money, including overdue accounts. The more insightful companies will recognise that credit is part of the sales package and will involve the sales people in any departure from the normal course of events. This means that when a customer does not pay, it is the sales people who go and try to sort it out rather than have some inflexible and inexperienced clerk from the credit department stuffing up the customer relationships. The best way of operating is for the finance or credit department to administer the system, but by working closely with sales, pass on to sales for action with the customer, any non-standard situation.

It also means that sales people may have to discuss overdue accounts, and will have to negotiate the provision of credit. They may have to be involved with discussions with customers aimed at providing more security against the credit risk. They may have to tell the customer that unless he pays his outstanding bills, the company will not sell him any more product.

Overall, the sales department must administer the company policy on credit. It should have a budget for average receivables and it should have a budget for bad debts. Many companies have discovered that the provision of extended credit which they used as a tool to get business in the late-1970s and early-1980s can cause enormous problems when interest rates go up, as they did in the late-1980s. They have found that it takes seconds to extend terms from 30 to 60 days, and years and some large bribes to get them back to 30 days.

The sales manager must know which customers are paying outside agreed terms and take the necessary action through his sales people.

Inventory management and forecasting

The other factor which has a large effect on the company's cash flow, and which sales has some influence over, is inventory. The inventory of finished goods is sales inventory; it is there for you to sell.

Every salesperson would like there never to be a stock out. However, to aim for such a situation would be a folly. The cost of inventory to assure above about 95 per cent filling of orders at the time they are requested starts to rise exponentially. Most companies will aim for about 97–98 per cent. To plan on 100 per cent would cost the earth. Customers understand this, surprisingly enough, and will judge you not on the fact that occasionally the goods are not available on the day they were requested, but on the quality and timeliness of the advice you give them about it. More and more companies are moving towards better inventory control systems, such as JIT (Just-in-Time) and Manufacturing Resource Planning.

Many customers are starting to keep records of how their suppliers perform on delivery of orders against when they were requested. Your sales people are given a delivery record and a rating. To avoid being caught on the back foot, you should take the initiative by keeping your own records and presenting them at your business review and development meetings.

The two best contributions you can make to inventory control are as follows. The first one is to only provide consignment stock if the customer takes a special product and is located in a remote place, especially if the product is imported and by shipping straight to the customer, you can save freight. Otherwise consignment stock will lead to the need for higher inventories overall. It also encourages customers to be lazy in their own inventory control.

The second major function of the sales force is to forecast accurately. Unless your own production scheduling people know what you, the sales department, are going to need for sale, which products, where and when, then they will find it very hard to satisfy you, or will need to carry excessively high inventories just in case they are needed.

Unless you are careful, the sales people will see forecasting as simply a form-filling exercise, and they will tend to just put down the same as last month. To avoid this, you need to keep reinforcing the importance of forecasts. Tell them how accurate the forecasts are. Tell them what the inventory levels are and the costs of maintaining them. Show them the imbalances and the costs of carrying excess inventories, and identify lost business as a result of having no stock. Question the figures they have put in. Check out in the field how they ask the customer what he thinks his forthcoming requirements might be. Ensure that they present that question to the customer in a way that the customer sees that it is important and gives more than superficial consideration to it. Check that the sales people are actually asking the right people.

The accuracy of forecasting is important enough that it should be included in the job description, and acceptable standards of performance should be defined. In other words, the sales manager must hold the sales people accountable for forecasting.

Name of account:

Account manager:

	1989	**1990**	**1991**	**1992**
Invoiced sales				
Less rebates —volume —promotional —other				
= net sales revenue				
Less cost of goods —packaging —freight —credit				
= contribution				
Less sales costs —invoicing costs —technical support —advertising				
= net contribution				
Less fixed cost allocation				
= net profit before tax				

Notes

1 Where actuals are not available, allocations may be made.
2 Cost of goods should be based on standard costs.
3 Sales costs, technical costs can be calculated as visits as a percentage of total visits multiplied by total sales or technical costs.
4 Fixed cost allocation should be provided by the accountant as a guide to how satisfactory the net contribution level is.
5 Make comparisons over time and between accounts.
6 Use the information for planning, as a profit diagnostic and in account negotiations.

Figure 13.2 Account profitability format.

14

Running effective sales meetings

Most people find sales meetings boring. That is because most of them *are* boring. Furthermore, in large part they are a waste of time. Yet they should be one of the most important events for both the sales manager and the team. The manager is able in these meetings to build team spirit, to communicate, to set objectives, to plan, to problem solve and to train and develop his people.

The sales meeting should be useful to the sales people too, providing them with a channel of communication, direction, recognition where it is deserved, leading to improved motivation and a feeling of involvement in the business.

The problem with most sales meetings is that they address just the last period's sales figures in a rather monotonous way, and perhaps some administrative details. It is necessary, of course, to review sales and other important figures against budget or plan, but don't devote the whole meeting to it.

Objectives of the sales meeting

- Review sales results and other important factors for control of your business.
- Communicate:
  - — changes in policy or procedures
  - — any marketing items
  - — status of supply and stockholdings
  - — elements from the advertising campaign
  - — overall company results
  - — any other specific items or notices.

- Obtain feedback from the sales force of trends, competitive activity, levels of demand, suitability of marketing programs, any problems or other items.
- Address any current issues, such as price rise, inventory problems, competitive challenges, windfall opportunities, introduction of new products.
- Building on some of the above items, train and develop your people.
- Reinforce previous training.
- Rekindle or build on enthusiasm, to motivate the team and individuals.
- Achieve necessary individual or group attitude change.
- Provide a meeting place and forum for exchange of ideas and views for the sales people, building team spirit and morale.

Preparing for the meetings

Hold them regularly, usually once a month, perhaps every two months depending on the geographic spread of your people and the amount of material you have to cover. To really demonstrate that you take these meetings seriously, set the dates for the whole year, and stick to them.

The length of the meetings may vary depending on what is going on. Most regular sales meetings last one or two hours, but you should hold some meetings which have much broader objectives and which could last from half a day to a whole day. Never take more time than you need in order to meet your objectives. If you incorporate a real training session, allow a full day.

In planning the meeting, consider:

- the location
- the audience
- the agenda
- meeting activities.

The location

The environment of the meeting can be of critical importance to success, especially if it is wrong! Similar comments to those made about locations for training are appropriate (see page 108). The room should be well lit, well ventilated and the projector and screen such that material can be easily read by all attendees.

A round table format is best for normal sales meetings, but if there are more than eight or nine of you in a meeting with a training component, a horse shoe arrangement is better. If there is no suitable meeting room at your offices, you would be better advised to hire a room for half-day or full-day meetings.

The audience

The participants will normally be all the external sales people. You should also include as many of the internal sales people as possible, given that someone will be required to answer the telephones. You might also invite individuals from other departments, such as marketing, distribution and technical. Know exactly why they are being invited and let them know what their role is to be. If it is to observe so that they can get a feel for what is going on in the market place, they will not be expected to interrupt all the time. If they are expected to give information, make sure that they know what they are expected to communicate and give them a time limit. Sometimes invitations to people from other parts of the organisation with which your people have little contact, such as finance, or people at director level, can be very useful.

Avoid involving senior people for the whole of the meeting, otherwise you may find that your sales people will clam up.

To a certain extent, the number of people present will determine some of the activities. For example, it is not a good idea to have role plays with more than six to eight people, because the others will get bored. In fact, when it comes to the training sessions you may hold as part of these meetings, you should make sure under normal circumstances that only your own people are involved.

The agenda

Every meeting should have an agenda, together with timings. It should be carefully planned to ensure that variety and interest are built in and that the meeting rises to finish on a high note rather than tailing away. Cover action items from the last meeting and administrative details early, and leave specific work sessions, problem solving and training towards the end. Get the sales results out of the way early.

Ask for agenda items from the team, and ask them what sorts of things they would like to be included in later meetings. Allow some time for questions and for general comments and grievances of a group rather than a personal nature (grievances of an individual nature should be taken up during quality time).

Meeting activities

This is the hardest part of organising a meeting, because you face the same problem as you do with many customers, namely how to gain attention and maintain interest. The more variety, novelty and creativity you can build in, the better. The more involvement of the participants, and the more visual the presentation, the easier it will be to retain attention. Make sure that you get through the administrative issues quickly and efficiently.

When you cover sales figures:

- set a strict limit on the time to be devoted to the figures
- have individual sales people review their own customers before the meeting and be able to comment on any variations from plan, either above or below
- do not spend any time on figures which are on target
- give recognition for figures which are above target, and try to get some understanding of the reasons
- for below-target performance, try to turn the negative into the positive by agreeing on a positive action to address the problem. If nothing can be done about it, don't spend time wringing your hands in anguish, move onto something where some positive action can be taken
- make your motto, 'recommendations not recriminations'.

If you need to impart information on new policies or new products etc., a lecture style will be needed, but it can be made more interesting by getting outsiders, either from other departments or even from outside the company, to address the meeting. Make sure they have good visuals and some hard copy to leave with the participants on the key points.

Getting people to participate

Participation of the group can be achieved in a number of ways. You can ask one of your sales people to brief the rest on how he achieved a particular good result, or to explain to the rest of the group a suggestion for how the sales group could operate more effectively. Nominate individuals to run parts of the sales meeting. When it comes to problem solving, divide the group into twos or threes and get them working on the problem. Use case studies, or role plays. Turn issues such as a price rise, or a stock out into a mini-training exercise. Get the team to nominate their view of how it should be handled, and take feedback until you all agree on an approach.

Getting your people to give a short talk on aspects of their job or the market can give them practice in presentation skills.

Reinforcement of product knowledge is very necessary but can become boring. One highly stimulating method is to run a quiz.

Either the sales manager or technical or product managers can put the questions together. Or even better, divide the group into two teams, and get each team to devise product questions for the other. Each team answers the questions posed, and scores accordingly. The sales manager acts as chairman and scorer, and the losing team buys the drinks for everybody. The advantages of doing product training this way are that the teams learn while they are making up the questions for the other team. It is a team exercise and builds team motivation; it saves the sales manager the time in setting the questions himself, and there is a friendly competitiveness which can and should be fun. This works very well as an evening exercise after dinner, especially at conferences.

Chairmanship

The success of a meeting will to a large extent depend on how well it is chaired. Strong chairmanship means keeping within the time limits overall, which might mean letting one subject go on a little longer if it is constructive, but then saving some time elsewhere. It means controlling discussions, not allowing digressions or irrelevant interruptions, making sure that everyone has a chance to contribute, stopping the conversation hoggers, knowing when to set a subject aside for a separate meeting, summarising points and registering agreed actions, encouraging open and frank comment but avoiding conflict and negativity. It is an exhausting job if it is done well.

You should allow some of your more senior people to have the opportunity to develop their skills in chairing meetings by delegating some or all of the task to them on occasions. It is an opportunity for you to assess their management potential and for them to start to develop skills.

A good way of holding interest is to hire training video films. There are excellent ones available and most of the large video training libraries have times when people can go and review films at no charge. Sales managers should attend some of these open days; it gives ideas for training and is an enjoyable way of spending a couple of hours.

When you do show films in meetings, make sure that they are appropriate for current needs, and are consistent with the training needs of the group. Do not just play the film, but try to build some simple exercise around it to ensure that there is some discussion and that the key learning points as they relate to the group have been made. Relate the film to your own situation so that the content is seen as practically relevant.

Leading discussion

One of the best ways to create understanding and bring about attitude change is through discussion, and the sales meeting is an ideal forum. The discussion needs to be structured to bring out the main points. The pace can be altered according to whether common understanding has been achieved. Feedback is immediate and indicates whether or not your objectives have been achieved. Participation and involvement of the whole group is more likely to lead to commitment, putting peer pressure on some of the waverers. Everyone learns without feeling that they have been taught.

The problem is that leading discussion requires quite a high degree of skill on behalf of the discussion leader. He must carefully plan what the outcome is to be, and then stimulate thought and discussion so that it seems as if the conclusion he wants is actually proposed by the participants. This is done by listening very carefully to the verbal and non-verbal language and then guiding the conversation by questioning.

The leader should start with some general questions which set the scene and which should not be contentious. In a sense there is some similarity with non-directive training techniques. The questioning should then lead in a firm direction, using a mix of open and closed questions. The open questions, the how?, what?, why?, where?, will stimulate more discussion; the closed questions will give commitment and indicate the degree of agreement. The closed questions will advance the discussion in a more definite way. Part of the skill of a discussion leader is asking the questions in such a way that a certain response is suggested, without people feeling that they are being manipulated or led in a direction they are opposed to.

When the leader asks a question and there is no response, he may feel under tremendous pressure to start speaking himself. However, there will be even greater pressure on the group to respond. It will be very rare for the first response to take more than 15 seconds to come, even if it seems like eternity. You can always make the question into an overhead-direct (see page 110), by nominating a person to answer.

Avoid the temptation in these silences to tell them what you wanted to hear. Wait for them to give the answer; it will be much more powerful. You must try not to twist what people say, but you may paraphrase it.

It will be important for you to summarise each point you wanted to reach agreement upon. You must make sure that your summary is a correct statement of the degree of agreement reached, otherwise you will destroy the trust and credibility on which successful discussion leadership depends. Your ability to do this will depend on your own listening skills.

Finally, although keeping to time schedules is important, flexibility is required in leading discussions. If a point is important and there needs to be more discussion before you can get to the point, then you will just have to invest the time. To cut it off may leave you further away from your objective than when you started.

Checklist for preparing for the sales meeting

1. Keep a file for the meetings. Include:
   - agendas
   - action points from each meeting
   - points arising in the meeting
   - items for inclusion on the next agenda.
2. Set the meeting dates up to a year in advance.
3. Decide which meetings you will use for other than routine business (at least half the meetings), and allocate a half or full day for these.
4. Before each meeting review the meeting file:
   - Decide which items from the file you must cover.
   - Put down a time allocation for each item.
   - Decide which other items to cover and set a time limit for them.
   - For those items which cannot be included, make alternative arrangements for covering them, such as fax, memo or telephone.
5. For each item set an objective.
   - For communications note the key message to get across.
6. Prepare the agenda:
   - Sequence items to get the administrative issues and the sales results analysis over first.
   - Vary the format for interest.
   - Move on to the more creative things as soon as possible.
   - Build in some activities and participation.
   - Arrange for any outside speakers; agree with them on the objective, time allocation and content of their session.

- Allow some time for questions, but avoid calling it 'any other business'; instead try to focus the questions towards a specific topic.

7 Circulate the agenda several days before the meeting.
- If there are any other important items suggested by other people, include them.
- You may also include items nominated at the start of the meeting, but only if they are important, appropriate and can be accommodated during the meeting without disrupting the existing agenda.

8 Arrange for the meeting room to be set up correctly:
- Book meeting rooms well ahead of time.
- Check any equipment, overhead projectors, video machines, screens.
- Arrange for white board pens, and pens and paper for participants if required.
- Arrange for refreshments.
- Issue instructions on messages and interruptions.

9 Include your internal sales people as often as you can, and involve them in the meeting rather than having them there purely as observers.

Checklist for conducting the meeting

1 Open the meeting.
- Welcome the team.
- Introduce and welcome any guests.
- State the overall objectives and summarise the content by referring to the agenda.
- Ask for any suggestions for the agenda, or any other questions.

2 Guidelines.
- Keep to timings overall, but be flexible on individual items.
- Create the right positive atmosphere.
- Encourage constructive participation.
- Treat all comments seriously.
- Do not reject any answer or comment out of hand.
- Never put someone down in front of the group.
- Be gentle with responses that are incorrect.

- Address the whole group, move your eyes around the whole room.
- Do not talk to the screen.
- Make sure any visuals are in print large enough to read.

3 Guest speakers.
- Introduce the speaker, by name and position.
- Give the title of the talk or session.
- State why that subject is being covered and tie it in to the current needs.
- State why this speaker is qualified to speak on the subject.
- Don't steal the speaker's thunder by talking about the subject yourself.

Checklist for leading discussion

1 Decide on the subject.
- Ensure it is appropriate to training needs.
- Ensure it is appropriate to the current business needs.

2 Set an objective for the session.
- What do you want to happen as a result?
- Knowledge? Skills? Attitude change?

3 Analyse the topic and construct a logical step-by-step sequence.
- Start with general points where you will get easy agreement.

4 Take into account the experience, attitude and skill levels of the group.

5 Plan how you will introduce the session.

6 Prepare any support material:
- Overhead slides.
- Written material, such as checklists or key points you want them to remember.

7 Prepare the discussion.
- Write out the main headings.
- Write down the main conclusions from each part of the argument.
- Decide what questions to ask to lead the discussion where you want it to go.

- Anticipate responses or objections and decide how you will handle them.

8 Arrange the seating so that you do not have 'blocks' of people with similar views, or two great mates who are likely to prefer to chat to each other, and so that discussion is encouraged.

Checklist for controlling meetings and coping with difficult situations

1 Sensitive issues and criticisms of the company and management.
   - Listen to what is being said and identify the real problem or grievance.
   - If necessary, probe.
   - Do not cut the subject off immediately.
   - Keep comments objective and unemotional.
   - Do not get drawn into the argument yourself.
   - Use the technique of 'non-reaction'.
   - Do not comment or give agreement unless your position is consistent with company policy, and you can sustain your position.
   - If appropriate, defend the company's stance and explain the background to the issue.
   - Be prepared to not allow any further comment in the meeting.
   - You may arrange for a later discussion, maybe on an individual basis.
   - Never let such comments destroy the fabric of your meeting.

2 Conflict between attendees.
   - Recognise that conflict is not necessarily a bad thing and that sometimes it can provoke useful discussion.
   - You must mediate if the emotional tone starts to rise, or if the comments become personal.
   - You should let the discussion continue only in so far as it is leading somewhere or is likely to.
   - Otherwise stop it and if necessary arbitrate, but fairly or objectively.

- You may also decide to defer further discussion to a private meeting involving the protagonists.

3 Maintaining interest.
- Try to invite some interesting people.
- Do not get bogged down with the problems of one individual.
- Use visual material.
- Build in exercises.
- Get people doing things.
- Have small discussion groups and then take feedback.
- Get everyone involved; draw out the quiet ones.
- Shut the conversation hoggers up.
- Build in variety.
- Vary the format.
- Vary the venue.
- Vary the chairperson.
- Control the agenda and keep to time.
- Summarise at the end of each session.

4 Keeping to the agenda.
- Do not let satellite discussions develop.
- Maintain a firm but quiet discipline.
- Refer to the agenda.
- If people get off the subject, bring them back to it gently but promptly.
- Take notes, especially of any action items.
- Concentrate all the time.
- Listen very carefully.

5 Getting discussions started.
- Do not talk too long yourself.
- State the subject matter and why it is being discussed.
- Ask stimulating and interesting questions.
- Ensure that any pre-meeting briefs have been sent out, so that participants can give thought to the subject or research it.
- Get everyone to make at least one suggestion.

6 Controlling digressions.
- Restate the subject matter and the objective of the discussion.
- Redefine the point at issue.
- Summarise the points discussed.
- Recap on the common ground and the agreements reached so far.

- Direct a question to the more positive contributors.
- Encourage people to build on ideas rather than find fault.

7 Closing the meeting.

- Summarise the key points.
- Reconfirm actions which either the group or individuals need to take.
- Stress the points of agreement.
- Reconfirm the next meeting details.
- Ask for any agenda items.
- End on a positive note.

15

Interrelating with other functions

Not only must the sales manager perform in his role within his own department, but he must also interact with a number of other company functions as head of his team or of the whole sales department.

As with production, the results of the sales team are immediate and visible. Because sales is such an important function for any company, the sales department is frequently under everyone's eyes.

It also means that the sales department is very vulnerable to criticism. In some cases it is justified and in some cases it is not.

The sales manager often has to do his selling, not to the customers, but to other departments in the same company.

Sales interacts with marketing, distribution, production scheduling or directly with production, with the technical department, with finance on matters such as credit, with information technology (what used to be called EDP) and research and development. In fact, there is some interaction with most areas of the company's operation. The function which has the most central role to play and which has a strong relationship with nearly every department is marketing. The relationship between sales and marketing is probably the closest and at the same time the stormiest.

In many organisations, the situation is exacerbated by three factors. Firstly, there is not a clear understanding of what is sales and what is marketing. Secondly, the job descriptions of both sales and marketing people do not clarify sufficiently where the responsibilities for various tasks lie, and do not give guidelines as to how the two functions should interrelate. Thirdly, more status is ascribed to marketing than to sales, with the result that some of the junior marketing people can become prima donnas.

There are a thousand definitions of marketing. However, in terms of deciding what should be marketing and what should be sales, it is helpful to look at marketing as being strategic, and sales as being tactical. Marketing is about deciding overall goals and strategies. It is about how we should run the business overall. Sales is about implementing those strategies with the customer. Marketing owns the markets or the products; sales owns the customers.

Running a business has a very real element of balancing a number of internally inconsistent factors. The plant will usually run much more efficiently producing a small number of products. Inventories reduce too. However, that may not suit the marketplace. Sales would like a full range to keep out the competition. These sorts of problems abound. Inevitably there is conflict, and this can happen in areas where both functions have an accountability. Marketing in its central position will remain the mediator.

Note that marketing is judged in most cases on financial results, such as ROI (Return on Investment) or net profit before tax, or contribution based on factory standard costs. As such, marketing will always control pricing strategy. So, if sales is responsible for the customer, and selling goods at a price, how can that work? The only way it can work is for marketing to make strategic price decisions, giving guidelines within which the sales department can operate. Sales should be consulted before pricing guidelines are formalised in the marketing plan. If sales considers the suggested prices are not realistic, then marketing must listen. The sales department, under the supervision of the sales manager, then administers these prices within the guidelines. If the guidelines are too strict, the sales managers will be constantly going back to marketing, which is not very practical. The marketing people must learn to trust the sales department's ability to manage price. The sales department has to show it has earned that trust. In fact, sometimes sales and marketing are both accountable for contribution.

The relationships that exist across an organisation rather than up a strict line reporting, are often known as 'dotted line', or 'matrix' or 'relational reporting'. As mentioned, they exist with not just marketing, but a number of other functions too.

It is always a good idea to define the important relationships of this type in a person's job description (see Chapter 3). The sales manager should also set down guidelines for communication. This becomes extremely important for information on deliveries, availability of product, credit management and order placement. Not only should there be strict guidelines as to how the channels should operate from the sales department to the outside on these matters, but also within the department. Furthermore, the sales manager should also make it clear what information he wants from outside the department, when he wants it, how and to which job function.

A tremendous amount of time is spent chasing things up which should have been communicated in the first place. Equally, prevention is better than cure, and having the right information at the right place and the right time may well prevent many of the problems which arise. We all know that customers will be far more accepting of a late delivery if we telephone them three days before the delivery was due to be made and advise them of a delay, as opposed to them calling us the day after it was supposed to be delivered and asking what has happened!

It is up to the sales manager to set up the information flow with other departments to achieve this.

Sometimes it will mean negotiating a compromise. The more the sales manager knows about how the company and other departments operate, the better placed he is to appreciate the problems of others but at the same time to find a workable compromise.

In his relationships with other managers, the sales manager is being compared. He should be aware of this and act accordingly. The better he manages his own department, the more respect he will gain. However, he also must learn to manage the peer relationships. He should be loyal to his team, without being defensive or protective. He should act in a way to build up the status of the sales department. Many other functions within the company do not understand what sales is all about. One of the ways to achieve a better appreciation throughout the company of the problems you face and what your job is all about, is to invite people from other departments to your sales meetings and conferences. It can be very constructive to invite both marketing and other personnel to selected training courses, either as observers or to participate.

It is a good idea to get some of the people whose actions affect customers, such as production or distribution or credit control, out to see the customers together with your sales people. Be sure that everyone is well briefed on the objectives of the visit.

At the same time the sales manager should go to lengths to find out what other people's jobs are all about. Are there ways the sales department could make their lives easier?

The sales manager should remember that a certain amount of conflict is inbuilt into the business system. In his relationships with others, he must try to build on the middle ground and adopt a leadership approach, rather than let the conflict get out of hand. It somehow does not seem to matter as much if we get angry with people within the company, we are all the same family, unlike the need to not lose one's temper with a customer. In fact, it is just as important to be assertive and not aggressive with what are in reality your 'internal' customers.

There is so much wasted energy and loss of productivity as a result of the petty bickerings and even open warfare in some companies. An excellent way of initiating better relationships across functions, is for sales managers to set up a number of meetings with managers of other functions, with an agenda where each of the two managers comes along to the meeting with five things he proposes he could do to make the life of the other manager easier, and five things the other manager could do to make his life easier. Then they sit down and talk about the lists and come up with some agreements as to how they could help each other.

Not only will the sales manager benefit immediately from better cooperation, but how he interrelates with other managers should be taken into account when the time comes to consider the next step up the ladder.

Checklist for a constructive relationship with marketing

The best working relationships between sales and marketing seem to be when:

- marketing provides clear marketing plans to the sales department
- agreement is reached that they are achievable
- the sales department interprets those plans into the actions required at the customer level
- agreement is reached with marketing that the plans are acceptable
- marketing provides flexibility in administering pricing within guidelines to the national sales manager, who then will delegate to his sales force or not, as he sees fit
- it is recognised that sales owns the customer
- marketing plays a supportive role to sales at the customer interface, and only acts with sales or with their knowledge and agreement
- there is open and regular two-way communication between sales and marketing through regular established channels

- marketing does not generally get involved with the day-to-day running of the accounts
- sales has a significant input to marketing to assist marketing in writing their plans
- there are clear channels for communicating with marketing on various subjects.

A flow chart of the sales/marketing interface is shown in Figure 15.1.

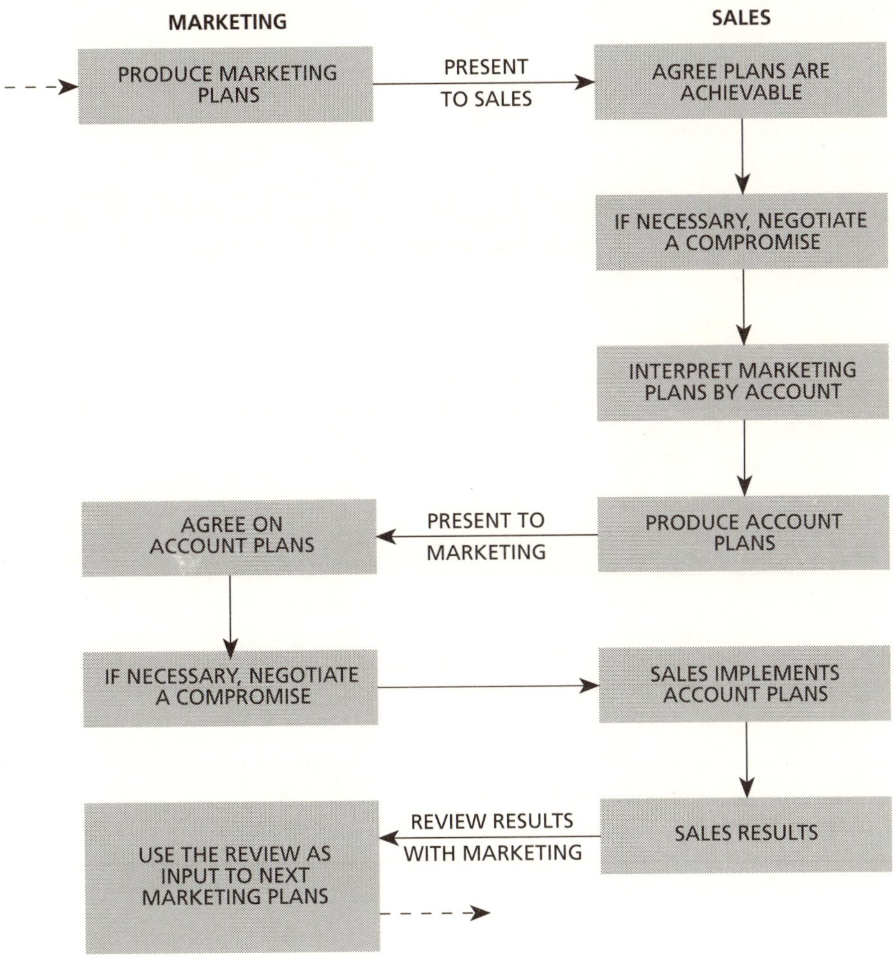

Figure 15.1 A sales and marketing interface.

For those sales managers operating in a technical area where there is a significant element of technical service, many of the comments about structuring relationships with marketing apply to technical service too.

16

Preparing for the next step

By the time the sales manager has digested and implemented the contents of this book, he will probably start to think about what he wants next in his career. There is a fairly common career path which goes from state sales manager to national sales manager. The ability to move from the national sales manager's position is somewhat more difficult. If, by the time you reach the position of national sales manager, you have already had some marketing experience, then you stand quite a good chance of moving to the position of marketing manager. From there you have a good chance to get to the top job. There would be more chief executive officers appointed from marketing positions nowadays than from any other discipline.

The problem is if you have no marketing training or experience by the time you get to be national sales manager. This is because to get that experience you would have to take a job that would be significantly below the level you have already achieved. There are not too many people prepared to take that drop, and not too many companies that are prepared to pay you the national sales manager's salary while you pick up some experience.

The best strategy if you really want to advance to the top is to get some marketing experience early in your career. The ideal time to do this is between a sales position and a sales manager's position. Otherwise, you should consider getting some experience in marketing before you move to the position of national sales manager.

Can you make up for not having the practical experience through formal training? It depends upon the industry, the company and upon you. There is no substitute for practical hands-on experience, but a good academic grounding can certainly help you score the job you want. However, it can never be guaranteed.

In principle, the younger you are, and the less experience you have, the more useful academic training can be. For example, a sales person who at the age of twenty-seven obtains an MBA has probably given his career prospects a significant boost relative to a similar sales person of the same age who has not got one.

However, a marketing manager with several years in his job, and now forty-five years old, is not going to change his job prospects much at all if he goes and gets an MBA. At this level some of the more practical shorter and more intense business courses would be of more value.

In the final event, it will depend on whether you are committed, as far as one can ever predict the future in this uncertain world of takeovers, to the company you are working for. If you are, then you should discuss the matter openly with your own boss, or even his boss, and if you have a human resource development group, with them too.

Ascertain their view of what you would need to do to get to the next step you are aiming for. Make sure you are getting straight answers and not being fobbed off. If it is perceived you are short on experience in some area such as marketing, try to see if you could get involved in some projects in order to gain experience. If you have your own job well under control, and have developed one or two people to the point where you can delegate some of your normal functions, you should be able to take on a project without giving up your current job.

This is clearly much easier to achieve in a company which takes human resource planning seriously, and has a good structured management system.

It is essential that in the same way that you will be having clear job descriptions and standards of performance and regular assessments for your people, you need the same yourself. If you do not have it, ask for it. Otherwise you will find that the other sales managers who in fact are not nearly as professional as you, have the same chance at the next job as you do.

While showing the company that you want your career to progress, you must at the same time be patient. Positions do not always appear when you would like them to. If, on the other hand, you are passed over, or a promise does not come to pass within a reasonable time frame, reassess the situation. Maybe the company is not being quite as honest with you as it should be.

The higher up the organisation you go, the more similar people's jobs become, irrespective of the industry or type of organisation they are in. The ability to manage people is common to all senior jobs. You will recollect that for top managers there is less of a need for technical skills, and a greater need for conceptual skills. However, the amount of interpersonal management skills remains the same (see Figure 11.1 on page 180). It is essential, therefore, to demonstrate that you are a very effective manager of your own people and that you are able to command the respect and cooperation of other managers in other disciplines within the company.

You cannot know too much about the company and how it operates. As a sales manager, the chances are that apart from marketing, the other area where you will be lacking in skills for a top job, will be in the financial area and knowing how businesses operate. This is an area where some formal training courses can help. In fact every account manager, let alone sales manager, should have some skills in this area in order to effectively manage large accounts and be able to relate to the senior executives of these accounts.

Fortunately, not every sales manager wants to get the top job or even the marketing manager's job. Many state sales managers do not even want the national sales manager's job.

The job of sales manager when performed well is an extremely demanding and very satisfying job in its own right. The job offers variety in terms of content; no two days are ever the same. It requires considerable skills, and it will continue to become more and more sophisticated, largely because of the changes in technology which give everyone so much more information to bring into the equation. Having said that, it is still true that the greatest contribution to success will still be getting the basics right. That is what this book has been all about. Doing your job well, knowing you are doing it well, and getting recognition for it, is a very motivating experience. We spend so much of our waking lives at work and although a healthy life has a balance of work together with play, social and family life, if you get satisfaction from your work it contributes to the quality of your whole life.

If this book has assisted you in this regard, then your investment in reading it will be well rewarded.